Break Beats in the Bronx

Break Beats in the Bronx

REDISCOVERING HIP-HOP'S EARLY YEARS

Joseph C. Ewoodzie Jr.

THE UNIVERSITY OF NORTH CAROLINA PRESS
CHAPEL HILL

This book was published with the assistance of the Authors Fund of the University of North Carolina Press.

 Designed by Sally Fry Scruggs and set in Utopia and Univers types by codeMantra. Manufactured in the United States of America. The University of North Carolina Press has been a member of the Green Press Initiative since 2003.

Cover illustration: DJ Ed at the PAL Lynch Center block party, summer of 1980. Photo by Ricky Flores.

Library of Congress Cataloging-in-Publication Data
Names: Ewoodzie, Joseph C., Jr, author.
Title: Break beats in the Bronx : rediscovering hip-hop's early years / Joseph C. Ewoodzie Jr.
Description: Chapel Hill : The University of North Carolina Press, [2017] |
Includes bibliographical references and index.
Identifiers: LCCN 2016053760 | ISBN 9781469632742 (cloth : alk. paper) |
ISBN 9781469632759 (pbk : alk. paper) | ISBN 9781469632766 (ebook)
Subjects: LCSH: Rap (Music)—New York (State)—New York—History and criticism. |
Hip-hop—New York (State)—New York—History. | Bronx (New York, N.Y.)—Social life and customs—20th century.
Classification: LCC ML3531 .E96 2017 | DDC 782.42164909747/275—dc23
LC record available at https://lccn.loc.gov/2016053760

For my late grandmother,

MERCY EDZII,

and

hip-hop historian

TROY L. SMITH

Contents

Figures and Table

FIGURES

TABLE

Introduction

"So, when did you fall in love with hip-hop?"

My father, my brother, and I were on our way to my aunt's house in the South Bronx, on Fox Street and Westchester Avenue. It was 1999. I knew very little about the Bronx. Since emigrating to the United States from Ghana only a few years earlier, all I had heard about the Bronx was that it was mean and dangerous. According to my friends in Canton, Illinois, the small, Midwestern town in which I had been living, it was "the ghetto." My father drove us down Westchester Avenue in our sky-blue Ford Windstar; we rode slowly in the narrow lane between the rusty steel pillars holding up the tracks of the 2 Train above us. Sitting in the back, I took in the bustle and commotion on the street. Teenagers wearing headphones, old men walking with canes, and young women pushing strollers made their way through the heavy traffic, unafraid of the vehicles that passed so closely by them. Horns honked from cars and buses and music blared from speakers on the sidewalks, as folks who were not selling or buying something hurried to where they were going.

The radio in our van was tuned to Hot 97, New York City's premier hip-hop station during the late 90s. We were not listening because we were fans of the music but because my father was trying to immerse us in the sounds of our new urban surroundings. Mesmerized by all that was happening outside our van, I was only half paying attention when, after a commercial break, the show's host Angie Martinez, introduced the next song. She must have mentioned the title, the artists, and maybe even the producer of the song, but I missed all that. All I heard were whirring sounds of helicopter blades. I turned to look up, but the only thing above us was the racing train. And then I heard what sounded like a man talking on a phone. I started to pay closer attention and realized the sounds were coming from the radio. The next few seconds were sounds of aggressive, guitar-like synthesizer. Then, just as the man on the phone hung up, pulsating drum kicks and snares dropped in. Simultaneously, another man's voice shouted, "WHAT WHAT WHAT WHAT WHAT," while a woman's voice smoothly sang the same word. I turned my gaze from the street to the car radio and looked to see if my dad and brother were listening, but they were oblivious, absorbed by the world outside. Using the remote control in the back seat, I turned up the volume a couple of notches. The first verse began,

> Ay yo! We light a candle,
> Run laps around the English Channel,
> Neptunes, I got a cockerspaniel.[1]

The words made no sense to me, but I was engrossed, especially by how the rhythmic delivery of the spoken words synchronically danced with the instrumentals.[2]

It was not the first time I had heard hip-hop, but this was the first time I noticed it. It was when I fell in love with hip-hop. As the song continued, I thought to myself, "How did they come up with this? Who thought to place words, poetry really, perfectly onto musical instrumentation this way? How did they get all the different sounds to work together so well? And how, where, and when did this happen?" At that moment, while riding in my family van, I did not realize the answers to my questions lay just outside the van's windows. I did not know that the South Bronx, the very place where I first took notice of it, was hip-hop's birthplace. I did not know that one of the founding figures of hip-hop had grown up just down the street from my aunt's house.

Nearly two decades after first hearing Noreaga's "Super Thug," I am still intrigued by the way hip-hop started. My objective in this book is to tell, or better yet retell, the story of how it began. Several scholars, in various fashions, have taken on this task, but as Jeff Chang writes, "There are many more versions of the story to be heard."[3] The version I present here combines never-before-used archival material with sociological analysis. It portrays the creative, conflictual process that brought about what we now know as hip-hop and shows that hip-hop was a result of serendipitous events, accidents, calculated successes, and failures that, almost magically, came together. It examines assumptions about hip-hop's beginnings and asks important questions that shed light on its evolution. How, for example, did the genre come to comprise four elements (DJing, MCing, breaking, and graffiti-writing), as it is often argued? Surely other social activities were available to its creators, so why did they focus on these four? Which others were excluded, and why? How did the four elements come together? Also, why did hip-hop begin in the South Bronx and not in any other borough, or any other city for that matter? Why did it begin with Kool DJ Herc? In addition to Kool Herc, Afrika Bambaataa, and Grandmaster Flash—"the Holy Trinity of hip-hop"—who else was involved? Furthermore, how did hip-hop's conventions develop? What impact did African American cultural traditions have on the music form? Was the Black Arts Movement, for example, necessary to its rise? *Break Beats in the Bronx* answers these and many other questions about hip-hop's beginnings.

Providing new empirical details, this book also unearths what occurred during a crucial span of time that has been surprisingly underexamined in previous studies: the years between 1975 and 1979. I argue that during this period the internal logic of the hip-hop scene was formed. To clarify how this internal logic coalesced, I rely on insights from the sociology of culture, especially contemporary scholarship on symbolic boundaries.

The book is divided into three parts, each comprising two chapters. Part I retells stories that are, for the most part, familiar to historians of hip-hop, with the objective of explaining what is often taken for granted. Chapter 1 addresses why hip-hop began with Kool DJ Herc. The second chapter investigates how Afrika Bambaataa and Grandmaster Flash entered the DJing world in the Bronx and how they shaped and distinguished that music scene from those in other parts of New York City. It also looks at DJing in Harlem, Queens, and Brooklyn and explores what made these scenes different from the one in the Bronx. The main objective, however, is to determine why hip-hop started in the Bronx and not in any other part of the city. Chapter 2's analysis of why hip-hop started in the Bronx rather than another part of the city traces the emergence of a new social and cultural entity.

Part II begins to fill in the often-omitted years, 1975–1979. It investigates how the emerging art form became strengthened through the creation of conventions. Chapters 3 and 4 discuss the role of MCs, the invention of the scratch, the role of flier-makers, the importance of routines, the coining of the term "hip-hop," and the pivotal role of the 1977 New York City blackout.

Part III explores hip-hop's endurance through the late 1970s. Its two chapters examine how some participants became popular figures and how newcomers fought to make a name for themselves. Chapter 5 examines the ways race and gender influenced status in the scene. Chapter 6 analyzes the way MCing replaced DJing as the easiest way to gain fame in the hip-hop world and examines how members of the Sugar Hill Gang, through more established institutions—the radio and record industry—made their mark. The narrative ends with participants in the scene reflecting on the way "Rapper's Delight" ushered in new rules and conventions.

These six main chapters include many names—of individuals, crews, and venues—so many that the reader might be overwhelmed. To help keep track of them, I have provided a glossary of names at the end of the book.

Histories of Hip-hop

All historical accounts of hip-hop begin with one person. Alex Ogg, for instance, opens *The Hip Hop Years* this way: "Unsurprisingly, many have laid claim to roles as kings or kingmakers of hip-hop tradition. Most students, however, find one name cropping up time and again. For all intents and purposes, hip-hop started the day Jamaican-born Clive Campbell, aka Kool Herc, first set foot in New York in 1967."[4] It is true: every published historical account of hip-hop's creation names DJ Kool Herc as its unequivocal founding father.[5] Some even identify a specific date and location as *the* starting point: a party Herc threw on August 11, 1973, at 1520 Sedgwick Avenue in the South Bronx.[6] This beginning is so familiar and ubiquitous that it seems needless to question it, but we must. Why did hip-hop begin with Kool Herc? What made him the right person for the task? Along with Herc, two other figures—Afrika Bambaataa and Grandmaster Flash—always appear in hip-hop origins narratives, and typically they are treated as the next logical steps in a preordained natural progression. How did these three young men, with different biographies, interests, and dispositions, become the foundation of the same social practice? And how did they become the leading voices?

After discussing these three figures, who often dominate the period from 1973 to 1975, historians of hip-hop often jump from 1975 to 1979, when the Sugar Hill Gang entered the scene. The years in between are frequently left out. Cheryl Keyes's *Rap Music and Street Consciousness* and Tricia Rose's *Black Noise* make no mention of what took place during those years. Jeff Chang's *Can't Stop Won't Stop* does, but only briefly.[7] Jim Fricke and Charlie Ahearn's *Yes Yes Y'All* is one of the few texts that substantively explores the history of hip-hop that occurred between the rise of the three pioneering figures and the emergence of the Sugar Hill Gang.[8] Providing rich firsthand accounts, Fricke and Ahearn's book supplies interview excerpts about the formation of and competition between crews, and audiences at parties. But much remains to be told. Beyond providing a more comprehensive account, a careful look into these omitted years helps us understand how hip-hop emerged because it was during these years that the scene's internal logic was formed. To use a cooking analogy, if the ingredients for hip-hop were gathered between 1973 and 1975 and the meal was completed by October

1979, then the cooking occurred between 1975 and 1979.[9] To ignore these middle years, therefore, is to ignore most of the action that went into the making of hip-hop.

I would argue that previous writers have ignored these pivotal years for two reasons, one practical, the other theoretical. The practical reason is that historians and journalists have simply not had access to those involved in the creation of hip-hop between 1975 and 1979 because most of them did not become famous. Books and articles have focused on the contributions of Herc, Bambaataa, and Flash, along with the Sugar Hill Gang and those who entered the scene afterward, because they are, for the most part, the ones who became public figures. Some forty years later, the rest are quietly living their lives. Unless one searches hard, one is unlikely to come in contact with the many other influential figures.

The theoretical reason for the neglect of the 1975–1979 period also explains why these lesser-known actors have not been sought out. The majority of the historical narratives in the current literature move from present to past. Most authors begin with what is currently known and then trace it back to its origins, or they look at what has become the most important component of hip-hop and trace its beginnings. We can see this approach in Tricia Rose's brilliant *Black Noise*. A classic text, this work covers much ground but describes aspects of hip-hop as being significant without explaining how they became so.[10] For example, she writes: "Alternative local identities were forged in fashions and language, street names, and most important, in establishing neighborhood crews or posses. Many hip-hop fans, artists, musicians, and dancers continue to belong to an elaborate system of crews or posses."[11] Rose's observations about crews are accurate, but her narrative does not explain why they became a part of hip-hop in the first place or how they were formed.[12]

So what are the benefits of examining these missing years? Examining them opens up the story to include the contributions of hundreds of others who were part of hip-hop's creation. It allows us to move from a heroic account toward a people's history of hip-hop. Moreover, shining a light on this time and this wider community allows us to view the lives—including the joys, pains, interests, inclinations, and dispositions—of a cohort of black and Latino teens who came of age during the 1970s in the Bronx. It becomes a way to understand what made them tick and what made them want to do what they did.

This book insists that we take a different historical approach, one that starts with the past to find how it made possible the present.[13] Too often, to use American sociologist Andrew Abbott's words, "We start with what we know emerged and then seek its origins. But history is lived [past to present]. Things emerge not from fixed plans, but from local accidents and structure."[14]

Along the way, this approach should offer a better sense of the material and symbolic resources participants used in creating hip-hop. In the current literature, authors prioritize either cultural and symbolic influences or structural and material ones. While these scholars do not refute one another's arguments, most historical accounts privilege one of these perspectives over the other. Cheryl Keyes's *Rap Music and Street Consciousness*, for example, presents a culturalist approach. Drawing on various sources, Keyes suggests that the hip-hop MC is, in many ways, similar to figures in Western African oral traditions. She cites the verbal dexterity of bards in Senegal and griots in Gambia as evidence of the African roots of hip-hop music. She explores how African culture, via slave culture, was translated into African American musical genres such as spirituals, gospel, the blues, and, eventually, hip-hop itself. And she describes the influence on hip-hop of African American artists such as Amiri Baraka, Nikki Giovanni, and Sonia Sanchez, all from the Black Arts Movement, as well as the Last Poets, Gil Scott-Heron, James Brown, and George Clinton. Drawing on Paul Gilroy's work to present a black diasporic intepretation of the genesis of hip-hop, she also points to the influences of Jamaican music and sound systems. of sonic expression.[15] While Keyes does not argue that hip-hop began with Senegalese griots or with Amiri Baraka, she does suggest that its roots lie in earlier forms of African, African American, and Caribbean culture.[16]

Authors privileging the materialist perspective focus instead on the social-structural conditions in which hip-hop was created. These kinds of narratives are present in Nelson George's *Hip Hop America* and Tricia Rose's aforementioned *Black Noise*.[17] More recently, Jeff Chang has zoomed in even closer on the site of hip-hop's birth, calling the Bronx a "necropolis," a city of the dead. He describes the devastating effects on the South Bronx of New York City's early-1970s financial crisis and the various social policies that turned the borough into the epitome of urban decay. He also gives a detailed account of the rise, reign, and fall of gangs in the area, as well as their damaging social effects.[18]

Both the culturalist and materialist approaches have their strengths. Those who focus on cultural resources draw interesting parallels between hip-hop and other black cultural art forms. Some authors, however, interpret the similarities that hip-hop shares with prior art forms as evidence that one causally influenced the other, a claim that perpetuates romantic notions of the similarities of peoples of African descent across time and space. Likewise, those who emphasize the importance of social-structural conditions correctly demonstrate that it was not likely for something like hip-hop to have emerged from such destitution. However, social-structuralist arguments are often ambiguous. In certain places, the writers appear to be claiming that hip-hop started in the South Bronx because life was bad and people had nothing else to do; elsewhere they seem to argue that hip-hop developed as a tool for social activism. Both claims are, as will be evident in the chapters that follow, only partially accurate.

Break Beats in the Bronx merges and clarifies these two lines of thinking. In expanding the historical narrative to include the omitted years and accounting for the roles of several more participants, this book illustrates how, at different junctures, early hip-hop participants drew equally on both material and symbolic resources.

Cultural Sociology, Symbolic Boundaries, and Hip-Hop

Throughout the history of sociology, *culture* has meant different things to different thinkers, although certain conceptions of it have dominated at particular times. During Talcott Parsons's heyday, for example, culture was equated with values. Drawing from his work, as well as others who came before him, sociologists of poverty, for instance, often explained economic inequality by suggesting that lower-class Americans had distinctly different cultures, by which they meant different values. Sociologists today still do not have a single definition for *culture*, but what they mean when they use the term is quite varied. Some still think about culture as values (ends toward which behavior is directed), but others conceptualize culture as frames (cognitive perception of self and surroundings), repertoires (strategies of action), capital (shared styles, tastes, and signals), institutions (organizations), or conventions (informal rules). All these definitions provide distinct windows through which one may perceive and understand culture, and each will have a place in the present narrative about hip-hop. But the works of scholars who view culture as the creation, maintenance, and transformation of symbolic boundaries will take center stage. Their ideas inspire the past-to-present historical approach that guides this work.

"Boundary" is not a new concept to sociology or other social-science disciplines. We see it appear as far back as Marx's distinction between the proletariat and capitalist classes in *Capital*. Likewise, Durkheim evokes it in his differentiation between the sacred and profane realms of life in *The Elementary Forms of Religious Life*. And in Weber's *Economy and Society*, the idea of social closure speaks to the relational process of boundary creation.[19] In recent years, the concept has captured the attention of social scientists spanning such fields as sociology, anthropology, history, and social psychology. An understanding of boundaries has allowed theoreticians to make important strides in explaining social distinctions that often are taken for granted, and it has integrated subject areas that once were separate.[20] In sociology alone, the study of boundaries (boundary works) has become an organizing principle that draws into closer proximity topics as diverse as social and collective identity; class, ethnic/racial and gender/sexual inequality; professions, science, and knowledge; and communities and national identities.

Several insights from this body of work can enrich our understanding of hip-hop's origins. To begin with, boundary works insist on inquiring into, rather than taking for granted, how an entity (e.g., a racial category, a profession, or a nation) took on certain features. Hip-hop's various components and attributes—i.e., what lies inside the boundary around hip-hop—are not inherent to it but are the result of processes that must be explained. How does one go about explaining how hip-hop took on its particular attributes? Scholars of boundary work would suggest investigating the interactions among actors involved in the making of hip-hop. It is in their interactions that we can observe how hip-hop became what it is. Research on boundaries also underscores that actors decide what to include and exclude in the boundaries not only on the basis of rational and strategic choices but also on the basis of deeply buried dispositions. It will become evident that I heed these insights in this project.

Andrew Abbott's work, more than any other in the field, explicitly frames my analysis of the way hip-hop emerged. His theory of boundaries comes from investigating how the profession of social work emerged. Fundamental to his approach is the dictum that "we should not look for boundaries of things but for 'things of boundaries.'"[21] In his view, discussing the boundaries of a thing presumes that a "thing" already exists. Talking about boundaries of ethnic groups, professions, or academic disciplines, for example, presumes that ethnic groups, professions, or academic disciplines already are formed and fixed entities. But how do they come into existence in the first place? This is, essentially, the question that drives this book. When we begin our account of hip-hop by establishing that hip-hop has four elements, we presume that hip-hop already exists. The question for me is, how did hip-hop come to exist and come to have four elements in the first place? When we search for "things of boundaries," Abbott argues, we realize that entities actually emerge from boundaries. "In this view," he declares, "boundaries are a logical correlate of thingness and vice versa. Therefore, indeed, saying that a set of closed boundaries exists is logically equivalent to saying that a social thing exists."[22] To illuminate how this approach might help in investigating hip-hop's past, it will be helpful to consider his specific empirical case.

According to Abbott, neither the occupation nor the phrase "social work" existed in 1870. But by 1920 not only was the occupation flourishing, there were professional societies and academic departments dedicated to it. How did this come to be? After an 1874 conference about social welfare activities, simple differences emerged between people who once had performed the same tasks. Among those in the psychiatric field, for example, the division fell along gender lines: male caregivers differentiated themselves from female caregivers, even though they did similar work. The men became psychiatrists and the women became social workers. Soon afterward, these differences became the basis for the creation of a new occupation. As the distinctions became more exaggerated, social welfare workers began to see themselves as occupying different occupational spaces. They created what Abbott calls proto-boundaries.[23] These boundaries were not rigidly set, but they represented the initial inklings of a new, distinguishable profession. From this empirical case, Abbott theorizes that "the making of an entity is simply the connecting up of these local oppositions and differences into a single whole."[24] I make a similar argument in my explanation of the way hip-hop emerged: Youth cultures already existed in New York City, but at a crucial point in the South Bronx in the early 1970s, local oppositions and differences emerged. When these sites of differences were connected, a new entity—hip-hop—began to emerge.

When, if ever, do proto-boundaries become real boundaries? And "when, if ever, does a set of relations actually count as a 'thing,' a substance, or an entity"?[25] Abbott would respond: "The central quality of an entity is endurance."[26] The endurance or recurrence of an entity often comes from some structure internal to it that permits it to recur. Proto-boundaries around social welfare activities became real boundaries and social work became a real occupation when a certain logic developed within it, when rules and conventions developed to make it "self-regulating, self-validating, and self-perpetuating."[27] In addition, according to Abbott's formulation, an entity becomes durable when it is able to "originate social action," when it becomes a "thing with consequences."[28] Social work became a more durable occupation when it started to become significant in the lives of both practitioners and clients. In much the same way, hip-hop began to gain traction when its rules and conventions made it "self-regulating, self-validating, and self-perpetuating" and when it began to direct the actions of those involved.[29]

Investigating how hip-hop was formed can actually also enhance our understanding of how boundaries are formed and maintained. Abbott's framework goes a long way in explaining this, but more work is needed to specify precisely how sites of difference actually emerge, how they are lined up, how they are "yoked" together, and how they endure. This project explores the intricacies of these processes. In rich historical detail, it shows how, within the context of actors' lives, several developments spurred sites of difference to emerge; how some sites became linked to others; and how, while some sites of difference were already in sync when they emerged, others required more alignment before proto-boundaries formed. My analysis also adds to Abbott's framework by clarifying how proto-boundaries become durable. I agree with his claim that the endurance of proto-boundaries is connected to the development of an entity's internal logic. But how, exactly, does this internal logic appear, and how does it ensure reproducibility and durability? Drawing on extensive data and referring to the work of other cultural sociologists, I highlight how and why actors became so deeply invested in hip-hop, as well as how and why they came to believe and participate in it.[30] Then, I show how, within the emerging hip-hop world, they developed their own ends toward which they directed behavior, their own cognitive perception of themselves and their world, their own strategies of action, their own styles, tastes, and signals, and their own social organizations.

The emergence of an internal logic, which allows the emerging entity to reproduce itself, is not the only way an entity endures, however. What more must entities do if they are to last? To this, Abbott replies, "They must be able to 'originate action.'"[31] Using empirical data, I demonstrate that entities endure when they come to matter in the lives of those embedded in them. For analytical purposes, I distinguish between conventions, which serve to direct behaviors within a particular world, and another set of structural forces that shape participants' lives outside those events. I refer to these additional structural forces as the cultural and social attributes of the entity. An entity becomes cultural when it instills in its participants a real or imagined distinction between themselves and the outside world, when it forms among them a sense of mutual connection and responsibility, and when it shapes the way they express themselves (e.g., through gestures, postures, aesthetics, and language).[32] An entity becomes social when it shapes the behavior of those participants even in aspects of their lives not directly related to the entity or other participants therein—for example, when it influences decisions about how to spend time, what to value, or how to serve the community.

Sources of Data

Some books present fresh evidence; others force the reader to look at old stories in a new light.[33] This one does both. The first two chapters, which are about the narrative's starting place, cover ground that has been explored in previous works. For this reason, I rely on already published empirical materials. To fact-check, confirm, and revise details of well-known stories, I use other secondary sources, including documentaries and published works on topics related to the South Bronx, music, and youth cultures in the 1970s. I also refer to books on the history of hip-hop, including journalistic writing, scholarly works, and memoirs. In addition, I scoured the Internet for blogs and websites devoted to hip-hop's founding years. In some cases, I wrote to the keepers of the website to ask further questions—my exchange with Mark Skillz was especially helpful. Moreover, I visited archives at Cornell University, Harvard University, and the Schomburg Center for Research in Black Culture.[34]

However useful the past-to-present approach might be, it alone cannot resolve the fundamental drawback in historical analyses of hip-hop—the omission of pivotal years. To tackle this problem, we need good data that can illuminate what took place between 1975 and 1979. Chapters 3 through 6 present fresh evidence that does just that. Much of the data for these chapters comes from two sources: the Museum of Pop Culture (MoPOP) (formerly the Experience Music Project and Science Fiction Museum Hall of Fame) in Seattle, Washington, and interviews conducted by Troy L. Smith. The first source includes 600 pages of transcripts from 61 interviews with DJs, MCs, breakdancers, and graffiti writers, as well as interviews with club owners, party promoters, journalists, and other actors who participated in or observed the birth of this art form.[35]

The MoPOP interviews, conducted primarily by Jim Fricke, often begin with descriptions of how the interviewees became part of the hip-hop scene. They provide a sense of who these actors were and what they did before their involvement with hip-hop. They also offer a feel of the social space in the South Bronx prior to hip-hop's emergence. When the interviewees speak of hip-hop's beginnings, they describe a wide range of inspirations and motivations for their participation in the new scene. They also give important details about other actors involved, the equipment used, the music played, and the venues where events were held. Many speak of the early stages of hip-hop—the successes, failures, consistent features, and fleeting trends. In doing so, they provide anecdotes about how individual actors met each other and created DJing and MCing crews. Moreover, the transcripts are rich with details about specific events. Some of the best passages are accounts of memorable parties and gatherings, as well as significant moments when new DJing and MCing techniques were introduced, new figures stepped onto the scene, and celebrated figures fell from grace. The interviews also include descriptions of moments of distress, violence, and death. The passion behind these recollections provides a sense of how meaningful these events were for those involved. Because the interviewees at times present different accounts of the same events, their varying perspectives allow for a multifaceted understanding. In some instances, they even contradict one another. The variations in their stories are especially illuminating because they force us to sort out and explain the discrepancies. In short, these interview transcripts provide invaluable empirical material for this study. Their weakness lies in their emphasis on basic narrative elements: character, plot, and setting. The questions Fricke and others asked focus on who was involved, when events took place, and where they took place. Very rarely does the interviewer probe below the surface to ask why things happened as they did.

I came upon my second major data source, interviews by Troy L. Smith, fortuitously. While searching the Internet for information about various actors and venues, I found that a number of answers to my questions were authored by Smith. His name was unfamiliar, but after some investigation, I learned he is a Harlem native and a devoted investigator of the beginnings of hip-hop. He lived through that era and spends much of his spare time working to keep the story of hip-hop's beginnings alive. He is known for his immense collection of audio tapes of early hip-hop performances and his interviews with lesser-known but important actors involved in the story. With his permission, I used all his interview transcripts pertaining to hip-hop's formative years, 1973 to 1979.[36]

Troy Smith's interview transcripts differ from those of the MoPOP. In addition to asking questions about who, where, when, and how hip-hop was created, he asks why it developed the way it did.[37] Beyond this, Smith challenges his interviewees over historical accuracy. Recognizing that factual inaccuracies are endemic to recollections of events, he often asks several individuals about contested components of the narrative. His camaraderie with the interviewees gives him the freedom to challenge those who provide less-than-accurate accounts. In addition, his status as a Harlem native allows him access to interviewee's stories about their roles in the making of hip-hop that they might exclude from conversations with outsiders. This is particularly obvious in responses from participants who were interviewed by both Smith and the MoPOP staff. In Smith's interviews, one finds candid, uncensored details that are, consciously or unconsciously, omitted from the interviews with the MoPOP. Because Smith's interviews have not been used in published works, some of these details have never been included in historical narratives about hip-hop. For these reasons, I draw upon his interviews more than I do upon those of the MoPOP.

A drawback to Smith's data is his closeness to the story. Because he is so familiar with the context and the meanings, names, places, and activities, he often glosses over what can seem foreign to an outsider.[38] While working on this book, I developed a relationship with Smith, who has graciously answered a great many of my follow-up questions. Over the course of our relationship, now over six years long, we have spent countless hours on the phone discussing various portions of the narrative. He has taken a number several of my follow-up questions back to those he interviewed so they could flesh out the story. On several occasions, he even put me in direct contact with them.

I had the pleasure of visiting Smith for the first time in July 2009. As we walked through his neighborhood in Harlem, he schooled me on some of the pioneering actors who grew up around the way. He pointed out where they lived, where they performed, where they went to school, and where they met to compose their rhymes. Every street corner had a story, and he knew it. Later we went to his apartment. Stashed in one corner of his dining room was his library of published books on the history of hip-hop. His computer's web browser had bookmarks for interviews, photos, conference presentations, lectures, newspaper articles, and anything else that speaks to the birth of hip-hop. In another corner lay his prized possession: a collection of tapes of recorded performances of early hip-hop parties. Comprising about 250 tapes (it is hard to imagine that anyone would have more), this collection gives an overview much of the music created between the start of hip-hop in 1973 and the recording and distribution of "Rappers Delight" in 1979—precisely the period I am concerned with here. After reading about these performances for over two years, I got to hear them for the first time in Smith's apartment. He enthralled me with more stories about the actors involved in the scene while playing the tapes.[39]

After meeting Troy Smith the first time, I hopped on the 2 Train and headed back to the Bronx. Soon after crossing the Harlem River and entering the Bronx, the train rose above the ground. With Afrika Bambaataa's "Planet Rock" thumping in my headphones, I stared out the window, wondering how the South Bronx streets looked three decades before. I imagined the burned-out buildings, with broken windows, paint peeling off their walls, and fire escapes dangling down their sides. Scattered about were all kinds of rubble. Dead cars with their tires stolen and their windows busted sat on street corners. Garbage cans lay in the middle of the streets, empty, surrounded by trash. Trees looked shriveled, dead, and what once had been green grass was now brown. Dust from the rubble and trash filled the air. I envisioned young men roaming these streets, alive and vibrant, some with cut sleeves to signify their gang membership, others just racing to finish their tags on a wall before they were noticed. Some women were hanging on the arms of their boyfriends; others strolled in cliques, giggling and carrying on, seemingly reveling in their youth, undeterred by misfortune even if later, during quiet moments, they lamented their luck in life. I imagined visible evidence of these young men and women all over. Someone had written "DECAY" in orange on a portion of a white wall, just in case no one had noticed the conditions in which they lived. I imagined turntables set up on the sidewalk of Prospect Avenue—or better yet in the park, Rainey Park—since it was such a nice summer evening. Kids were swinging on what was left of the playground equipment, while teens gathered to hear what the DJ had to offer. Some of the older folks poked their heads out of their windows to keep an eye on the children. Others sat on the stoops of their apartment buildings to enjoy the summer breeze. The train was in Grandmaster Flash's territory, so I became excited about what I would encounter if I could travel back in time. My anticipation of an old-school hip-hop jam came to a disappointing end, when, waking up from my daydream, I realized I had reached my stop.

Luckily, the memories of hip-hop's early days need not exist only in a daydream. We also need not rely solely on historical fiction like the television series *The Get Down*. With this book, we can journey back to the 1970s and to the South Bronx neighborhoods to rediscover these early years of hip-hop.

PART I

The Beginnings of a Boundary

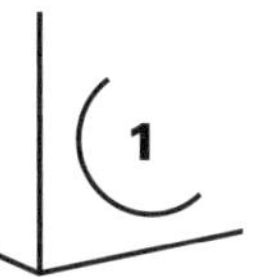

1 Herc: The New Cool in the Bronx

There is an age-old story that hip-hop began at 1520 Sedgwick Avenue in the South Bronx on August 11, 1973, at a party hosted by Cindy Campbell. As the story goes, Cindy's main motivation was to supplement her paycheck from the Neighborhood Youth Corps so she could buy new clothes for school. She rented the recreation room in her apartment building, bought some Olde English 800 and Colt 45 beer and soda, and asked her brother, Clive (known as Kool Herc), who had been DJing house parties for three years, to perform. Cindy created handwritten fliers using index cards and spread them around her neighborhood to advertise the event. At the door, she charged twenty-five cents for the ladies and fifty cents for the guys. Word is, about one hundred people showed up.

According to several accounts, the party did not start well. As would have been done in Kingston, Jamaica, where the Campbell family was from, Clive began by playing dancehall music. But he was not in Kingston. Nor was he in Brooklyn, where Caribbean immigrants would have enthusiastically appreciated his musical taste. This was the Bronx, and people wanted something different, not dancehall or even what was on the radio. "They didn't want to hear the smooth songs that Frankie Crocker played on WBLS and Hollywood played in the discos, records like 'Love Is the Message,'" according to Dan Charnas's version of the story. "They preferred songs with long breakdown sections . . . like 'Get Ready' by Rare Earth, which had a drum break that lasted two full minutes."[1] So, like any good DJ, Clive switched up his style. Instead of dancehall music, he played soul and funk records; and instead of playing songs in their entirety, he played the portion of the song with the most percussion. Just as he had hoped, this strategy turned the party out. He went from the most danceable, high-energy peak of one song to that of another so the dancers would never feel a lull. His playlist probably included the funkiest parts of songs like "Cold Sweat" by James Brown or "Scorpio" by Dennis Coffey. Herc kept the music at that high tempo the whole night, and

FIGURE 1.1 DJ Kool Herc party flier.

the partygoers loved him for it. This, according to several scholars, was the beginning of hip-hop.

It is not a myth that this event occurred. A 2008 episode of the PBS Series *History Detectives*, hosted by sociologist Tukufu Zuberi, proved that it did. In the episode, Zuberi travels to the Bronx and interviews several people who attest to the event having taken place. He also meets Marcyliena Morgan, director of Harvard University's Hiphop Archive, who produces a copy of Cindy's flier (figure 1.1). Zuberi affirms that the party happened but concludes, "was it the birth of hip-hop? That's probably too big a statement."[2]

Before Herc, DJs who lived in the South Bronx and in other parts of New York City threw parties in parks and community centers. So in a sense, there was nothing special about the 1520 Sedgwick Avenue party. Why, then, does it mark the beginning of hip-hop, especially since some aspects of hip-hop existed before that event? Equally important, why does it begin with Herc, and not any other DJ? These questions motivate this chapter. Answering them forces us to take a hard look at something historians of hip-hop often take for granted. Some of the stories in this chapter, especially those about Herc, have been published elsewhere.[3] I rely on them, but I supplement the empirical details with important analyses that shed new light on what we already know.

I argue that hip-hop begins with Herc, but not because of any extraordinary or unique abilities he possessed. It starts with him because he played an important role in a complex interactional process that spurred hip-hop.[4] That is to say Herc's role in this process is not just about who he is. As one writer puts it, historical explanations are not "really about individuals qua individuals or even individuals taken as a group or type, but rather about the conditions that make particular individuals particularly important."[5] In this case, it is as if the socioeconomic circumstances of the Bronx in the 1970s, combined with the social life of South Bronx youth, came together in Herc's life to spark something new.[6]

The narrative about Kool Herc that I offer differs from others in a subtle but significant way: it does not position Herc as a founder or a heroic figure. Here, he is merely a teenager who happened to stand at the intersection of various social forces that pushed him into the limelight. To put it differently, Herc did not *intend* to invent hip-hop. When gang culture died down during the early 1970s, it left a vacuum that DJing filled. It provided a new way to gain a name, and, for various reasons explored below, Herc was the first person to use DJing to gain local clout. As a participant in other social scenes, he was able to amalgamate DJing with other activities and thereby to set in motion the making of a new social and cultural entity.

To lay the groundwork for this argument, I explore the socioeconomic background of the South Bronx prior to the 1970s. Afterward, I construct two narratives—one about graffiti-writing and another about DJing and a particular form of dancing that accompanied it—to delineate some of the vibrant activities that were part of the broader youth culture in the South Bronx even before Herc came on the scene. With both of these efforts, I characterize the *place*, as geographers use the term, in which hip-hop was birthed.[7] Beyond noting the dire economic conditions of the Bronx during the 1970s, as previous authors have aptly done, I also point out the *space* and the social consequences of urban decay, and the meanings the inhabitants gave to it. More importantly, for the purpose of this book's narrative, I highlight the range of intangible cultural practices that were present before anything called hip-hop.

Of course, the three activities, graffiti-writing, DJing, and dancing, were not the only popular activities at the time. I focus on them because they provide a useful gauge of what existed before hip-hop and also because they are essential to the genesis of hip-hop. Some may view the selection of these three activities as arbitrary, or as a form of the present-to-past approach I criticized earlier, since my selection is based on a retrospective knowledge of the way hip-hop unfolded. These are fair charges, which bring up a broader question: where should historical narrations begin when we seek to use a past-to-present approach? If we are to follow this approach explicitly, we risk falling into a trap of perpetual regression in time because, really, there is no beginning to the past.[8] I construct these storylines because they provide a context for the contingent initial encounter that set in motion hip-hop's creation. Instead of assuming that hip-hop began with these activities, I explain how, within the specific context of the South Bronx, they entwined with one another to spur something new. I illustrate how and why actors selected and combined certain existing tangible and intangible resources to create what would become hip-hop, and I pay particular attention to Herc's role in the process. Through this discussion, I portray what historical sociologists often refer to as *conjuncture*: "the coming together—or temporal intersection—of separately determined sequences."[9]

Urban Decay

In the early 1970s, the Bronx, especially the South Bronx, became known nationally and internationally as the epitome of urban decay. When sociologists found that poverty rose by 40 percent in the top five U.S. cities during the 1970s, that the number of people living in high-poverty areas grew by 69 percent, that the concentration of poverty was most pronounced for African Americans and Puerto Ricans, and that some of the sharpest increases were in the Northeast, they were, in many ways, describing the South Bronx.[10] What happened to the South Bronx, and why? Social scientists have established that various factors cause the rise and concentration of inner-city poverty, and that concentrated poverty itself leads to other social ills (see figure 1.2, below, for a summary). Using what they found, let's explore the case of the South Bronx.

From 1890 to 1930, the population of the South Bronx grew from around 89,000 to more than 1.2 million.[11] Historian Evelyn Gonzalez contends that the South Bronx attracted many new residents, especially second-generation Jews from Eastern Europe, because it was a haven for upward mobility. To begin with, according to another scholar, it offered decent housing. Many recent immigrants left the crowded tenements of East Harlem and the Lower East Side for the Bronx's newer and more spacious apartments surrounded by parks, tree-lined boulevards, and open land.[12] These apartments also boasted the latest urban architectural designs and featured modern amenities such as elevators, telephones, electric lights, and steam heat. Additionally, the Bronx offered efficient transportation. Beginning in 1900, with New York City's construction of a new transit system, two subway routes connected the Bronx to the rest of the city. Thanks to this inexpensive rapid transit, many could afford to live in the Bronx and still have easy access to

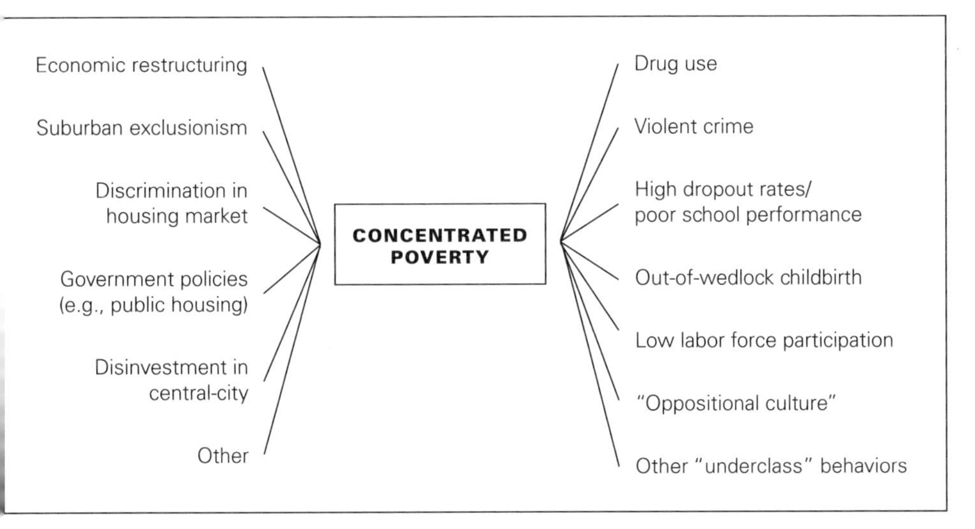

FIGURE 1.2 Causes and Consequences of Concentrated Poverty, from Edward G. Goetz, *Clearing the Way: Deconcentrating the Poor in Urban America* (2003). (Used with permission from Urban Institute Press [Rowman & Littlefield Publishers])

Manhattan. This made the Bronx, which consisted of diverse neighborhoods, "one of the fastest growing urban areas in the world" and earned it nicknames like "the banner home ward of the city" and "Wonder Borough."[13] By the late 1920s, it also was home to cultural institutions such as Yankee Stadium, the Bronx Zoo, New York University's University Heights campus, and Fordham University.

The demographic makeup of the borough began to change a few decades later, however. By the 1960s, the population of the South Bronx was no longer two-thirds white; it was now two-thirds black and Puerto Rican. Several policies fostered this change. Federal Housing Authority Loans and Veterans Administration Programs, along with the suburban housing boom and ineffective urban renewal planning, provided financial incentives for whites to leave the Bronx.[14] Blacks and Puerto Ricans from other parts of the city poured into the Bronx, especially the South Bronx, then the least expensive area of the borough, increasing its population from approximately 145,000 in 1950 to 267,000 in 1960. The children of these new black and Latino residents would create hip-hop. Even though they existed in different racial categories, they were bound together by the poverty they faced. Most of them had been displaced by Robert Moses, who used Title I of the Housing Act of 1949 to remove tenants from their "slums" in other parts of the city, especially in Manhattan, to make room for middle-class housing projects.[15] Others,

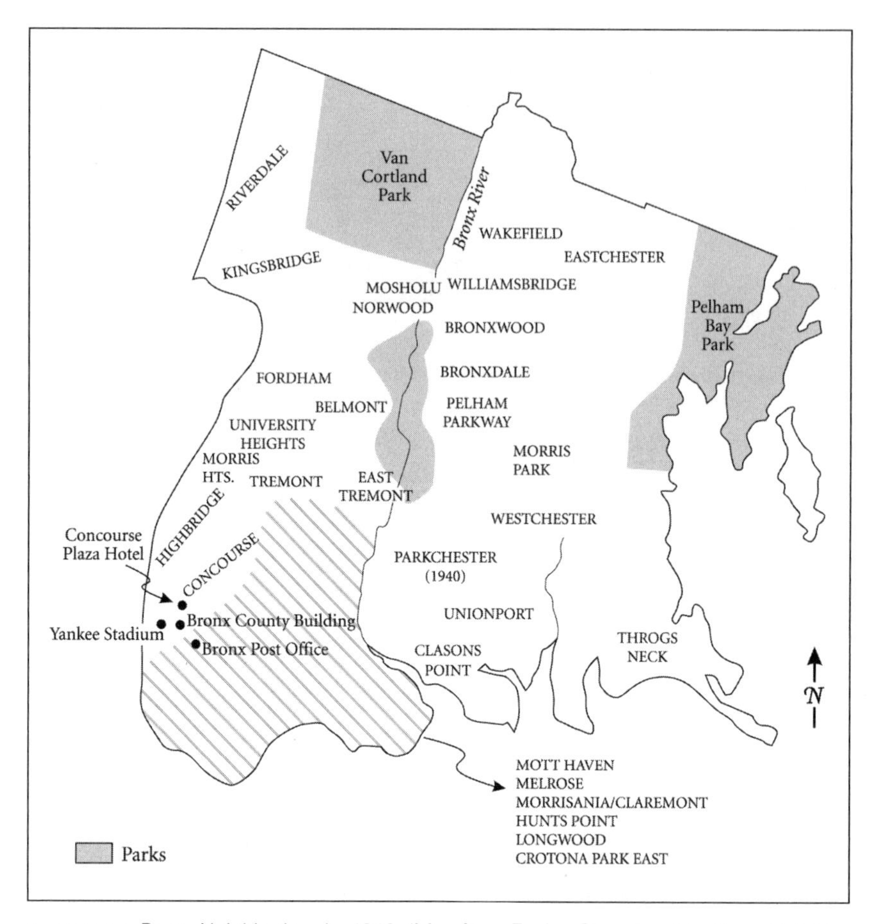

FIGURE 1.3 Bronx Neighborhoods, 1940. (Map from Evelyn Gonzalez, *The Bronx* [2006]; used with permission from Columbia University Press)

in particular southern blacks and Puerto Rican immigrants who came with fewer financial resources, opted for the Bronx. They could afford it there because the city subsidized the rent in those areas.[16] Because of these measures, some of the poorest residents in New York City began to concentrate in the South Bronx.

Attempting to control the exodus of middle-class families from the Bronx to other boroughs and the suburbs, city officials implemented policies such as the Mitchell-Lama Law and the Rent Stabilization Law of 1969. The former provided tax incentives and subsidized mortgages to private landlords in exchange for lower rent for people earning a modest living, while the latter set limits on rent. “The Mitchell Lama housing was a disaster for the borough,” Evelyn Gonzalez explains, “[because] its co-ops siphoned off white

FIGURE 1.4 Urban decay in the South Bronx. (© Joe Conzo; used with permission)

[middle-class] families from housing that was still sound, leaving vacancies to be filled by poorer blacks and Puerto Ricans, themselves often displaced or moving away from the worsening slums, and thus spread[ing] the blight and the segregation farther."[17] The Rent Stabilizing Law failed because landlords did not profit from their rent-regulated buildings and thus did not maintain them; instead they allowed their buildings to deteriorate.[18] In the South Bronx, they even burned them down.

Between the mid-1960s and the mid-1970s, the South Bronx lost approximately 43,000 housing units, the equivalent of four square blocks a week, to fire. From 1973 to 1977, property owners set 30,000 fires in the area. The borough became plagued by vacant lots and abandoned buildings.[19] Another city policy brought about this destruction. Welfare recipients who sought better housing options would not receive reimbursements for their moving expenses unless they stayed in the same place for at least two weeks. The only exception to this rule, which was often posted in large print at welfare offices, was for tenants who had been burned out of their apartments. In such cases, tenants would immediately be moved to the top of the waiting list and would be eligible for a grant of $1,000 to $3,500. Some argue that this exception motivated rampant arson.[20] Bob Werner, a police officer who served South Bronx neighborhoods during the early 1970s, believes that landlords paid for their buildings to be torched in order to collect money from insurance companies.[21] Still others contend that the fires were less the work of arsonists than of social policies that promoted "benign neglect" and "planned shrinkage," essentially pulling resources out of communities considered pathological. For instance, between 1972 and 1974, four fire companies in the Bronx were closed. Each had served 60,000 people.[22]

The concentration of poverty in the South Bronx can also be attributed to the loss of manufacturing jobs—a trend that was hitting the rest of New York City and many other American urban areas.[23] Job loss was worse in the Bronx, however, because new tax laws introduced by the city—including new corporate income-tax regulations and increases in permit and inspection fees—had a more damaging effect on businesses there.[24] While in 1959 the Bronx had 2,000 manufacturers, by 1974 there were only 1,350 and the number of jobs they supplied had decreased by one-third: 600,000 jobs disappeared.[25] Consequently, the average per capita income dropped to $2,430, just half the New York City average and 40 percent of the nationwide average, and welfare rolls swelled correspondingly.[26] The number of welfare recipients in the Hunts Point neighborhood alone went from 11,000 in 1962 to 53,000 a decade later.[27] These recipients, parents of those who became part of hip-hop, made do with what they had. Their strategies for surviving poverty would become a cultural value for their children, one that would serve them well as they created their own means of enduring urban decay.

Such an intense concentration of poverty, according to some scholars, takes on causal significance of its own and leads to various forms of social ills.[28] This, too, was evident in the Bronx. As socioeconomic conditions deteriorated and brought along a sense of hopelessness, crime rapidly increased: reported assaults quadrupled between 1960 and 1969, and burglaries increased sixteenfold. The 41st police precinct, serving Hunts Point-Crotona Park East, led the city in murders and crime from the 1960s onward.[29] Heroin usage also increased. On Charlotte Street in the South Bronx, "They sold drugs like they were groceries," one resident recounts. "So many people were ODed, we used to see them all the time in the hallways and the vacant lots."[30]

Another blatant manifestation of the concentration of poverty in the South Bronx was gangs.[31] After the violent summer of 1959, New York City had witnessed a steady decrease in the number of active gangs: from 248 in 1961 to 184 in 1962 to 130 in 1965, according to the police department.[32] This trend reversed in the 1970s, however. "Without much notice, it seems, street gangs have again become a problem in New York," reads a 1972 *New York*

Magazine article, "this time on a scale and with a potential for violence that may be unprecedented—the near certainty of gunplay and a high probability of mindless, trivially motivated homicide."[33] In the South Bronx, the rise of gangs was particularly noticeable. The gang organizations, which members called clubs, included, from least to most powerful, the Liberated Panthers, the King Cobras, the Majestic Warlocks, the Ghetto Warriors, the Flying Dutchmen, the Young Sinners, the Young Cobras, the Young Saints, the Young Saigons, the Roman Kings, the Turbans, the Brothers and Sisters, the Latin Aces, the Peacemakers, the Dirty Dozens, the Mongols, the Javelins, the Bachelors, the Savage Skulls, the Savage Nomads, the Black Spades, the Seven Immortals, and the Ghetto Brothers. Some, like the Majestic Warlocks, were affiliated with other larger organizations, while others, like the Black Assasins, remained independent.[34] They divided the Bronx into sections and each gang controlled its turf.

If gang life was a negative marker of urban decay for some, it was a positive institution for those who participated. For thousands of young men and women, these clubs were an important part of life and often formed their primary social identity.[35] Take the case of D.S.R., a member of the Savage Nomads: After an unfortunate incident in which he fell out of the window of a high rise (he believes he was pushed), D.S.R. lay unconscious in a hospital for eleven days. When he awoke, he did not know where he was or what had brought him there. "A couple of the Nomads came to the hospital," he recalls. "I knew them right away, and then my memory started coming back. After them doing that, you know, bringing my memory back and everything, I could never leave these guys."[36] He pledged complete allegiance to the organization. As sociologist Charles Cooley would describe it, "[his] very [self], for many purposes at least, [was] the common life and purpose of the group."[37]

Club members often viewed themselves as latter-day Robin Hoods, a positive solution to the dire environment. For instance, they provided security services for tenants who lived in apartment buildings located in especially dangerous sections of the Bronx, and in exchange, the building superintendents gave them a room in the basement to use as their clubhouse. "They [also] protect[ed] the neighborhood," says Joan Butler, a community worker intimately acquainted with the operations of the gang organizations: "There [were] so many empty buildings, people [could] go in to attack you. But [now] we . . . [had] protection. The Savage Nomads [were] always there."[38] Moreover, at times the gangs banded together to protect themselves from unwarranted harrassment from the police. To Manny, president of the Turbans, "The police department [was] the biggest gang out here."[39]

The clubs also ruthlessly guarded their territories in a manner more brutal than had ever been seen. One South Bronx Catholic priest compares gangs of the 1970s to those of previous decades: "In the late 1950s and early 1960s, you had gangs, the West Side Story stuff. Those young men came [into the Bronx] with families. They rumble[d] and you appeared, they'd scatter. They were afraid. The gangs of the 1970s were pathological. They engaged in random violence for no reason."[40] While gangs of the 1950s used puny homemade zip guns, the new organizations, according to *New York Magazine*, provided a "factory-made piece for every member—at the very least, a .22-caliber pistol, but quite often heavier stuff: .32s, .38s, and .45s, shotguns, rifles, and—I have seen them myself—even machine guns, grenades, and gelignite, an explosive."[41] The gangs terrorized their neighborhoods. They preyed on the elderly, drug addicts, storeowners, undercover police, unaffiliated youths, and each other.[42] "The Nomads . . . were a very terrifying group of boys[,] believe me," says Butler; "they would attack anybody, it didn't matter to them as long as they could do an attack. . . . Some of the store [owners] said they moved out of the neighborhoods because of the attacks."[43] The gangs' reign did come to an end, but not before deadly battles and shootouts among themselves and with the police. Led by the Ghetto Brothers after the death of their beloved leader Black Benjie, the gangs came together to sign a peace treaty sometime in 1972.[44] The organizations slowly dissipated, although the personalities, attitudes, and behaviors remained in the Bronx. The sensibilities that were part of gang culture—group loyalty, organizational structure, territoriality, fashion sense—also remained in the Bronx and would become important resources for hip-hop's creators.

For those who believe that the concentration of poverty causes other social ills, the logical response is to dilute it and thereby mitigate its effects by removing the poor from poverty-stricken areas. No one relied on this logic more than Robert Moses. As mentioned earlier, Moses used the Housing Act of 1949 to remove thousands of poor people from the "slums" in which they lived. Often, however, his efforts only deepened the concentration of poverty. For one thing, he destroyed communities, along with whatever networks and coping strategies they relied on to survive their economic conditions. For another, his efforts usually benefitted the lower-middle class and left behind the poorest of the poor.

One example of his slum clearance approach is the way he managed the construction of the Cross Bronx Expressway. Ernest Clark, the consulting engineer, described the project this way: "When I first looked at this project, I thought, 'How the hell are we going to get across here?' It was probably one of the most challenging highway projects that had been constructed, or even conceived, up until that time. I dare say that only a man like Mr. Moses would have [had] the audacity to believe that one could push [the expressway] from one end of the Bronx to the other."[45]

Besides its technical difficulty, the proposed project faced a more serious obstacle, which was that it would destroy a mile of apartment houses—"forty-four [apartment houses], fifty-four structures of brick and steel and mortar piled [in total] fifty, sixty and seventy feet high and each housing thirty or forty or fifty families."[46]

Protests began when, on December 4, 1952, residents of East Tremont Avenue received an order, signed by Moses, to relocate in ninety days to make way for the construction of the expressway. This notice came as a shock to the residents not because news of the expressway was a surprise but because they had heard it so many times they thought it was just a rumor or a joke. It was unimaginable that their neighborhood would be destroyed to accommodate a highway. Unlike other neighborhoods bulldozed for previous Moses-led projects, theirs was not a slum. It was among the most populous and vibrant parts of the Bronx. "The neighborhood was very dense," one resident recalls, "everybody lived out on the street and spent a great deal of the time [there]. In the summer, the kids would play till it got dark." He adds, "Parents would sit out in folding chairs and watch, and gossip. There were always women leaning out of the window who would comment on what you were doing, and ask about the family."[47] Arthur Schemer, another resident, remembers the neighborhood fondly: "I enjoyed the people that I grew up with. Everybody knew each other. You could not walk five steps without meeting someone that you knew. We had a lot of things in common. We were all in the same type of situation. It was just a happy memory. That's why I think I was so angry when this thing occurred."[48]

Moses biographer Robert Caro adds:

> If it was desperately important for the people who lived in East Tremont that their neighborhood be saved, it was also desperately important for the city of which that neighborhood was a part. For a hundred years, East Tremont had performed a vital function for New York. . . . It had been a "staging area," a place where newcomers who had lived previously in America only in slums, successful at last in their struggle to find a decent place to live, could regroup, and begin to devote their energies to consolidating their small gains and giving their children the education that would enable them to move onward and upward.[49]

None of this mattered to Robert Moses. For him, the South Bronx stood in the way of the most direct truck route between the northeastern states and the rest of the country.

Reluctant to leave their beloved community, members of thirty-one civic, religious, and veterans organizations banded together to form the Cross Bronx Citizens' Protective Association to protest the construction.[50] Residents from other neighborhoods whom Moses had evicted protested as well, but this one, according to William Lebwohl (one of Moses's attorneys), was "more bitter and personal" than those of the past. Community members, New York City politicians, senators, and the mayor were called upon to help the community, and many responded. East Tremont's Congresswoman Isidore Dollinger, State Senator Jacob H. Gilbert, Assemblyman Walter H. Gladwin, East Tremont's Councilwoman Bertha Schwartz, and Comptroller Lazarus Joseph all pledged their support.[51] Their goal was not to halt construction of the expressway altogether. They sought only to reroute one mile of the expressway so it would circumvent the neighborhood. And there was a feasible alternative, according to engineer Edward J. Flanagan. The route could have swung down two blocks, even one block in some places, to pass by the edge of Crotona Park instead of going through the East Tremont neighborhood. Lillian Edelstein, along with several other housewives, consulted other engineers to draft the technical details of this alternative route, including its cost to the city.[52] They found that the alternative route would involve the destruction of six brownstone tenements housing nineteen families and the Third Avenue transit depot, while Moses' route required the demolition of "fifty-four apartment houses, ninety-one one- or two-family homes, and fifteen one-story 'taxpayer' buildings housing sixty stores, for a total of 159 separate buildings."[53]

The engineers estimated that the demolition of these buildings would cost $10,000,000; moreover, the loss of real estate taxes brought on by the relocation of 1,530 families would amount to $200,000 per year. Newly elected mayor Robert Wagner initially supported the alternate route, as did several others. Despite their efforts, Moses proceeded with his plan. His success in forging ahead was a reflection of how much political capital he wielded, though he was not an elected official.

The Cross Bronx Expressway lies one block from 1520 Sedgwick Avenue. During and after construction of the highway, the neighborhood changed.[54] "While it was painful for those who had to move, it was also painful for those who [had to] stay," writes historian Jill Jonnes. "The demolition and ensuing excavation for the roadbed generated tremendous chaos in the contiguous

FIGURE 1.5 Mayor Robert Wagner (*right*) joined by Robert Moses (*left*) and Frank Meistrell (*center*) on a housing project tour, 1956. (Photograph by Walter Albertis; courtesy of the Library of Congress)

streets."[55] Debris and residue from the construction littered the streets. Robert Caro describes the scene: "After seven o'clock [in the evening], the residential streets of East Tremont are deserted, roamed by narcotic addicts in gangs like packs of wolves. Even on East Tremont Avenue, by nine o'clock most of the stores are closed, the lights out, huddled behind steel cages and

FIGURE 1.6 South Bronx teen taking part in neighborhood cleanup. (© Joe Conzo; used with permission)

iron bars. The streets of East Tremont are carpeted so thickly with pieces of shattered glass that they shine in the sun. Garbage, soaked mattresses, bits of broken furniture and, everywhere, small pieces of jagged steel fill the gutters."[56]

Even with this devastation, Borough President Herman Badillo believed that the South Bronx could have been saved, were it not for "the worst mistake of them all," the construction of Co-op City.[57] Under the leadership of Robert Moses, this 15,832-apartment community, the largest apartment development in the United States and the largest cooperative apartment development in the world, was intended to aid the housing crisis. But it backfired. Moses's plan was a classic "domino-effect" slum clearance initiative:

> Because the principal barrier to urban renewal programs was tenant relocation, new housing should be built where there were no tenants: in vacant areas of the city. After it was built, tenants from slum areas should be moved out of the slums—out of whole slums at once—into the new development. The areas they had vacated, now empty, should be razed and new housing should be built there.

> Then residents of another slum area should be moved into that new housing, their area razed and rebuilt, tenants from still another slum move in—until all the city's slums had thus been replaced with modern housing.[58]

Unfortunately, not all residents of the South Bronx could afford to move to Co-op City, especially poor blacks and Puerto Ricans. In less than a year, the South Bronx's middle class left.

The borough's poverty and chaos provided the social context for hip-hop's creation. The children of those who remained in the South Bronx were among the poorest of the poor. Although few material resources were available to them, they had an abundance of symbolic resources, most of which were strategies their parents had developed for dealing with urban decay.

Two Story Lines

The youth of the South Bronx lived through dire urban decay, but that was not the sole feature of their lives. Like young people everywhere, they partook in social activites. Hip-hop arose from those social activities. In this section, I fit into a much larger narrative two of the most popular social activities of the South Bronx's early-70s youth and draw out how they helped those who became part of hip-hop's creation.

GRAFFITI

Robert Reisner, one of the foremost scholars of the 2000-year history of graffiti, describes it as a dialogue between the anonymous individual and the world. He and other historians agree that the intent of most graffiti before the 1960s, in content and visual aesthetics, was to communicate a thought in a literate and readable manner.[59] However, during the mid-1960s, a different form of graffiti began to emerge in racially segregated neighborhoods in Philadelphia, when writers used graffiti to mark the territories their gang controlled. In addition, they started to mark the territory of competing gangs as a way of challenging the latter's authority. With an increase in segregation in many U.S. cities during the post–civil rights era, these territorial markers visually depicted the boundaries of such neighborhoods. Like gang culture, the practice of graffiti was in many ways a means for Philadelphia's youth to cope with and respond to urban decay. Ley and Cybriwsky provide an example of such graffiti use in Philadelphia: "North of Fairmount Avenue and east of the jail, there is a sharp break from a biracial population to a solidly black neighborhood. Despite a large number of vacant and cleaned rubble-strewn lots, the intensity of graffiti increases for this part of the territory of the Moroccans, one of the larger and more violent North Philadelphia gangs. At Corinthian Avenue their territory abuts abruptly against the white neighborhood of Fairmount, and there is very little graffiti transgression across this boundary."[60]

While 1960s graffiti carried an implicit political motive, it differed from earlier forms of protest graffiti because it did not promote or defend a cause or protest an action.[61] Instead, writers sought primarily to articulate their aggression toward other groups and to support their own group. With one or two individuals representing an entire gang, they transformed the rules of graffiti that had existed for hundreds of years. For example, the use of names changed drastically. "The personal name, or pseudonym, broke out of its traditional small scale with its use in territorial graffiti," explains historian Jack Stewart.[62] Writers wrote their names in bigger and bolder ways than people had done previously. Also, the "association of the person with a larger cause, one's turf, helped to break down the timidness, fear, and need for secrecy that seems to have been an emotional part of writing one's name in a public place up to that time."[63]

Perhaps influenced by the large-scale graffiti of gang members, another breed of graffiti emerged: loner graffiti. The goal of loner writers was to get their names onto as many places as quickly as possible. Soon, rivalries among peers turned into a citywide quest for notoriety. Two criteria for gaining status arose: the quantity of hits (or writings on public surfaces) and the difficulty of access to the places where the graffiti was written. Several writers rose to the top: TITY PEACE SIGN, for spraying his name on the back side of an elephant in the Philadelphia Zoo; BOBBY KIDD, for spraying a police car while his friend distracted the policeman; and the most famous of all, CORNBREAD, who gained notoriety for spraying his name on the wing of a TWA jet. At the airport, he also added to the welcome sign so it read: "*CORNBREAD* WELCOMES *YOU* TO PHILADELPHIA."[64]

The location of graffiti work gained increasing significance for both territorial and loner writers. To the territorialist, markings on the borders of gang territories were perceived as courageous, especially when they infringed on the territories of rival gangs. Also, territories yet to be claimed by particular gangs were seen as areas of contestation. Here, one could observe more combative graffiti. According to Ley and Cybriwsky, "The graffiti in these central blocks change from self-reinforcing autographs to aggressive epithets directed against the other gang."[65] For loner graffiti, location also acquired greater meaning and, in some ways, altered the criteria for status: "Between a location difficult to access but with a limited audience, and another that was risky or difficult to reach but affording a large audience, the latter became more desirable to hit."[66] Because of this, public transportation became a popular target. Both buses and subways in Philadelphia became saturated with graffiti in the early 1970s, so much so that city councilman Joseph L. Zazyczny proclaimed to the newspapers that his city was the "graffiti capital of the world."[67] However, graffiti would not be confined to Philadelphia. It would soon find a home in New York City.[68]

In the mid-1960s, graffiti was not a big problem in New York City's subway system. And where it was present, graffiti existed only in poor neighborhoods where territorial markers represented gangs such as the Ghetto Brothers, the Savage Nomads, the Savage Skulls, the Seven Immortals, and the Galaxies. Loner graffiti writers were rare, but that soon changed. Territorial marker– and loner-graffiti practices took shape in New York City much as they had in Philadelphia. Those not involved in street gangs became graffiti writers. Jack Stewart explains: "Graffiti gave these early writers something to be involved with instead of gang membership. From the beginning it seemed to be a preferable, or acceptable, alternative for many of them. At first they were just considered 'loners' by the gang members, but as long as they didn't make the mistake of hitting other names on the gang clubhouse they weren't bothered very much."[69] TAKI 183, one of the early loner graffiti writers, confirms Stewart's assessment: "Well, it was what you do when you're sixteen, you know. Other guys go drinking, break into cars. We'd go out writing at night.[70]

In the depth of economic hardship, graffiti-writing emerged as a way for aimless youth to pass the time. Stewart notes: "They had seen the tension reach the flash-point in Harlem and the South Bronx. Neglect was very real to them, and many of them suspected that it was all that they could look forward to."[71] BAMA I, a New York City loner-graffiti writer of the era, remembers the pervasive desperation: "The sixties kind of died, and things started to get a little settled. But in the neighborhoods, the ghettos, in the outback areas, where people [were] forgot about, a lot'a tension was still happening. Whereas, OK, now we have equal rights and you can do this and you can do that, but still, I come home to this. I have to put up with certain things. I still have problems getting a good education. . . . I still get drugs thrown at me. . . . I mean people walking up to me in the streets showin' me how to use a syringe."[72]

Graffiti, then, was a powerful and colorful response to societal neglect. The writers used their names, their graffiti names, to hit back. In *The Faith of Graffiti,* Norman Mailer describes the meanings of graffiti for the writers: "An object is hit with your name, yes, and in the ghetto, a hit equals a kill. You hit your name and maybe something in the whole scheme of the system gives a death rattle. For now your name is over their name, over the subway manufacturer, the Transit Authority, the city administration. Your presence is on their presence, your alias hangs over their scene. There is a pleasurable sense of depth to the elusiveness of the meaning."[73] So the values and repertoires available in the Bronx during the early 1970s, even the ones that came from youth cultures, were deeply connected to the dire socioeconomic circumstances.

In New York, the graffiti world operated according to the same rules that held in Philadelphia. Writers gained respect based on the number of hits, the difficulty of the location of hits, and the visibility of hits. However, one distinction between the two cities was the addition of numbers, often the house numbers where the writers lived, to the names of the New York City loner writers. In New York City, the following writers were among the best-known: GREG, CAESAR, BRONSON, PHIL T. GREEK, CHE 159, CAY 161 (at 14, the youngest writer of this bunch, most of whom were 16 years old), his writing partner JUNIOR 161 (the first to experiment with writing large scale letters), BABY FACE 86 (credited by some with the first use of the crown),[74] RICAN 619, FRANKY 135, DUTCH 135, JESUS 137, RAT 1, CHEW 127, his partner TREE 127, RALPH 611, FJC IV, RLM II, CLIFF 159, FRANK 207, CLOUD 160, ACE 137, C.A.T. 87, and EL MARKO. But the most legendary of them all were TAKI 183 and his writing partner JULIO 204.

TAKI 183 started writing his name in Washington Heights in 1969. The following year, with a summer job that allowed him to roam through different parts of the city, his hits spread beyond his neighborhood. "You see, I used to be a messenger, I was sixteen, my first job, a delivery boy, and I used to go all over the east side, that's what made me so popular." As he traveled the city, he began to spread his tag all over, even in affluent neighborhoods. "I used to write in the areas where influential people would see it, like I would go into a fancy building—I used to deliver cosmetics. All those guys that write for newspapers, they all live in nice neighborhoods but in some affluent areas as well. So they would see it and they'd say 'AW God,' but they'd write about it the next day."[75]

TAKI received the ultimate reward when, in July 1971, *The New York Times* wrote a profile of him entitled "'Taki 183' Spawns Pen Pals." When asked why he wrote, he responded: "You don't do it for the girls, they don't seem to care. You do it for yourself. You don't go after it to be elected President."

FIGURE 1.7
Taki 183 spray painting his tag. (Photographer unknown)

He described the respect he received from his peers: "I don't feel like a celebrity normally . . . but the guys make me feel like one when they introduce me to someone. 'This is him,' they say. The guys know who the first was." And, when told that it cost 80,000 man-hours and about $300,000 to clean up the tags on the subway, he answered: "I work, I pay taxes too[,] and it doesn't hurt nobody. . . . Why do they go after the little guy? Why don't they go after the campaign organizations that put stickers all over the train during election time?"[76] The fame he received from this article inspired other writers. As Stewart explains, "Graffiti became for the youth of the city like a big lottery with a real prize of fame literally at their finger-tips. As any graffitist will tell you—fame is the name of the game."[77] With emboldened motivation for participation, several social conventions were established, ones that dictated "the materials to be used . . . the abstractions to be used to convey particular ideas or experiences (such as the use of bubble letters or 3-D letters) . . . the form in which materials and abstractions will be combined . . . and the appropriate dimensions of a work."[78] Markers and spray cans were stolen, not purchased. A writer could not cover the work of another writer. Writers often belonged to social groups consisting of master writers and "baby writers" or protégés, and female writers were welcomed into these groups. Names, or tags, became aesthetically detailed, as writers shifted from hitting the inside of subway cars to hitting the outside. By 1973, creating graffiti was a vibrant activity.

As in Philadelphia, graffiti writers in New York realized that their pieces could travel throughout the city if they were put on modes of public transportation, commercial road vehicles, and delivery trucks.[79] Eventually, writers found the ideal home for their work: New York City's subway system. Writers initially went to subway stations simply to tag on station signs because people looked at those signs the most. Then they moved to writing on station walls, inside subway cars, and finally on the exteriors of the cars.[80] Soon stations began to serve another purpose as well. According to Jack Stewart: "Some of the stations became like a clubhouse for them. The West 168th Street Station became an early center . . . because the A and the AA trains, B trains, and the Number 1 trains stopped there. The West 96th Street IRT station, where the Number 1, 2, and 3 trains stopped[,] was also an early popular spot where the writers liked to gather. . . . [T]he abandoned 91st Street station on the Number 1 line quickly became covered because they could work there undisturbed and the station was never cleaned."[81]

Naturally, teens of the South Bronx were aware of New York's graffiti competition, and soon some of them began to exert influence in the graffiti world. Perhaps the most famous of all Bronx writers was Wayne Roberts, popularly known as STAY HIGH 149.[82] Born in Virginia, Roberts moved with his family to Harlem in the mid-1960s and eventually to Grand Concourse in the Bronx. He received his graffiti name from a friend who used it to describe Roberts's marijuana habit. In addition to creating large pieces that covered an entire side of a subway car, STAY HIGH developed a character—"The Smoker"—that became part of his signature: "I was a child of the 1960s who watched a lot of television. One of my favorite shows was a show with Roger Moore, which featured a Saint stick figure in the beginning of the show. I expanded on that idea by facing the character in the opposite direction, added the smoking joint, and thus, the smoker was born."[83]

Fame came as Roberts's work traveled throughout the city. Like TAKI, who inspired him, STAY HIGH was a messenger who put his name everywhere he went. Besides making his name ubiquitous, he and writers like PHASE 2, BAMA, SNAKE, and STITCH transformed the aesthetics of lettering. Roberts perfected the art of producing large, bold block letters, which made him one of the most recognized of all writers. And he was relentless in maintaining his status: "I bombed so much that I slept, ate, and bled graffiti. I became an addict for it every night, painting in a train yard, lay up, or some place in the city. The biggest high, however, was seeing it run all through the city. There was nothing like it! I was up on the trains so much that the heat was coming down on me; the vandal cops found out who I was, so I needed to find an alias."[84] He created a new tag name, VOICE OF THE GHETTO, but other writers recognized the work as that of STAY HIGH. When *New York Magazine* published an eight-page essay about subway graffiti in 1973, STAY HIGH was prominently featured.[85]

Like gang culture, the world of graffiti writers had its own rules and ways of being. From the adoption of pseudonyms and the formation of teams to the visual aesthetic, their world was rich with symbolic resources that became valuable to the creators of hip-hop. Similarly, the world of DJs and dancing provided important resources.

DJING (AND DANCING)

Scholars of DJing believe it began on Christmas Eve of 1906, when Reginald A. Fessenden, a colleague of Thomas Edison and Lee DeForest, transmitted the first radio waves between the United States and Scotland from Brant Rock, Massachusetts. After this first step, several enthusiasts saw possibilities in radio for communication and entertainment. Radio was perfected for these purposes by Charles D. "Doc" Herold, Thomas E. Clark, Dr. Elman B. Meyers, and Dr. Frank Conrad, whose weekly shows, sponsored by local record stores, began commercial broadcasting.[86] As radio became an important medium for communication and entertainment, the individuals behind it became equally important.[87] Particularly significant was the DJ's role as selector of the music to be played on the radio, for in doing so, he had the power to popularize certain songs.

Almost immediately, DJs faced threats from musicians, music publishers, and record labels, because playing songs on the radio for free public consumption undercut the market for live music.[88] But these challenges could not curb the DJ's rising popularity. For example, on his show *Make Believe Ballroom,* Martin Block garnered 4 million listeners, making radio a viable instrument for advertising.[89] Black radio DJs became important because they marketed products to urban black listeners while also popularizing black music.[90] Their showmanship on air inspired early hip-hop MCs.

In 1947, when a DJ first stepped away from the broadcasting booth to play records in front of a live audience, it was in a small town—Otley, West Yorkshire, England—and the DJ was Jimmy Savile. He and other DJs in northern English towns—who became known as northern soul DJs—developed several aspects of the art of DJing that would, in time, make their way all the way to DJs in the Bronx. According to historians of DJing Bill Brewster and Frank Broughton, "What northern soul brought to the DJ was obsession. Because it placed an incredible premium on musical rarity, it made him into an obsessed and compulsive collector of vinyl. It taught him the value of playing records no one else owned, of spending months, years and hundreds of pounds in search of that one unheard song which would bring an audience to its knees."[91] This obsession with records would continue across many generations of DJs, eventually including of the South Bronx. In addition, and more than previous DJs, northern soul DJs insisted on generating a physical response to the songs being played. The audience did not have to dance in any particular way, but if they were not moved somehow, the DJs were not doing their job. This new role of the DJ spread quickly to other cities. In Paris, the same development occurred during World War II when live bands were prohibited. In response, DJs played jazz, for a live audience. At about the same time in London, consumption of jazz music was combined with opium and marijuana use for long nights of partying and revelry. New York City already had a lucrative jazz scene, but it soon became the haven for club and discotheque DJs.

As the sixties came to a close in New York City, and in the backdrop to the Stonewall Rebellion, a DJ named Francis Grasso set a new standard for DJing. He played at the Sanctuary—a former Baptist church at 8th Avenue and West 43rd Street in Hell's Kitchen that had been converted into a club. As one observer puts it, "Grasso took the profession out of servitude and made the DJ the musical head chef."[92] Earlier DJs, like Terry Noels, whom Grasso replaced, had controlled the flow of a night by selecting specific records to be played at specific times. The power to affect the mood and energy of a crowd remained in the records, and the DJ hoped the songs would do what he or she intended. DJ Francis, by contrast, insisted that the power to influence the crowd lay in his hands, not in the songs. He believed it lay in his ability to manipulate any record and thereby get the people on the dance floor to feel what he wanted them to feel. He was in control, not the record. This sentiment was an important step in the development of DJing, and it was key for the making of hip-hop.

Even with modest equipment, DJ Francis perfected beat mixing, a skill that gave DJs unprecedented creativity. He also used the "slip cue" to start records exactly at the point he wanted. This allowed him to create seamless transitions from one song to another that created the effect of musicians changing tunes without stopping or even missing a beat.[93] With these techniques, DJ Francis enhanced the danceability of the music he played and serendipitously created the modern DJ. Moreover, the decreasing danceability of rock and roll, due to "the bloated self-aggrandizement of its 'progressive' era," urged a shift in the kind of music DJs played in urban clubs.[94] DJ Francis featured the rhythms and drum parts of music created by the pop artists his predecessors had played, such as the Rolling Stones or Led Zeppelin, and also included artists such as James Brown, the Four Tops, and Kool & the Gang. This in combination with recreational drugs and a keen sense of sexual liberation gave rise to the musty, sweat-filled disco culture of 1970s New York.

Francis Grasso's approach to DJing represented a break from the way earlier DJs had performed. While most ruptures "are neutralized and reabsorbed into . . . preexisting structures in one way or another—they may, for example, be forcefully repressed, pointedly ignored, or explained away as exceptions," historian William Sewell Jr. notes, more significant ones, such as Grasso's, "touch off a chain of occurrences that durably transform previous structures and practices."[95] (A few years later, DJ Kool Herc initiated another significant shift that sparked another creative process.) Following Grasso's lead, other DJs added more innovative techniques. His disciples, and the places they would be best known for, included David Mancuso at the Loft (he set the standard for sound reproduction at dance clubs and was meticulous in selecting songs that created an atmosphere);[96] Nicky Siano at the Gallery (considered the first commercial DJ, he perfected the use of sound and high-energy performance to draw a large crowd);[97] Larry Levan and Frankie Knuckles at the Continental Baths (after serving his tenure at this upscale gay club, Knuckles moved to Chicago and participated in the creation of house music); Walter Gibbons at Galaxy 21 (Gibbons was especially known for emphasizing rhythm and drum patterns);[98] Tee Scott at Better Days (at this famous black gay club, Scott focused on longer overlaps between soul records and live music);[99] and David Rodriguez at the Ginza (known for discovering new records, he was also greatly influenced by Nicky Siano). Together, these DJs made their mark by shaping the way audiences physically responded to music. They made the DJ an essential figure in dance culture. As one writer explains, "This was when [the DJ] . . . became a god to his dancefloor. This was when he learned his vocabulary of mixing techniques, and this was when the industry recognized him as the person best placed to create dance music rather than just play it."[100]

Grasso's disciples, and the swanky spots they played, inspired a boom of discotheques that swept across New York City's outer boroughs. "It's hard to give a firm number on how many discotheques there are in New York," Bob Casey, founder of the National Association of Discothèque Disc Jockeys, explained to the *New York Sunday News*, "because every Joe's Pizzeria in town is now hooking up a couple of turntables and calling itself a 'discotheque.'"[101] As one venue spiraled off another, discos became a craze and brought the DJ along with them. Some of the popular disco DJs outside midtown Manhattan included Pete "DJ" Jones in the Bronx, DJ Hollywood and DJ Eddie Cheeba in Harlem, Grandmaster Flowers and Maboya in Brooklyn, and the Disco Twins in Queens. In the Bronx, specifically the South Bronx, a parallel DJ scene was sparked by those too young—DJs of twelve and thirteen years of age—to enter discos in other parts of the city.

The first of the great South Bronx DJs was Clive Campbell, aka DJ Kool Herc. His sense of what made a good DJ was not only informed by what was happening in midtown Manhattan. The conception of the DJ in Jamaica, where he had been born and raised, was also part of his cultural toolkit.[102] In Jamaica, he lived near a Trenchtown dance hall. He recalls: "We used to be playing marbles and riding our skateboards, used to see the guys bringing the big boxes inside of the handcarts. They used to make watercolor signs and put them on lightposts, let people know there's going to be a dance coming."[103] Clive Campbell was too young to enter the party, but he heard the music emanating into the streets. At such a young age, he was unable to understand DJing techniques, but the power and significance of the sound stayed with him.

When his family immigrated to New York City in 1967, Clive sought to assimilate into the urban youth culture and turned to the radio. "When I first came here in '67, I was listening to a lot of white stations . . . DJs like Cousin Brucie. So I was singing a lot of white music—until I got turned onto WWRL [New York's top black music station], surfing the stations, picking up the Temptations and different groups."[104] This station expanded Clive's musical palette. The more he listened to the sounds on WWRL, the more he came to identify with them. The music on the radio became as meaningful to him as the reggae and dancehall music he had left behind in Jamaica. When he started DJing in the recreation center of his building, he combined what he had observed from going to parties, what he had heard on the radio, and what he remembered from the Trenchtown DJs.

What is often considered Kool DJ Herc's major contribution to DJing was simply an adherence to, perhaps, the longest-lasting DJing orthodoxy. Here is his description of how this came about: "I was smoking cigarettes and I was waiting for the records to finish, and I noticed people was waiting for certain parts of the record. . . . The moment when the dancers really got wild was in a song's short instrumental break, when the band would drop out and the rhythm section would get elemental." Following the DJ's cardinal rule—that such energy should be encouraged—he looked for ways to highlight these particular segments of the songs.[105] "Forget melody, chorus, songs—it was all about the groove, building it, keeping it going."[106]

FIGURE 1.8 Tony Tone and Kool Herc at the T-Connection, 1979. (© Jamel Shabazz; used with permission)

Kool DJ Herc called this highlighting technique the "Merry-Go-Round." His mixing was very basic. "There was no attempt to cut each record into the next or to preserve the beat. Instead he just faded from one record to another, often talking over the transition," explains DJ Grand Mixer D.ST, an attendee at Herc's parties. "Herc didn't cut on time or nothing like that . . . his variety of music, the songs that he had, it was very clever. It was a combination of the old and new. And it moved the crowd."[107] Despite this simple technique, Herc's DJing resonated with many South Bronx youth who saw him perform, because he had created a new style of playing records that was unique. And in response to his style, a new form of dancing emerged, one strikingly different from the disco dancing popular in Manhattan. Nelson George describes it as a "medley of moves" that grew out of the "shuffling, sliding steps of James Brown; the dynamic, platformed dancers on Don Cornelius's syndicated *Soul Train* television show; Michael Jackson's robotic moves that accompanied the 1974 hit 'Dancing Machine.'"[108] We can add to these diverse influences were karate moves from kung fu movies and the showmanship of the Harlem Globetrotters, both popular among South

Bronx youth.[109] This new dance style, initially called burning, later on came to be called *breaking*.[110]

To burn someone, according to Cholly Rock, an early b-boy, was to "get the best of them, to embarrass them." Imagine a pantomime comedic act set to music. "You might do something where you're dancing and you make like your screwing their head off while you're dancing. . . . We take a dude's head off and I have my partner play football with it! You know, 'Hike!' Throw the head down after the touchdown or pass it around." This was what turned into what would be called up-rock. "'Uprocking' [became] part of Burning," Rock adds. "If somebody got burned on the dance floor, it could have came while he was uprocking."[111]

Word of a new DJ named "Herc" spread quickly around the neighborhoods. After his party at 1520 Sedgwick, he could no longer go back to the recreation center. Instead, he threw parties outside or in bigger venues such as the Police Athletic League on 183rd Street. Disco Wiz, an early follower, remembers, "I first heard Kool Herc's sound check and heard of his parties through friends and acquaintances. I went to his party and was blown away by what I saw."[112] People attended Herc's parties for different reasons. Some went because little else was happening in the neighborhood. "See[,] in the South Bronx we really had nothing to do," notes DJ AJ, then a teenaged resident of the Bronx. "There was no movie theatre—everything we did was like something just to make a little bit of excitement. . . . [W]hen people seen Kool DJ Herc, it was like some excitement, and it drew a crowd."[113] Disco Wiz adds: "We weren't socially accepted at disco joints [in Manhattan]" (and as noted above, many were too young to enter). "I was looking for an outlet to express myself. I was young, thuggish, and just looking for something to do besides getting in trouble. . . . [W]hen Kool Herc finally hit the scene, we started getting the buzz. . . . [T]he beats and the bass thumpin,' it was something that really blew me away, more so than any other music I'd ever heard in my life."[114] Others, like Sha-Rock, a young woman from around the way, went to enjoy the sound system. "The atmosphere was awesome, cause Herc had a system, and if you were really into music . . . that was everything. . . . Just to hear the bass was like everything," she recalled.[115] And for several others, it was the music iteslf that caught their attention. "He used to play a lot of records that you couldn't buy in the store," DJ AJ explains. "He played a lot of James Brown, Melvin Sparks, the Incredible Bongo Band, Baby Huey, a lot of real interesting break beats."[116]

For all these reasons, Herc became one of the main sources of entertainment for South Bronx youth during the early 1970s. Grandmaster Caz, an avid Herc follower, describes how hearing him changed his life:

> The turning point—which made me go from pedestrian to driver, I like to call it—was in 1974. I went to a party, a indoor party, at a club called Hevalo, and I saw this DJ named Kool Herc. He was the DJ. I mean he was it. Everything that I heard and saw all came together that night when I saw him DJing. I saw how it's really done and what it's really about. . . . I said, "Now that's what I wanna do. . . ." That night in 1974 when I went in that club and I saw Herc, I knew that day on that's what I want do for real, you know? Not as a hobby. I wanna be a DJ.[117]

Linkages: The Beginning of a New Social and Cultural Entity

The history of DJing in the South Bronx differs slight from the history of DJing in Manhattan. Coke La Rock, Herc's childhood friend and DJing partner, explains: "See, growing up, [in the late 1960s] DJs were not popular. They were the last guys on the totem pole when it came to respect when we were growing up. A nigga will put his foot in your ass, take your records, take your money and your sodas and beer[,] and tell you 'have a nice day'! The only cats that got true respect in the streets were the pretty boys, the boys that were getting money, if you could fight, and the ball players. Those were the four popular cats coming up."[118]

It was not until the 1970s that DJs became popular in the Bronx. Coincidentally, this occurred around the same time that gang activities started to die down. Because of this, some scholars argue that DJing began to replace gang culture as a way for young people, especially young men, to gain social clout. If the decline of gang culture demonstrated social disorganization among South Bronx youth, then the rise of DJing began the process of social reorganization.[119] Jeff Chang, for example, argues that DJs ushered in a "new cool," one that overtook the reputation that gang leaders had enjoyed.[120] It was not given or predictable that DJing would become a new means of earning social status, especially in light of the fact that only a few years earlier DJs were not well regarded. So why did this happen? The answer highlights the difference between graffiti-writing and DJing as sources of social status and reveals Herc's important role in hip-hop's creation.

First, the DJ stood at the center of a social practice sweeping the country—disco. Even if DJs were not popular in the Bronx, they were in much of the United States. As the popularity of discotheques spread beyond Manhattan to the Bronx and the other boroughs, the high social regard for the DJ followed. In contrast, graffiti did not become a national phenomenon; its popularity was limited to New York City and, perhaps, Philadelphia.

Second, DJing became a means for gaining social status in the South Bronx because a DJ's name could spread quickly. In contrast, graffiti writers had to put in long hours over several weeks before anyone noticed their tags. Because of this, Herc surpassed the popularity of writers such as EL MARKO 174, PHASE 2, SUPER KOOL 223, and BLADE, who had been practicing their art much longer. In addition, the DJs' fame transcended the subculture to which they belonged and reached all members of the South Bronx community; by its very nature, the craft of the DJ brought people together in a social setting to provide an escape from the destitution around them. Young and old alike knew who the DJs were, especially since they performed in public spaces like community centers and and parks. Moreover, DJs were viewed as productive members of the community, because their parties gave people something to look forward to. DJs were lauded while graffiti writers were seen as destructive and were repudiated by the community and the law.

Third, DJs were able to earn money for what they did. Few other social activities—at least legal ones—generated money. This was especially significant, considering the difficult economic situation of the time.

Kool Herc did not step into his role as a DJ having considered these factors, but he became among the very first to gain popularity as a DJ in the Bronx. How did this happen? To begin with, Herc had access to a powerful set of speakers. His father, Keith Campbell, was an avid music collector and the sponsor of a local band for which he had purchased a new Shure PA system. Initially, Campbell did not let his son touch the new system. But behind his father's back, Herc learned how to wire the speakers for maximum volume, something his father had yet to figure out. For this, Campbell gave Herc permission to use the system for throwing his own parties in the park. Kool Herc was not the first to bring a sound system to a park, but his speakers were louder than most, so they drew more attention.

Furthermore, the music that Herc played earned him a following. For Tony Tone, one of the early followers, this was what made the difference. "I was a DJ before I knew about Herc," he explains. "I was working in a record store. Nobody was playing what Herc was playing. Nobody was playing 'Gypsy Woman,' and other stuff that Herc was playing. I was playing what was on the radio; I was playing what was at the record store."[121] Unlike radio DJs and other neighborhood DJs who played popular music, Herc's parties featured soul and funk records that weren't necessarily being played on the radio. He played this type of music because, as a partygoer himself, he had seen his DJ friends John Brown and Shaft try them out on their audiences. Importantly, the records he played were those his parents collected, so during his first few parties he simply played their records. Because audiences responded so positively to the borrowed music, Herc searched for more of it at local record shops. And the more he played soul and funk music—for instance, the Incredible Bongo Band's infectious, conga-infused beats in songs like "Apache" and "Bongo Rock," James Brown's "Give It Up or Turn It Loose," or Dennis Coffey's "Scorpio"—the more he attracted the attention of his audience.

Why did this music capture the attention of South Bronx youth? One potential explanation is that the music differed from disco music. Because the most popular (black and Latino) music of this time, the early 1970s, was composed for Manhattan discos clubs, the youth of the Bronx rarely identified with it. Disco music—which Nelson George describes as a "rigid formula of rhythms and instrumentation . . . [comprising a] redundant blend of hi-hat drum patterns, swirling string arrangements, Latin percussion breaks, and moronic lyrics"—simply did not appeal to them because it was played in venues they could not enter. So, they rejected what they were refused and declared that "Disco sucked."[122] Herc provided an alternative by playing music that was at once familiar and new. The older soul and funk music was familiar because it was what their parents played at home. But, by highlighting the funky breaks in these songs, Herc made them new. He made partygoers hear their parents' records as music of their generation; it became their own.

Another explanation for how Herc gained high status as a DJ in the South Bronx was, quite simply, his large physique. His size mattered because it allowed him to avoid the harassment often aimed at DJs due to the negative reputation they once had suffered. After all, only a few years before, DJs had been viewed as "the last guys on the totem pole." As a tall young man, an athlete, and a weight lifter, he easily escaped harassment from former gang members. "They [the gang members] respected us; we respected them," Herc explains. "We didn't need no colors [gang affiliation] to be on our block to be recognized or put fear in people's heart, stuff like that. When they come to the party, they know if they mess with us, we was gonna have our business. If you step to me, you're gonna have problems."[123]

Herc's popularity as a DJ might also have come from his amalgamating DJing with other social activities. Prior to becoming Kool Herc the DJ, he was CLYDE AS KOOL the graffiti writer. "I used to run with a graffiti crew called the Ex-Vandals," he recalls. "It was PHASE 2, SUPER KOOL, LIONELL 163, STAY HIGH 149, EL MARKO, and SWEET DUKE, a lot of graffiti artists. We used to meet up there—it was like a meeting ground." These meetings were not limited to conversation about graffiti, however. "We'd all talk about where we tagged, when we bombed, and all that; we used to dance."[124] His crew of graffiti writers was not unique. Many other crews included dancers as well; so when Herc became a DJ, the graffiti crowd came to his parties. As a DJ, CLYDE AS KOOL dropped the first part of his graffiti name and added Herc, short for Hercules, a nickname he had received because of his stature. But why did a DJ need a pseudonym? Up to this point, it was not part of DJ culture to adopt another name—for instance, DJs in Manhattan discos used their given names. One explanation is that for Clive Campbell DJing and graffiti-writing spilled into one another. The DJ in him borrowed from the graffiti writer. Herc's use of a pseudonym as a graffiti writer, to preserve his anonymity, became entwined with his persona as a DJ. For a similar reason, all subsequent participants in the South Bronx DJing scene—DJs, B-Boys, MCs, flier makers—also took on pseudonyms, a convention that continues to define hip-hop today.[125]

Naturally, dancing became an important part of the burgeoning DJing scene. According to ethnomusicologist Joseph Schloss, the audience at Herc's parties was already accustomed to dancing at public gatherings. "Since early hip-hop jams took place in the same spaces as street drumming—sidewalks, parks, public beaches, and schoolyards—the experience of dancing to an extended, Latin-style percussion break played by a deejay in a park would have been extremely similar to the experience of dancing to live drummers in that same park."[126] Like his choice of records, the overall setting of Herc's parties was simultaneously familiar and new. All the energy was focused on the dance floor and the dancers—the youth who had come for the "Merry-Go-Round"—became personalities in their own right. Moreover, the type of dance generated by Herc's music and his style of DJing gradually became a fundamental facet of hip-hop.[127]

Herc acknowledged the presence of the dancers at his performances and dubbed them "b-boys" (and later "b-girls"), short for "break boys" and "break girls," not only because they waited for the break beat of songs but also because their movements alluded to the street term "to break," meaning to "go off," to reach a breaking point.[128] He did not see the dancers' popularity as rivaling his own; rather, each enhanced the other—DJing became a more durable activity because Herc welcomed graffiti writers who became b-boys. This, perhaps more than anything else, distinguished the South Bronx DJing scene from those in other parts of the city.[129] Alien Ness, a b-boy of the era, explains how Herc catered to the dancers: "What he would do was[,] in the midst of playing his records, when the break was coming, he would grab the mic and just like let everybody know. He'd chant 'B-boys are you ready, B-girls are you ready.' And that would just get all the dancers, all the B-boys and B-girls, that would just get them amped and ready. . . . And when that break beat dropped, everybody hit the floor. Everybody went bananas. It was crazy."[130] Cholly Rock describes how he would, after he gained a following, enter b-boy circles:

> I would come in the party and I would hear some B Boy records being played. I would see the circle already going and I would come in with a Cortefiel or Bomber on, whatever and I was one of the first people around the way with my name on my jeans. The words CHOLLY ROCK! coming down one side and the other side of my pant leg had a Black Spade with TZK for The Zulu Kings. So now we are in the circle at the Jam, and I would walk in there and part the circle. I would hear people saying here comes Cholly Rock and some cats would see me and leave and I would take over the circle and go the f— off and it would get bigger, because "Cholly Rock is here." Let me be clear, I am not the only one who experienced that. If you were "A1," you were treated like that! I would Uprock first. There's a move and I don't know why they do it but they call it the Cholly Rock, it's actually named after me. After I'm uprocking, when the go-off part of the song comes, I go down and I start spinning. My thing is I can spin like a top! You ask Pow Wow he will tell you, "Yo Cholly would get on the floor and he would just be spinning and spinning!" Then I would come back up and zoom right back down. Then after spinning I would do some routines. Then I would fly in the air and land on my back and come up like I was rising from the dead or I would spin and stand on my toes and then do the Baby thing like Clark Kent! Brothers would see I'm going off and no one would come into that circle.

While Herc took pride in providing the best music for the dancers, it soon became evident that his parties were exciting also because of the breakdancers themselves. "The hippest music out was what Kool Herc was playing—'Apache,' 'Mardi Gras,' 'It's Just Begun,'" recalls Richard Cisco, an attendee of Herc's parties. "These certain records that everybody was b-boying off of. What propelled it [the DJing] was all the b-boy action."[131] B-boys enhanced the durability of the South Bronx DJing phenomenon even further by coming up with new ways of moving to the music, a dance style that was specific to the local scene. And from this mode of dancing came a posture, known as the "b-boy stance" (raised shoulders, arms crossed tightly, head often tilted to one side), which the all party-goers adopted.

Moving from small community centers to larger and better-paying venues, such as the Twilight Zone on Jerome Avenue, Herc formally partnered with b-boys for his parties, and they soon became a permanent part of these events. His crew the Herculords included Coke La Rock, DJ Timmy Tim, Clark Kent the Rock Machine, the Imperial JC, Blackjack, LeBrew, Pebblee Poo, Sweet and Sour, Prince, and Whiz Kid and the Nigger Twins.[132] This crew gave Herc's South Bronx DJing more traction, since now the audience could be entertained as much by the dancers as by the DJ.[133] In the eyes of one of Herc's early followers, Theodore, having the crew also made Herc standout from other DJs in the Bronx. "[Other DJs] didn't have all that," he explains. "Herc had all of that. DJ D, [for example], had a nice system, and they might be playing some breaks. But Herc had Coke La Rock on the mic with the fucking echo. . . . If you went to a party and you seen D on one side and Herc on the other side, you would've probably ended up on Herc's side."[134]

Herc's stardom resulted from the enthusiastic reception to his music, for there was no inherent value in the breaks he played other than that assigned by the audience. In a sense, the audience made Herc special.[135] They exerted agency as they "enunciat[ed] aesthetic judgments that influenc[ed] [the] performers' [in this case the DJ's] selection of songs."[136] As the audience adjudicated between Herc's musical experimentation, they began to establish what kinds of practices and boundaries would define this new scene. For example, audience rejection of the dancehall music that Herc played during his sister's back-to-school party forced him to try other kinds of music. If they had embraced dancehall music, the story being told here would be a different one. In contrast, the crowd's enthusiasm for Jimmy Castor's "It's Just Begun" encouraged Herc to play it repeatedly, making it one of the anthems of the time. As Nelson George explains, this song, and others that were accepted, "didn't become hip-hop classics in a vacuum. DJs played them, and often unearthed them, but it was the dancers who certified them. It was their taste, their affirmations of certain tracks as good for breaking, and their demand to hear them at parties that influenced the DJs and MCs who pioneered hip-hop's early sound."[137] How does such synergy between a DJ and his audience happen? Here is one theorist's answer:

> When a producer . . . produces products adjusted to the taste of his audience . . . it's not [necessarily] that he has tried to flatter the taste of his [audience]. . . .
>
> The correspondence that is established *objectively* between the producer . . . and his audience is clearly not [always] the product of a conscious pursuit of adjustment, conscious and self-interested transactions and calculated concessions of the demands of the audience.[138]

Herc's musical taste and that of his audience did not converge simply because the DJ sought to please his audience. The correspondence occurred because of a "common system of references" among all those participating in the scene. To put it differently, the merging of preferences between the DJ and his audience signified that both were drawing from shared points of reference. In this instance, part of Herc's musical taste aligned with that of his audience because his parents and his audience's parents all listened to similar soul and funk records. A result of historical accumulation, this common set of references lay at the very foundation of the making of hip-hop.[139] Herc is important to hip-hop's history because his DJing highlighted this commonality.

Therefore the role of Herc's audience cannot be underestimated. Attendees at his parties were mostly black and Puerto Rican young men and women stuck in the abyss of poverty. In sharp contrast to youth in prior decades who received attention and mentorship from adults in the neighborhood—those living in the Patterson Houses in the Bronx, for example—the youth of these same neighborhoods, now rampant with heroin addiction and facing social isolation, were raising themselves.[140] While the youth of the 1950s and 60s were allowed to take their musical instruments home from their high-school music classes so they could practice, the youth of the early 1970s had neither music classes nor instruments. While the youth of the 1950s and 60s attended after-school sports programs supervised by CCNY basketball star Floyd Lane and former Knicks player Ray Felix, the youth of the early 1970s strayed aimlessly in the streets.[141] While in earlier decades these neighborhoods had their share of gang activity and social ills, the 1970s were markedly different. Mark Naison explains that, "except in rare cases, neither gangs nor illegal activities led to deadly violence [during the 1960s]. . . . Even those who acted outside the law seemed to operate within a powerful communal consensus."[142] In the early 1970s, though, it was almost as if the laws of the city, or the country, did not apply in the South Bronx. Utterly neglected, the youth found it deeply meaningful that this new DJing scene was built on their own musical and aesthetic preferences. Because of this, hundreds of young people invested themselves in the music and faithfully attended the parties.

It is true that hip-hop began with Herc, but it simplifies the story to see him as the singular or sole progenitor of hip-hop. Herc did not invent the various components that would become the new social and cultural entity known as hip-hop. Nor was he significant because he single-handedly brought together components of hip-hop that already existed. Though Herc clearly made important contributions, the context was also important. Herc represents the beginning of hip-hop, or, as described by another pioneering figure, DJ Disco Wiz, "the main hip-hop entrepreneur," because of the serendipitous merger between the social and cultural conditions in which he lived and his (socially constituted) personal characteristics. He was perfect for the times, and the times were perfect for him.

2 South Bronx DJs vs. Other DJs

After Herc, Afrika Bambaataa and Grandmaster Flash were the next two DJs to become well known in the South Bronx. It was not inevitable, as hip-hop folklore would have us believe, that Bambaataa should follow Herc, and that Flash should follow Bambaataa. After Herc, others attempted to use DJing to gain fame, but none approached Herc's level of success, partially because they did not follow his DJing style—their styles tended towards those of Manhattan DJs. This chapter investigates how and why they, like Herc, achieved fame among their peers, and why these three defined the South Bronx DJing scene.

The first section of the chapter traces Bambaataa and Flash's beginnings in hip-hop. Using biographical portraits of Bambaataa and Flash established in previous hip-hop historiography, I draw attention to the unique skill sets and dispositions they brought with them. But I add to what we already know by providing more intimate details about their lives gleaned from MoPOP's interviews with Afrika Bambaataa and Grandmaster Flash. By revisiting their biographies, I highlight the range of symbolic resources from which hip-hop was created. While chapter 1 addressed the influence of macro-level structural forces (i.e., socioeconomic context) and meso-level institutional and cultural forces that converged in the creation of hip-hop (i.e., gang organizations and youth culture), this chapter delves into micro-level influences (i.e., family life, dispositions, repertoires, and worldviews) that played a role in its formation.

The chapter's second section looks at DJing scenes in Harlem, Brooklyn, and Queens. The stories it includes, for the most part, have never been published and thus have not been part of popular narratives about the emergence of hip-hop. The scenes in Brooklyn and Queens were more mature than the one in the Bronx, and their DJs fashioned themselves after Manhattan DJs. Because non-white DJs dominated the music scenes in Harlem, Brooklyn, and Queens, the much younger South Bronx DJs looked up to them and, in several instances, even apprenticed with them. At the same time, though, because these DJs were more connected to Manhattan discos, South Bronx DJs defined themselves against them.

I have been referring to various DJing "scenes" in New York.[1] Before moving on to consider Bambaataa and Flash, I'd like to pause here to explain how I'm using the term "scene." The concept is akin to that of the "subculture," which gained prominence in both American and British cultural studies during the late 1970s and early 1980s.[2] Subcultures, especially among youth, are often viewed as deviant because they reject mainstream (and, implicitly, "adult") culture.[3] In this work, I opt for the term "scene" instead of "subculture" to minimize the connotation of deviance.[4] (Graffiti writers, for example, were viewed as deviant and thus were part of a subculture. DJs were not.) When fully developed, a scene is a social arena in which actors gather to express themselves about something that matters to them, to establish conventions regarding those expressions, and to compete for fame and notoriety. In this sense, scenes are related to Pierre Bourdieu's concept of "fields."[5] Like Howard Becker's "art worlds," scenes often need various kinds of members.[6] In the DJing scene, there are actors who have financial interests (i.e., club owners); those who must be present for the show to go on (i.e., the DJs); and those for whom the show exists (i.e., the audience).[7] In John Irwin's theorization, most of which I endorse, scenes are places and spaces where people enter, often voluntarily, for "direct rather than future gratification."[8] Therefore, scenes rely heavily on intense interaction. They often occur in public and visible places but are reserved for those who actively invest value in the given thing or activity that animates the scene—for instance, music, exercise, or sports. In what follows, I demonstrate that hip-hop became a scene in the South Bronx because its DJs distinguished themselves and their sound from DJing scenes in other parts of New York City. I also offer a sociological explanation of how social and cultural entities begin.

Bambaataa

Afrika Bambaataa is a towering, eccentric figure in the history of hip-hop, even more so than Herc. His real name, Lance Taylor, was until recently a mystery—some scholars incorrectly list Kevin Donovan as his real name. Taylor was born in Manhattan to parents who had emigrated from Jamaica and Barbados. When his family moved to the Bronx, they settled in an apartment on the ground floor of the fifteen-story Bronx River Projects. He was raised by his mother in a home rich with ideas from the international black cultural and liberation movements. Influenced by his family's faith—many were practicing Muslims—and by the beliefs of his uncle Bambaataa Bunchinji, a black nationalist, he became attuned to black politics. As he recalls, "Hearing the teachings of the Most Honorable Elijah Muhammad, Malcolm X, Minister Farrakhan, the Black Panther Party, and seeing a lot of the struggles that was going on all around the world through television, with the Woodstock era, the Flower Power movement, the Vietnam War, Lyndon B. Johnson—all that gave a lot of hope to this area to do something for itself."[9]

Bambaataa has repeatedly mentioned that another major influence besides his uncle was the 1964 film *Zulu,* a reenactment of the intense 12-hour battle fought in 1879 between a few hundred British soldiers and 4,000 Zulu war warriors in South Africa. "At that time we was coons, coloreds, negroes, everything degrading," he remarked. "Then I see this movie come out showing Africans fighting for a land that was theirs against the British imperialists. To see these black people fight for their freedom and their land just stuck in my mind. I said when I get older I'm gonna have me a group called the Zulu Nation."[10] Perhaps following his uncle, or perhaps paying homage to Mbata Bhambatha—a Zulu chief of the amaZondi clan who led a rebellion against the British to protest tax increases—he called himself Bambaataa. As a graffiti writer, he used different variations of this name: BAMBAATAA, BAM 117, and BOM 117. The sociocultural sea changes of the 1960s and his family's political orientation were foundations of his sense of self, which he would bring with him into the burgeoning DJing scene in the South Bronx.

A teenager of his time and place, Bambaataa was involved in gang culture.[11] By the age of thirteen, he had become initiated into the Bronx River Projects division of the Black Spades street gang in the Southeast Bronx. Though a young member, he quickly earned the respect of Black Spades leaders by fearlessly traveling through the territories of rival gangs. He rose to the rank of War Lord in his chapter and in this role was responsible for increasing membership and expanding the gang's turf. As War Lord, he placed himself in the center of the most intense episodes of gang violence:

> Little wars could start if you just look at another person or woman wrong, or you stepped on somebody's sneaker or their shoe. Or you just made a bump, or touched a person at the wrong time or the wrong place, or even if you said certain words that another group didn't like, that could have led into a full-fledged war, and violence could have sprung up all over the Bronx and it could have spread into

FIGURE 2.1 Afrika Bambaataa. (© David Corio; used with permission)

Manhattan and then into other parts of the city because the Black Spades, the Savage Nomads, and the Savage Skulls had chapters throughout the whole city and even in other states and towns.[12]

Bambaataa was successful in his post. As a leader, he brought together various chapters of the Spades in the Bronx and started new chapters in other boroughs. He took pride in his ability to organize and expand his gang's territories. Nonetheless, the activities of the gangs were, in many ways, at odds with the tenets of his Muslim faith and the teachings of the black political organizations he admired. So in 1972, he welcomed an opportunity to break away from gang activity.

When the gangs came together to sign a peace treaty putting an end to the violence their neighborhoods had become accustomed to, Bambaataa was in the room. A fervent believer in the peace talks, he thought of several ways to move the message forward. He knew that even though all the major organizations had agreed to seek peaceful resolution to conflict, they would not necessarily all abide by the treaty. Moreover, even if the organizations lived up to the terms of their pact, there was little guarantee that individuals would put an end to violent behavior, so he assumed responsibility for ensuring that the peace treaty would accomplish what it had set out to do. He sought to do so through DJing.

Because of Herc's rise to stardom, DJs were becoming the new standard for cool, and several former gang members, like ex-Black Spades Kool DJ Dee and Disco King Mario, quickly went in that direction. However, they did not follow Herc's "break-centered" DJing technique; instead, they preferred the "song-centered" DJing technique used by DJs outside the Bronx. Bambaataa also became a DJ, but his transition was not so sudden: "I started DJin' in 1970 . . . well, not with the two turntables and the mixers[.] [W]hat we had is that you went and got your mother's set or your father's set. You had one guy that was set up on this side of the room, and I was set up on another side. We had a flashlight, so if he was playing the Jackson Five's 'I Want You Back,' when his record was going down low, he would flash at me, and that would give me the time to put on maybe 'Stan' or 'Everyday People' by Sly and the Family Stone. And that's how we started DJin' back and forth before they came with the two turntables and a mixer."[13]

Bambaataa sought to do more than just entertain his audience, though. It was time to take all that was in his head—the speeches of Malcolm X, the beliefs of the Nation of Islam, and the rhythms of James Brown—and externalize it, institutionalize it in an organization he controlled. The following year,

Bambaataa formed the Bronx River Organization, which became known, simply, as "the Organization." This was its motto:

> This is an organization.
> We are not a gang.
> We are a family.
> Do not start trouble.
> Let trouble come to you, then fight like hell.[14]

Even as Bambaataa explicitly distinguished his organization from gangs, it is obvious that his desire and ability to organize came from gang culture, and presumably he organized and led in a similar manner. (If there were no similarity there would have been no reason to state that his organization was not a gang.)

Given his reputation as a former Spades War Lord, Bambaataa already had a following, so his parties attracted considerable attention. Although he had neither high-quality speakers nor a unique technique, he did have an immense and eclectic record collection. About his taste in music, he says, "I have to give credit to my mother. She had a taste for sound that was extraordinary." In saying this, Bambaataa points to what sociologist Tia Denora describes as "mixing text with context."[15] For him, music's importance went beyond the beats and the melodies; he also understood the events of his biography and the development of his sensibilities through music. He explains:

> [My mother] turned me on to knowing about Edith Piaf, Barbra Streisand, Janis Joplin. I also learned about the Rolling Stones, as well as James Brown. She bought the first 200 records. . . . I think her first record was 'Too Many Fish in the Sea,' by the Marvelettes. And after her first 200, I bought the next million. I was also into the African sounds of Miriam Makeba, the Calypso sounds of Harry Belafonte, the Mighty Sparrow, Lord Krishna, Calypso Rose. Who else was there? Jazz sounds of Les McCann, Don Cherry, Herbie Hancock. I heard it, you know, all type of things from back in the day. Even stuff from the '20s."[16]

Like northern soul DJs before him, Bambaataa prided himself on collecting and playing the most obscure records. More than anyone, he diversified the sound of the South Bronx DJing scene. Some of the music he introduced to his peers includes "Jam on the Groove" and "Calypso Breakdown" by Ralph MacDonald, "Dance to the Drummer's Beat" by Herman Kelly, "Champ" by the Mohawks, the themes from *The Andy Griffith Show* and the *Pink Panther* films, and *Trans-Europe Express*, an album by the German electronic group

Kraftwerk.[17] Even though his music was eclectic, it was in sync with Herc's DJing style, because, like Herc, he accentuated portions of the record that fueled breakdancing. "Bambaataa used to play the wildest records in the whole entire world," recalls one former b-boy. "He played stuff like Bugs Bunny—it's got a beat on it. Everybody was breakdancing to that."[18] Another early follower describes Bambaataa's musical taste: "I'll be honest with you. I hated going to Bam's parties. Bam would be playing the break beats and then would jump off and start playing calypso, or playing some reggae, or playing some rock. I was like, 'What is Bam doin'?' . . . He'd take an Aerosmith record, 'Walk This Way,' and slow it, or speed it up."[19]

His taste also amalgamated ideological stances of the time. Jeff Chang puts it best: "In the community, political positions on integration, violence, and revolution could harden into matters of life and death. But through his mother's record collection—an eclectic shelf that included Miriam Makeba, Mighty Sparrow, Joe Cuba, and Aretha Franklin—Bambaataa developed a different kind of perspective. In the rhythmic pull of James Brown's 'I'll Get It Myself' black-power turn or Sly Stone's 'Everyday People' integrationist dance, these positions lost their rigidity."[20]

Things were going well, until his cousin, Soulski, was killed by police. According to the local newspaper, the *New York Amsterdam News*, the police shot at three young men driving a 1968 Mercury because they had a gun. Allegedly, the three men, one of whom was Soulski, shot at the police and then ran into the wooded area of Pelham Parkway. The chase resulted in the deaths of two young men and left the third in critical condition. The tragedy revived some gang activity. A youth organization that included former gang members immediately declared war on the police officers who patrolled the Bronx. A month later, another fourteen-year-old was shot by Bronx police. These two events brought Bambaataa to a crossroads. While gang members urged him to join in their retaliation against the police, community leaders encouraged him to allow the justice system to run its course. To make matters worse, the courts quickly acquitted the police officers involved in both shootings. Given what they viewed as an unfair ruling, more of Bambaataa's peers joined together to strike back against the police department. Bambaataa was tempted, but he declined to take part, for he knew it was a battle they could not win. Nonetheless, these incidents motivated him to continue expanding "the Organization." He was convinced that only members of his community could improve its living conditions. Bambaataa trusted the outside world less and less and believed increasingly in the teachings of self-determination espoused by Elijah Muhammed and the Nation of Islam.

A few months before Soulski's death, Bambaataa had won an essay-writing contest sponsored by the New York Housing Authority. His reward was an all-expenses-paid trip to India. Unfortunately, he was unable to go on the trip because he failed to follow through with required pre-travel procedures. He won again the following year, 1975. This time, the prize was a trip to Europe and Africa. Like many of his peers, Bambaataa had never left the United States; for him, traveling to the African continent was a dream come true. He visited Nigeria, where he discovered Fela Kuti's music. For Bambaataa, Kuti exemplified the way to combine political ideology and music. If ever there was a link between the beginning of hip-hop and African musical traditions, this was it.

When Bambaataa returned, it was clear to his peers that the journey had influenced him immensely. He now went solely by the name Afrika Bambaataa, and "the Organization" was renamed "the Universal Zulu Nation" and dedicated to DJing, breaking, and activism, with particular attention to ameliorating violence among young people. Bambaataa's dancers—Zambu Lanier, Kusa Stokes, Ahmad Henderson, Shaka Reed, and Aziz Jackson—were now called the Zulu King Dancers, and others who held leadership positions in the Zulu Nation were known as Shaka Kings and Queens. Lucky Strike, one of the members, recalls his participation in Bambaataa's organization: "What he talked to me about in the Zulu Nation was about finding yourself, who you are. . . . They were teaching me things about my culture that I never knew and things I never learned in school."[21]

However, these messages were not well received by all of his peers. Bambaataa recalls: "You had members who were like, 'What is this? Stop all this Zulu thing. Some of [the former members of] 'the Organization' didn't like what we was doing."[22] They left to start their own organization—the Casanova Crew— but Bambaataa and his crew remained strong. They consistently packed the Bronx River Community Center.

Flash

Grandmaster Flash, born Joseph Saddler Jr., is today the most popular of hip-hop's three "founding fathers" because he had the most commercially successful career. He is also the only one among the three to have published a memoir, which provides intimate details about his childhood and the way he became part of hip-hop.[23] Flash's story is particularly interesting because he was from the Bronx but spent his early years in the Throggs Neck neighborhood. Therefore Flash was not *of* the South Bronx in the way Herc and

Bambaataa were. Because of this, the skills and dispositions he brought to South Bronx DJing were not rooted in the socioeconomic context of the South Bronx. Nonetheless, they aligned with the logic of the emerging scene.

From early on, Joseph Saddler was fascinated with records. One Tuesday afternoon, when he was about seven years old, he climbed on a dining room chair to reach the records on the top shelf of his father's closet—that is where his father kept his favorite James Brown records. Carmetta and Penny, his older sisters, were home but in their bedroom. His mother, Gina, and another sister, Lilly, were at a doctor's office. His father was at work. None of his siblings quite understood why Joseph messed with his Dad's records, especially since he always received some sort of punishment when caught, sometimes corporal. "It was something I just had to do," he would explain to them. He was not quite tall enough to reach the records on the top shelf even if he stood on his toes with his arms stretched as high as they would go. Desperate, he hopped up to grab one of the records. Unfortunately, the record next to the one he managed to get his hands on was knocked to the floor, and it shattered. It was Billy Eckstine's 'Jelly Jelly,' an old 78 shellac disc. Just as he gathered himself to pick up the pieces, his father entered the door shouting, "Who's in my closet? Who's messing with my records?"

Joseph Saddler Sr. worked at Penn Central Railroad. He was returning home from work early that day. As soon as he opened the door, he saw his record closet open and his son on the floor picking up pieces of a shattered record. Usually he gave Joseph Jr. whippings for touching his records, but on this occasion anger overtook him. He grabbed his son by his neck, dragged him from the closet, and slapped him across the face.[24] A boxer and runner, Saddler Sr. was physically fit and knew how to hit. The strength of the blow threw the young boy across the room. Joseph Jr. lost consciousness. When he awoke, it was to a terrifying scene. "Mommy was screaming and Lilly was crying," he recalls. "There was blood all over the front of my shirt and [my ears were ringing.]" Apparently, when his mother, who returned home shortly after the incident, try to intervene in the beating, Joseph Sr. hit her with a skillet. This was not the first time his father had hit his mother, but it was by far the worst incident. The neighbors called the police. "The cops knew where we lived, and by then, my father knew the drill—he skipped out before they came, leaving them to deal with Mommy. Disappearing back into the street life, back into the bars and boxing gyms he loved more than home."

This incident marked the dissolution of his parents' marriage. Joseph Sr. eventually moved out and took his record player and most of his records. "Maybe his leaving really was about me messing with his records—the man did love his music," Saddler Jr., wrote years later. "Maybe my father was jealous—I was mommy's favorite and he always said she spoiled me. Maybe he wanted out—having a family, especially a son, never seemed to make him all that happy. Or maybe he was just mean." Despite his disdain for his father, Joseph Jr. learned from him the importance of records. He had a few records of his own, but he did not have a record player on which to play them. He was desperate and wracked his brain to figure out ways to hear the music. On one occasion, he made the record spin by putting it on the wheel of his bicycle. Then he got a needle from his mother's sewing kit and held it in the groove of the record. The music did not come out as he had hoped, but he heard something. The next step was to figure out how to amplify the sound.

A few weeks before Christmas 1965, Joseph's mother came home with a record player and a few Nat King Cole records. Joseph was thrilled. Now he could play the records as much as he wanted without any repercussions. "I remember listening to Nat sing 'The Christmas Song' over and over again. No violence. No drama. No yelling." As he sat watching the needle run through the groove, he became mesmerized by the way the system worked. Between the thin lines lay the sounds of drums, guitar, vocals, and bass lines, and he was determined to get them out. He no longer loved playing records simply because he liked hearing the music; he also wanted to understand the technology of the record player. This fascination with the technical aspects of record playing, born mostly out of necessity, stayed with him and guided him when he became part of the South Bronx DJing scene.

The family got along well without Saddler Sr. until Joseph's mother, Gina, began showing signs of mental and emotional instability. The beatings she had received at the hands of her former husband had begun to take a toll. "One minute everything would be okay, and then she'd be screaming at the top of her lungs. . . . And it wasn't just screaming either. Mom got violent. Never to me or my sisters, but to anyone else who caught her on the wrong minute," Joseph recalls.[25] Things quickly went from bad to worse. The neighbors frequently called the police, and when they arrived, Gina fought with them. On several occasions, an ambulance came and she was hauled away in a straitjacket. Eventually, she was hospitalized, and Gina's sister took the kids in. When it became clear that their mother could no longer care for them and would likely remain hospitalized indefinitely, the children were separated from their mother and placed in a series of foster homes around New York City. The children disliked their foster homes so much that they often ran away, met at a park, and headed back to their real home, the Bronx. Each time, white vans would pick them up and return them to their respective foster homes, but soon enough they would leave again. Frustrated with this behavior, a case worker separated Joseph, Lilly, and Penny from Carmetta and placed them with a family in Millbrook, New York. Although it was only eighty miles from the Bronx, to them it felt like they had moved to a different country.

For five years, from 1966 to 1971, they lived in Millbrook and went to Greer School. It was home, but not quite *their* home. For Joseph, the worst part was that he did not have access to the music he loved. "Kids were into music, but it was stuff like the Byrds, the Beatles, and Jimi Hendrix. That stuff was cool, especially Hendrix, but as funky as the radio got was the Isley Brothers, and the Temptations, and Aretha, and I already knew that stuff backwards and forwards." Still, he never passed up the opportunity to serve as the DJ at high-school dances.

The children returned to the Bronx when their mother was released from Pilgrim Psychiatric Center. The reunited family moved to the South Bronx. Even though Joseph was happy to be with his mother again, he had to readjust to yet another life. Gina had become a strict Christian who insisted that all her children follow in the path of Jesus. The two older daughters were now Jehovah's Witnesses, and they dragged their younger brother to Kingdom Hall for worship. And their Aunt Mary, who, before foster care, watched them when their mother was not well, took them to the synagogue from time to time.

Outside the home, Joseph faced a similar challenge. He was unfamiliar with his environment, not only because he had been away for a few years but also because he no longer lived in Throggs Neck. He now lived on 163rd and Fox Streets in the South Bronx, a block away from the police department's 41st Precinct Station House on Simpson Street, nicknamed "Fort Apache." In this neighborhood, the Savage Skulls, the Black Pearls, and the Black Spades ran rampant, and junkies roamed the littered streets. "Just like Greer had been a whole other world for me, now the Bronx was a whole other world all over again. 'How come you sound like you're white?' the other kids would ask. I'd been away when my peers were learning how to walk, talk, and act on the streets. The Greer school kept me innocent." Joseph attempted to fit in by joining a gang, but he quickly dropped out: it was not his thing. From the perspective of the gang leaders, he was not their type either. He then tried his hands at writing graffiti. "Because of the trains, [graffiti-writers] were known and respected all over the city. They had to be, dangerous as it was. You couldn't help but bow down for what it took to be out there." He wanted the same notoriety, so he started tagging. His graffiti alias was FLASH 163.

The first part was a nickname he had received from his friend Gordon Upshaw. They both liked Flash Gordon, the cartoon character, and since his friend was already named Gordon, Joseph went by Flash, which also fit because he was a fast runner. Following convention, he added 163, the number of the street he lived on. Saddler's graffiti name provides another example of how South Bronx DJs' use of pseudonyms—as discussed above, a unique attribute among New York DJing scenes—came from their affiliation with graffiti culture. Unfortunately, Joseph was not good at graffiti. "When I saw [my tag] on the wall, it looked like shit. I couldn't get the letters to make the same shapes comin' out of the spray can. I couldn't get the spacing down so that it looked right." His tags would be crossed out by other writers and labeled HOT 110, which signified that he was not to be taken seriously. "Maybe God didn't want me to be a graffiti artist," he concluded, "But that didn't mean that I didn't feel those dudes. They spoke to me louder than ever, just not in my language. I had to find a language of my own."

Flash returned to the two interests that had remained constants in his life, music and electronics. As he got older, his passion for the latter increased: "I had this habit of wanting to know how the internal workings of things operated. Like I would take apart my sisters' radios, hair dryers. I'd go behind the washing machine. I'd go in my mother's stereo in the living room, you know? And I was getting beat for all these things, so in me doing this, my mother decided to send me to technical school."[26]

He went to Samuel Gompers Vocational and Technical High School in the Bronx. There, Flash could ask all the questions he wanted about how stereos operated. "Other kids there might have been passing the time, but I loved it. The teachers had answers. They knew the functions of all the colorful boxes, bubbles, and blobs inside the phonograph." They also challenged him to build things. For one assignment, he had to create a tube amplifier from scratch. Then he set his ambitions even higher, setting out to build an entire sound system. He did not have money or a job, so he roamed about junk yards searching for parts.

Out and about looking for what he needed, Flash befriended E-Z Mike, who introduced him to Monkey George and OJ: "One of the things that made us tight was music. Those guys were into the same jams I was. I remember OJ playing the Ohio Players' *Fire* LP for me[,] and I thought I'd died and gone to heaven. Truman hit me with the Jacksons' *Lookin' Through the Windows*, and Mike saved the best for last with Stevie Wonder's *Innervisions*; the sounds Stevie spun out were strange and lovely and went straight from my ear to my heart."

Flash's new friends were also dancers. In fact, the first time he saw someone break was E-Z Mike. Flash developed a few moves and tried to join Mike's dance crew, but he got rejected. He was not good enough. Again, his attempt to be part of the newly emerging social activities among his peers failed, so he went back to electronics. Eventually, though, this interest collided with the DJing scene when Flash attended a Herc and Bambaataa jam.

On his way back from school one day, Flash overheard a conversation between two neighborhood friends who sat across from him on the train. "You missed it," one exclaimed to the other. "This girl Cindy threw a birthday party over on Sedgwick Avenue. Her brother's a slammin' DJ with a killer sound system. You woulda been all over that ass!" What made the party so special, he continued, was that the DJ did not play the whole record; he played only the part that everyone wanted to hear. Intrigued by what he heard, Flash sought out the next Kool Herc party.

That party took place on May 25, 1974, at Cedar Park Recreation Center. Flash walked about ten blocks to get there. As he got closer, sounds from Herc's system became audible. "I was two full blocks from the park jam[,] and it was only an hour into the night, but, already, it was loud. Really fucking loud. I could name the tune he was playing; it was 'The Mexican' by Babe Ruth. . . . I had never heard sound—let alone music—that loud in my whole life." As he got closer, he began to feel the sound reverberating in his body. "There must have been a thousand people getting down to his music. Folks from four to forty, sweating and bouncing, breakin' and popping, doing the pancake and getting buck wild." The older folks busted out their old-school dances while the younger crowd showcased their breakdance moves. When he got close enough to the front, he saw the person responsible for it all: responsible for this approach to playing music; responsible for taking people out of their hardships, however brief; and responsible for allowing the kids to be kids and run around and act silly. "Herc stood six [feet] and some change. With his Afro and the butterfly collar on his AJ Lester leisure suit turned up, he looked even bigger. He was a god up there, the red and blue party lights behind him pulsing away on that big thumping beat." Flash inched closer to observe what Herc was doing, how he chose his records, how he played his records, when he played which record. "By the end of the party," he remembers, "my whole universe had shrunk down to one single thing." He was going to be a DJ. He and his friends became avid followers of Herc. His friends went to jams to dance and hang with the girls, but Flash went to observe the DJ, his techniques, his relationship to the crowd, and the equipment he used. He was obsessed with figuring out how DJing equipment operated.

When he became a DJ, he called himself Grandmaster Flash—the "Grandmaster" title came from a famous DJ in Brooklyn, Grandmaster Flowers. Flash sought to use his technical knowledge to make a mark in South Bronx DJing: "My thing was, to every great record, there's a great part. This is what we used to call 'the get down part.' This is before it was tagged 'the break'; it was called the 'get down part.' And this particular part of the record[,] . . . unjustifiably, was maybe five seconds or less. This kind of pissed me off. I was like, 'Damn, why'd they do that?' You know? So in my mind, in the early seventies, I was picturing, 'Wow, it would really be nice if that passage of music could be extended to like five minutes.'"[27]

Moreover, Flash wanted to extend these breaks without stopping the music. He wanted to be able to move from one break to another without altering the rhythm because, when observing Herc, he noticed that "sometimes he would get lucky and have the sync right, but other times, he'd go from a slower record—say at 90 beats a minute—to a faster one that was bouncing at 110." This was not ideal for the dancers. "If you looked at the crowd that moment between the songs, everybody fell off the beat for a few seconds. They'd get back on it again, but in those few seconds you could see the energy and the magic start to fade from the crowd."

Flash developed a way of mixing music that would extend the break and maintain the rhythmic flow. He called it the "Quick Mix Theory."[28] Before officially debuting it, he experimented with it at little park jams with his friends E-Z Mike and Disco Bee, who were breakdancers. "I wasn't there yet, but I knew if I could tweak the peak of the beats, I could do a whole lot more than the average DJ. Doing it better than the average DJ meant I could distinguish myself and even outdo Herc—he was still the man to beat." People started to know about Flash, just from the little DJing he was doing, and he started to gain a following. Among his fans were former gang members. To ensure that Flash had what he needed to continue throwing parties and thereby perfect his skills, former Black Spades who followed him "got" two Thorens TD-125C turntables from someone at Hunt Points Palace and gave them to him.[29]

In the summer of 1975, the new technique was ready. Flash had the right records, and, to make sure he knew where the funky breaks began, he marked their starting points on the records with a pencil. After hours of practice, he mastered all the different components of the Quick Mix Theory: the punch phase (also known as the "Clock Theory")—isolating short segments of one record and rhythmically "punching" them over the sustained beat of another record; the spin back—prolonging a break beat by reversing the rotation of

FIGURE 2.2 Grandmaster Flash at the wheels of steel, 1999. (© Mika-photography; used under the Creative Commons Attribution-Share Alike 3.0 Unported license)

the record; and the scratch phase—making a transition from one record to another by scratching while simultaneously maintaining the beat.

The day finally came to debut his DJing inventions. It was in early July at 23 Park on 166th Street and Tinton Avenue. In front of an exuberant crowd, he performed his new techniques. He was a bit nervous and wanted to make sure he executed all the moves perfectly, and he did. He transitioned from one break to another with the scratch phase. He punctuated jam favorites with the punch phase and, with the spin back, made certain break beats last longer than they ordinarily do. He knew he was killing it. With a big grin on his face, he glanced quickly at the crowd, expecting to see them going wild. He was disappointed; most were staring right back at him. They were dumbfounded. Instead of dancing, they were curious about what he was doing and how he was doing it. Flash put his head back down again and kept mixing, trying to focus on the techniques and catch the breaks at the right spots. Then he took a second look at the people. Again, most of them were looking up at him. This was not what was supposed to happen. They were supposed to be dancing.

Instead of fueling the dancers' energy, his new technique made the crowd stop dancing because what he was doing was so novel. They were intrigued by the way he seamlessly shifted from one funky beat to another without interrupting the beat. Because they were used to the sudden rhythmic interruption when a DJ moved from one song to another, Flash's technique, which was supposed to allow for smoother dancing, actually, and ironically, disrupted their routine. The audience stopped dancing to look up at him to see how he was doing it. It was not the kind of attention Flash sought. In fact, because his technique stopped the dancing, he would be considered a failure, since a DJ's sole task is to keep people dancing. Utterly embarrassed, he hurried through the rest of his routine and got offstage.

After this flop, Flash decided to give up DJing. He stopped going to the parties held at the nearby parks; he stopped messing with records; and he stopped playing around with his stereo. He was done, until an elderly woman who lived around the corner from him, Ms. Rose, noticed his absence and approached him to ask where he had been. He explained that he was no longer interested in DJing because his event did not go as he had hoped. While sympathetic to his feelings, Ms. Rose encouraged him, even insisted that he continue DJing. To further lend her support, she set up an appointment for Flash to meet Pete DJ Jones, an older disco DJ in the South Bronx. At the meeting, Jones convinced Flash not to give up. He even invited him to play at one of his parties in the park. Flash accepted. It was the biggest stage he had ever performed on. At the event, he mustered the courage to try his technique once more. Jones, observing his skills, responded with the kind of excitement that Flash had initially hoped for. He was so impressed that he took Flash on as a mentee and invited him to play in twenty-one-and-older clubs with him even though Flash was not old enough to get into these venues on his own. With Jones, Flash's love for DJing was rekindled, and he gained valuable performance experience. He also learned an important lesson about DJing. "It's not about you, Flash," Jones told him. "It's about the energy that *they* [the audience] got. They give it to you . . . you give it back to them stronger and again and again and again. That's how it works."

After his "internship" with Jones, Flash returned to the Bronx scene. He was more popular now as a DJ, but he still had to prove himself to the younger break-centered DJing scene. Flash's name travelled throughout the South Bronx neighborhoods, but he was not nearly as well known as Bambaataa, let alone Herc.

Other DJing Scenes

There existed in Brooklyn, Queens, and Harlem, in neighborhoods with socioeconomic conditions similar to those in the South Bronx, other DJing scenes that predated those in the South Bronx.[30] (The three scenes differed, but Brooklyn and Queens overlapped with one another a great deal.) Prior to the 1970s, DJs in these locales performed in parks and local clubs. The DJs in Brooklyn, Queens, and Harlem enjoyed followings that were even larger than those of Herc or Bambaataa. They were not as popular or as established as the ones in Manhattan, but they were more popular than the South Bronx DJs. Unlike those in Manhattan, they were mostly non-white—predominantly African American, Caribbean, and Latino; and, unlike the South Bronx DJs who were in their mid-teens, they were in their late teens and early twenties. How else did these other scenes differ from those in the South Bronx? More important, why do we not consider these other DJing scenes to be the site of hip-hop's creation?

One of the first well-known DJs from Brooklyn was Grandmaster Flowers, whose given name is Jonathan Cameron Flowers. Raised in the Farragut Houses project, he started DJing in junior high school in 1967 at places like the 243 Club on Flatbush and Myrtle Avenues. He also played at Washington Park during Labor Day West Indies parades, often going up against beloved West Indian musicians. While they played steel drums, Flowers blasted club music on his turntables. He was known for his diverse taste in music and his ability to hold a crowd's attention even playing music they had never heard. One early follower remembers: "Everyone would play the 'A' side, but Flowers would play the 'B' side as well."[31] Perhaps more than that of his contemporaries, Flowers' taste in music drove his performance. "Flowers was sort of like a Jimi Hendrix," another Brooklyn DJ notes. "[H]e would do everything and you were always learning from him." Harlem DJ Reggie Wells, a great admirer of Flowers, adds, "[Flowers] was incredible, what he used to do, he would play with a record; he would take the bass out of a record; he could turn the vocals down and bring them back in. . . . That man was creative with mixing. Not everybody can do that."[32] For other DJs in this scene, music was not always the most important concern.

Nu Sounds, a DJing group from the East Elmhurst neighborhood of Queens, were different from Flowers. They valued the sound system more than the music that came out of it. Inspired by the 1974 motion picture *Earthquake*, which used Sensurround technology, Ricky Grant and his brother, who made up Nu Sounds, built what they considered to be the "best sound system in the city." They called their invention "earthquake speakers." "When we said we had 5000 watts of power pushing our system, that was no exaggeration," J.D.—the MC for Nu Sounds—confirms.[33] Their obsession set the audio-technology standard for their scene. Donny Lawrence, popularly known as Dance Master, also helped to establish the importance of the sound system in the Brooklyn and Queens DJing scene. He did not build his own system but instead employed the services of Richard Long, a respected technician who had earned a master's degree in mechanical engineering from the California Institute of Technology and built the sound systems at Studio 54 and the Loft—both popular spots in Manhattan. Donny was the first to have the mobile versions of Richard Long's Bertha speakers. By the mid-1970s, he had moved up from playing in the parks to playing at swanky Manhattan disco clubs like Paradise Garage and Silver Palace.

And then there was DJ Plummer. He did not become interested in DJing until his early 20s, after graduating from college in 1972.[34] He worked at an audio store called Audio Exchange (later renamed Harvey Sounds) in Brooklyn, where he mingled with sound engineers who frequented the place. Plummer recalls: "I did not know what I wanted to do, didn't have a career or anything in mind, but I picked up on a lot of the technical aspects of the equipment we were selling. A lot of sales engineers would come in so I would listen[,] and I would have a keen interest in some of the stuff. I don't remember the sequence of events but I met this guy who often came into the store and bought equipment and we hit it off. We called him Action Jackson."

Jackson was a handyman who was technically savvy enough to build anything. He and Plummer became fast friends. Jackson introduced Plummer to the party scene in Brooklyn. Plummer had often heard the parties advertised on the radio while in high school, but because he was raised in a strict military family, he had never been allowed to attend them. Jackson convinced Plummer to check out a DJ named Maboya at Riis Beach. "I got really interested and went down there one time. . . . I never heard him before that day, but all I could see was this sea of people on the beach just dancing, rocking, and having a good time to this mostly Caribbean music played by him." Though impressed by Maboya's command of the crowd, Plummer was more interested in Maboya's equipment and the way it was set up. He and Jackson immediately noticed that the DJ did not properly wire his system. "Maboya was running a couple hundred feet of zip cord (18-gauge wire) for power [;] we knew that was part of the problem why his sound didn't sound anywhere near as good as it should. Plus[,] he just didn't have the right equipment for outdoors at the beach." Plummer knew that with Jackson's help he could put out a better sound than Maboya's. This was what motivated him to become a DJ—not the music, not the crowd, not the fame, but the sound.

Plummer and Jackson put their money and their minds together to build a sound system. First, they built six- and seven-foot folded horn bass enclosures. Then they purchased 18-inch Cerwin Vega speakers that could manage

500 watts in each. Finally, they put together a rack of Phase Linear power amplifiers. In addition to creating a powerful sound system, Plummer wanted to improve upon Maboya's music transitioning. Instead of playing one song after another as Maboya was doing, he wanted to mix the songs the way DJs in Manhattan's gay clubs did. There, the DJs used two turntables and a mixer to fade one music track into another. To replicate this, Plummer and Jackson bought an inexpensive semi-professional Tascam mixer. They had little idea of what music they would play, but, whatever it was, they knew it would sound good.

When their system was ready, Action Jackson and Plummer went back to Riis Beach to play alongside Maboya one Sunday afternoon. The agreement was that Maboya would go on first and Plummer would follow. Plummer recalls, "Everybody [was] coming around [to see Maboya] and looking at our equipment and wondering, 'Who the heck are these guys and what the heck is all this equipment?' We had not played anything yet." Maboya went on and, as usual, did his thing. "Maboya is Panamanian so he really had more of a Caribbean aspect to his music," Plummer recalls. His followers responded enthusiastically. Then Plummer's turn came. The crowd had no idea what to expect from the rookie DJ, but when he turned on his system, they were immediately blown away by the sound. What he played did not really matter to them because his system brought out musical detail they had never heard. It rendered with uniformly good resolution the hi-hats, drums, bass, and vibrant horn sections of the records Plummer played. The sound was not only louder but also crisper. It was as if the musicians were performing right in front of the crowd. "I have to say I felt bad about it later on," Plummer remembers. "When we turned our system on, the difference was like night and day[;]. . . the quality was unbelievable." He explains further: "The one thing Jackson and I agreed to after we heard Maboya and after listening to a couple of other folks, we agreed that some people had loud systems but they distorted the sound. See, they would just turn their system up so loud that they would become distorted and hurt your ears. We said that we are going to make sure our sound is loud but very clean and not distorted. We can turn it up so loud that you can walk past our bass speakers and your pants leg would ruffle but your ears would not be ringing at the end of the night." Plummer put on a good show that night. Although his musical selections were not noteworthy, his remarkable sound kept the audience dancing.

Afterward, he became the talk of the town. "I remember the next day Frankie Crocker saying on the radio program that there was this guy down there at Riis Beach named Ron Plummer and that 'you could hear the music coming off the bridge.' And that was where I got my name, 'Ron Riis Beach Plummer,' from.'" This brought Plummer to the attention of party promoters all over Brooklyn. They all wanted to book him, and his sound system, at their spot. Now at the center of the DJing world in Brooklyn, Plummer had to learn more about music. He followed the career of the great disco DJ Larry Levan, whom he had met through Richard Long, in order to stay abreast of the most recent popular music in Manhattan clubs. Plummer also joined David Mancuso's record pool so he was able to receive demo records directly from companies, especially those coming from Philadelphia—such as MFSB's anthem "Love Is the Message."

While in high school, the Disco Twins, a DJ duo from Queens, frequented Plummer's store, Harvey Sounds, to watch demonstrations on how to wire sound systems.[35] This knowledge helped them tremendously when they became DJs, and they helped raise the prominence of the sound system. They also befriended Richard Long (through their mentor Curtis Forte), who supplied them with top-notch sound equipment. "Sometimes [Long] would get stuff to test it[.] [H]e would say, 'Hey, try this out and bring it back.' Something like that," Reggie explains.[36] With brand-new equipment to experiment with, the Disco Twins always had the sharpest sound, and thus they were able to compete with other prominent players in the scene. They were also known for their showmanship—running around turntables or spinning records behind their backs—but everyone came to hear their speakers.

Beyond the eccentric music, as in the case of Grandmaster Flowers, and the sound system, as in the case of Plummer and the Disco Twins, this scene was also popular for the way the DJs talked over the music. Many say this practice began with KC Prince of Soul, Grandmaster Flowers' MC. But KC says he was just imitating Hank Spann from New York City's WWRL radio station: "Hank used to say, '*Put your foot on the rock, pat it and don't you dare stop now. This is Hank Spann wheeling and dealing from now until . . .*' And everything Hank would say, I would write it down. And I'd get my tape recorder and imitate what Hank would say."[37]

Harlem's DJ Hollywood, the forerunner of the club scene in Harlem during the early 1970s, was even better known than KC for talking over the records he played. Hollywood left home in 1971, at age 14, because, as he put it, he did not see eye-to-eye with all his mother's rules.[38] He lived in after-hours clubs in Harlem and supported himself by running errands for the clubs' patrons. A constant during parties, he became a fan of a DJ named WT: "[WT] had the two turntables and a mic mixer, with no cueing; see, what he would do was, between the records, as one went off and the other came on, he would talk. I really liked his delivery." Listening to WT's performance night after night, Hollywood imagined himself moving the crowd as the DJ did, so he mustered the courage to try it. Through his networks, he secured a couple of gigs, but initially he lacked the skills to stand out. As part of the DJing circuit, he met many other, more experienced DJs who mentored him. A DJ named Boojangles, for example, opened up Hollywood's musical taste and taught him how to mix. "He played soul and disco stuff. Stuff like 'Knock on Wood' [by Eddie Floyd], 'Melting Pot' [by Booker T. and the MGs], and Johnnie Taylor's 'Who's Making Love,' stuff like that." What interested Hollywood most, however, was not the actual DJing techniques; it was the talking over records. Hollywood recalls: "I was a singer before I ever became a DJ. I had a natural flair for talking over the records. Before me, everybody was just announcing. I had a voice. I used to like the way Frankie Crocker would ride a track, but he wasn't syncopated to the track though. I liked Hank Spann too. . . . Guys back then weren't concerned with being musical. I wanted to flow with the record. As a singer[,] that's what you're supposed to do. I guess I had a natural awareness of when to start talking and when to stop talking over a record."

When Hollywood began to gain a name, it was, as he had hoped, more for his voice than for his DJing skills. His parties were jam-packed, so he was able to sell recordings of his DJing sets: "I would record them onto 8-track tapes, and sell them for like 12 bucks a pop. I went around to barbershops and restaurants; I went anywhere where there was a bunch of brothers with money, that's where I would be at, selling my tapes." The tapes made his name travel even more quickly. By 1972, those who could afford it were paying up to $200 for a copy, and he became *the* DJ in Harlem. Kurtis Blow, an early follower who would become the first rapper to sign a contract with a major record label, describes DJ Hollywood's fame:

> Hollywood was "all city"[;] he could play anywhere he wanted in the city back then. Hollywood had a golden voice, he had a round and fat voice; he had tonality, tonality almost like a singer—he had singing routines where he would sing, *"Got a word from the wise, just to tranquilize, your mind your body and soul. We got a brand new rhythm now, and we're gonna let it take control. Come on y'all let's do it. Let's do it'*. . . . That was Hollywood, he was the master at the crowd response but, his voice . . . his voice was golden, like a God almost—that's why I wanted to be an MC!"[39]

In a conversation with hip-hop historian Mark Skillz, Hollywood explains how his rhyming skills evolved:

> One day in 1975, I was at home playing records, and one of the records I pulled out was the *Black Moses* album. It was not popular at the time. So, there I was listening to this album, and I put on a song called "*Good Love 69969*." Isaac Hayes was singing this part that went, "*I'm listed in the yellow pages, all around the world; I got 30 years experience in loving sweet young girls*." That record stopped me dead in my tracks. You see, before that record[,] I had been doing nursery rhymes. But after that record, I was doing rhymes. And not only was I doing rhymes, but I was talking about love. This was another level. I thought to myself, "What if I take what he's doing and put it with this? What would I get?" I got fame, that's what I got. I got more famous than I could've ever imagined. Everybody bit that rhyme. I would go to jams and people would be saying that rhyme, and none of them, not one of them, knew where it came from. It blew my mind.[40]

Eddie Cheeba was another well-known and respected DJ in Harlem.[41] He was inspired to become a DJ because he saw his sister's boyfriend mixing records and was fascinated. He practiced for a few years at home but eventually quit his job at a bank to take on DJing full-time. He played paying gigs here and there, but it was not until he landed jobs at spots like Charles Gallery, Hotel Diplomat, and Small's Paradise that he gained recognition in the Harlem scene. Like everyone else involved in the Harlem DJing scene, Cheeba knew about DJ Hollywood. Their paths crossed in 1975, when they played together at Club 371, a venue frequented by Harlem gangsters like Nicky Barnes and his crew. Eddie recalls, "It was Hollywood and DJ Junebug downstairs and me, Reggie Wells, and DJ EZ Gee upstairs. I'm telling you, we had them people running up and down those steps all night long."[42] The two main DJs, Cheeba and Hollywood, worked well together, so the club owners kept them both as their house DJs.

Reggie Wells and DJ Junebug also contributed to the success of Club 371. Reggie played in clubs and on the radio, but his rhyming added to Hollywood was doing. A typical Wells rhyme would might go something like this: "*This is the man with the golden voice, that talks more shit than a toilet bowl can flush, do more gigs than your grand momma wear wigs, got more clothes than you should wear pantyhose, yes baby sexy lady I hear ya hummin' I see you comin,' come on momma with your bad self, keep a pep in your step ain't no time for no half steppin.' It's W-E- double L-S, the world's exciting and most long lasting sound . . . WELLS . . . if you hear any noise, it's just Reggie Wells and the boys."*[43]

Junebug, a Puerto Rican and thus the only non-black among the DJs, was, in terms of technical skills, the best among the four. Kurtis Blow, on numerous occasions, has called him the best DJ he has ever seen.[44] With the DJ lineup of Cheeba, Hollywood, Wells, and Junebug, Club 371 became quite financially successful. Because the club earned so much, it paid its DJs well, providing them all they wanted, including a budget for their wardrobe, cars, and drivers. In Harlem, these four were on top of the DJing world.

Sites of Difference and Proto-Boundaries

A 2014 documentary titled *Founding Fathers: The Untold Story of Hip Hop* argues that the DJs in Brooklyn, Queens, and Harlem should be considered the creators of hip-hop. The filmmakers base this argument on the stylistic similarities between the Bronx DJs and those in the other boroughs—if what South Bronx DJs were doing was similar to what these other DJs were doing, then, since the scenes in Harlem, Brooklyn, and Queens had been established much earlier, they ought to be considered the beginnings of hip-hop. I disagree. I maintain that hip-hop began in the South Bronx not because of the similarities but because of the differences between Bronx DJs and other DJs.

Some, like Grandmaster Flash, claim that the difference between South Bronx DJing and DJing in other boroughs lay in the genres and styles of music played. For instance, the music played by Pete DJ Jones (and those outside of the South Bronx), the argument goes, was "sterile disco music," while Herc's music (and that of those in the South Bronx) was the "obscure funky, funky, funky music."[45] In some ways, this is true, but such a dichotomy is far too simple. There is historical evidence (that I provide below) to clarify and support the distinction that Flash, among others, makes. But it is important to note that this distinction, this sense of an "us" versus a "them," whether real or imagined, represents one of the initial glimmerings of the new entity. Even if empirical evidence proves that, in fact, participants in the South Bronx DJing scene had musical tastes similar to those in DJing scenes elsewhere in New York City, the Bronx DJs perceived a difference, and this imagined difference is one of the bases on which participants in the Bronx scene began to distinguish themselves.[46]

The truth of the matter is that DJing scenes outside the South Bronx included disco music and Top 40 records, but they also included funkier sounds. Plummer clarifies: "Now you had a lot of the Philadelphia stuff that was coming of age at that time. People were doing the hustle dance. Flowers had a broad range of stuff, but he played a lot more funk and rock than anybody else. . . Although I mixed in James Brown, Cameo, Gap Band, and lot of music similar to that kind of stuff[,] . . . I mainly stuck to a lot of the Philadelphia stuff in the beginning."[47] At Club 371, Cheeba, Hollywood, Wells, and Junebug also played songs like "Soul Makossa" by Manu Dibango, "Galaxy" by War, "Do You Wanna Get Funky With Me" by Peter Brown, and "Super Sporm" by Captain Sky.[48] Thus, according to historian Mark Skillz, "The differences [in choice of music] weren't major."[49] In his view, drawing the distinction along musical lines is hardly convincing, because, "at that time[,] damn near everything in black music was called disco." There was more to the distinction between the South Bronx scene and other scenes than merely the records they played. He explains further:

> Whereas Kool Herc called his set the "merry go round" (when he played break after break after break after break), cats in Brooklyn and Queens—i.e., Master D, the Smith Brothers, Grandmaster Flowers, King Charles, Disco Twins, Infinity Machine, and many others—were playing rhythm-and-blues and funk and soul records. They didn't specialize in rare and obscure records with five-second breaks like the Bronx cats did, but they did spin records like "Phenomenon Theme" and "Ashley's Roachclip," and when the break came on they kept it going. Not by scratching or cuttin,' but they extended the break.[50]

In other words, the difference, at least musically, between the South Bronx scene and the scenes in Harlem, Brooklyn, and Queens lay not necessarily in the kinds of records they played. It lay in *the way* they played the records. DJ Hollywood notes: "People talk about me not being hip-hop; well, it's because I spun the whole record. When the 'get down' part [or the break] would come on, I would keep it going. Herc and them guys, they practiced playing the obscure parts of records."[51] By focusing on the break beats, the South Bronx DJs separated themselves from the rest of the DJing world. This distinction is what sociological theorist Andrew Abbott would call a *site of difference*.[52]

Other sites of difference existed as well. While DJs outside the Bronx played in bigger, more established venues, the Bronx DJs, at least at the beginning, tended to stay in the Bronx and played in venues that were much smaller. DJs outside the Bronx also received a lot more money for their gigs. Eddie Cheeba comments: "Most guys back then only got $175 or $150 with a sound system to play a gig. You know what I'm saying? We got $500 an hour—without a sound system."[53] Their audiences were also not the same. "I was a club DJ downtown. . . . You had to be an adult to get into the places I played," Pete DJ Jones explains. "Therefore some guys talk about Flash, Herc, and Bambaataa because they were park DJs. . . . Anyone can go to the park, there was no age limit, but they were too young to see me."[54] The party-goers in the Bronx also dressed differently. Grandwizard Theodore, a member of the scene, remembers: "When we tried to get into Hollywood's parties, they would be like, 'Oh no! you have to have on suit jackets and shoes' and all that."[55] South Bronx partiers, by contrast, wore PRO-Ked sneakers, jeans, and mock necks to jams.

The South Bronx scene further distinguished itself by the way the audience responded to the music they heard. "I remember going to Club 371," said DJ Tony Tone, a member of the South Bronx scene, "and standing in the middle of the place, and a record with a break came on, and we started breaking, and [DJ] Hollywood . . . got on the mic and said, 'There will be no diving on the floor in here!'" Tone continued: "He stopped the music and got on the mic and said, 'get out of here with that on-the-floor bullshit' [referring to the way Tone was breakdancing]. . . . Go down the block to Flash's party with that."[56] Reggie Wells and other Harlem DJs rejected breakdancing outright because, to them, it just did not make sense. "One reason that there was no breakdancing there was because, for one thing, you couldn't dance with a young lady, and be spinning on the floor. Girls were not going for that."[57] Hollywood adds, "All that diving on the floor shit, naw, that wasn't happening. See, while you down there on the floor, some smooth cat has come along and stole your girl."[58]

I have identified five sites of difference that distinguish the DJing scene in the South Bronx from the scenes in Harlem, Brooklyn, and Queens: 1) break-centered DJing versus song-centered DJing; 2) dancing with a partner versus competitive breakdancing; 3) larger, more established, and more lucrative venues versus smaller, less established, and less lucrative ones; 4) twenty-one-and-older audiences versus twenty-one-and-under audiences; and 5) formal attire, including suits and dresses, versus casual clothes, including jeans and sneakers. These differences, by themselves, could not, and did not, generate a new social and cultural entity.[59] It was "only when they line[d] up into some kind of extended opposition along some single axis of difference" that something new, like hip-hop, arose.[60] Hip-hop emerged in the Bronx, and not in any other borough, because these various differences coalesced in the Bronx scene—that is the crucial point. The differences between the DJing scenes are themselves not surprising. When the parties thrown by Herc, Bambaataa, and Flash became popular, and the DJs themselves became well-known in their neighborhoods, the differences between the DJing scenes, and their respective clubs, began to merge. Some of the linkages occurred because actors made them happen; others fell in line on their own.

Herc began playing only the break beats of records when he realized that the audience waited to dance to particular segments of a song (site of difference 1). With his "Merry-Go-Round" technique, he was able to highlight just what they wanted to hear. Bambaataa, and especially Flash, improved upon and expanded this break-centered DJing style. The way they played music at their parties spurred a unique dancing style, what Herc called breaking (site of difference 2). The people who came to the South Bronx parties and developed this dancing style were in their early teens. They could not get into bars and clubs, so South Bronx DJs threw their parties outdoors, where everyone could attend, or in community centers, where there was no minimum age requirement (sites of difference 3 and 4). And among these young people, it was more acceptable, and perhaps more affordable, to wear jeans and sneakers than suits and dresses (site of difference 5). When this happened—when the youth of the South Bronx combined all the ways the party and DJing scene in their neighborhood differed from the party and DJing scenes in Harlem, Brooklyn, Queens, and Harlem—they created the beginnings of a symbolic boundary, a proto-boundary. That was the start of hip-hop.

The next step in our narrative is to understand how this embryonic form endured. A proto-boundary becomes a symbolic boundary similar to the way a group becomes a category, as Rogers Brubaker theorizes.[61] A proto-boundary is something loosely drawn but which has the potential to become more durable and stable. In other words, even though the merging of these sites of difference was enough to cause the foundation of something new, it was not enough to make certain that this new something would endure.

A proto-boundary endures when, within it, there emerges an internal logic, or structuring rules and conventions. I demonstrate how conventions emerged in the budding hip-hop scene in the next chapter. For now, let me quickly highlight the way Herc, Bambaataa, and Flash began to shape the rules of hip-hop. Because they were the first three DJs to gain a following in the South Bronx scene, their styles came to represent it. DJing as they did became a way to gain a name, or symbolic capital: accumulated prestige,

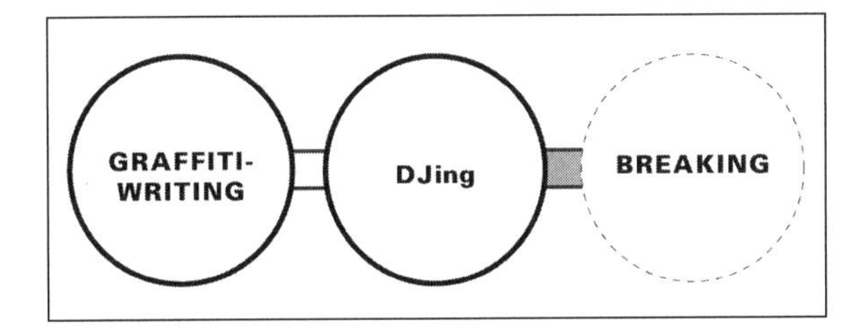

FIGURE 2.3
The Intersection of Graffiti-Writing, Breaking, and DJing.

celebrity, consecration, or honor. For example, Herc's large speakers, along with his use of the "Merry-go-round" technique to extend funky breaks, became the model for a good b-boy party. Bambaataa expanded the limits of the music that could be played: anything goes, if and only if the DJ could find the break. (These two DJs also made b-boys and girls a permanent part of their performances.) Flash's focus on seamlessly moving from one record to another, using his Quick Mix Theory, became a mainstay. All these attributes set the standard for the South Bronx DJing scene.

The continual strengthening of the proto-boundaries around this scene depended on competition among the three main DJs. If we adopt Charles Cooley's perspective, competition, or as he puts it, conflict, is simply another phase of cooperation, something that is "healthy and normal" in any social process.[62] Herc, Bambaataa, and Flash, along with the crews they formed, became identified with the neighborhoods in which they lived and threw their parties. This territoriality harkens back to the diffused gang culture. Herc resided on Sedgwick Avenue, near Jerome Avenue and Cedar Park; Bambaataa lived near Westchester Avenue and White Plains Road; and Flash lived a little further south, around Westchester Avenue and 163rd Street. They were all within a seven-mile radius of one another, and competition arose among them because the youth living in these locales wanted their respective neighborhoods to be known for throwing the best parties. The three DJs, each striving to be the best, invested more and more of their time in DJing. This intense engagement in the music combined with the competition among them became the source of their creative power—one of the things that sustained the newly forming entity. To quote Bourdieu, "the permanent struggle within the [scene] [became] the motor of the [scene]."[63] Herc, Bambaataa, and Flash are essential to the history of hip-hop because, as performers, they were the first to see value in what they fought over.

The initial stage of the development of this new social and cultural entity is visually represented in figure 2.3.

This figure and the others that follow will provide a way to keep track of the activities that make up the scene. They show how the social status of participants depended on the changing significance of each activity. DJing sits at the center because it provided the greatest social status (higher than graffiti-writing or breakdancing). Breaking was more strongly connected to DJing than was graffiti-writing—hence the dark line linking breaking and DJing. Because breaking had a stronger connection to the central activity of DJing, it offered more symbolic capital than graffiti-writing did. The popularity of the activities among the youth in the South Bronx also mattered. At this stage, graffiti-writing and DJing were thriving social activities with their own social regulations—hence the solid circle. Breaking was not as popular, as denoted by the dotted circle. However, overall popularity did not necessarily correlate with importance within the South Bronx DJing scene. Although graffiti-writing was more popular than breaking, breaking was more influential to the scene. The following chapters explore the ways each of these activities increased or decreased in popularity, how their relevance to the scene changed over time, and how these changes affected the accumulation of social status. They also trace how new activities came to be part of the scene.

PART II

The Development of an Internal Logic

3 Creating Conventions

At this juncture of the established narrative of hip-hop's early history—circa 1975—most historians jump to 1979, when the Sugar Hill Gang released "Rapper's Delight." One reason for this omission is lack of data. Herc, Flash, and Bambaataa, have been interviewed on numerous occasions, so there is an abundance of information about their contributions to the creation of hip-hop. In contrast, the stories of participants who came to prominence immediately after the three "founding" figures are known only to people who participated in New York's DJing and emergent hip-hop scenes during the second half of the 1970s. Thanks to the work of Troy L. Smith and to the MoPOP's *Oral History Project*, accounts of hip-hop can now include more information on these previously obscure years.

The stories I feature from here on include details about the South Bronx and the making of hip-hop that, for the most part, have not been published. If the three key figures mark the beginning of the process and "Rapper's Delight" represents a snapshot of the finished product, then exploring what happened in between illuminates the dynamics of formation. Looking at these years reveals how the dispositions and creativity of various actors (not only the now-canonical figures) molded hip-hop out of many possibilities and steered it toward being the particular social and cultural entity it became.

This chapter and the next feature stories about how the scratch technique was invented; how MCs became part of the scene; how DJ and MC crews were developed; how parties were thrown; how security crews came to play a significant role when parties grew violent; how hustlers became part of the scene; how battles between crews went down; how changes in youth fashion influenced the competition for fame; how former graffiti writers transformed into flier makers; how performance routines and showmanship became part of parties; how selling performance tapes influenced the race for popularity; how the 1977 New York City blackout affected the growth of hip-hop; how the term *hip-hop* itself became the name applied to cultural entity taking shape; and how other sub-entities grew out of DJing. Chapters 3 and 4 also identify several secondary figures who contributed to the making of hip-hop. Their stories show how people from different walks of life with various skill sets, dispositions, and world views entered the scene, the unique contributions they made, and the way their peers received those contributions.

By exploring these omitted years, these two chapters add to our understanding of how a new social and cultural entity emerges, how a loosely formed boundary becomes a self-perpetuating entity. While part I of this book described the beginnings of a new cultural phenomenon, part II describes the way it coalesced. While the former showed how sites of difference developed and proto-boundaries formed, the latter addresses how a certain set of relations and proto-boundaries became long lasting. These chapters show that boundaries endure when an internal logic develops within them and when that logic becomes cultural and social.

In passing, I have likened the internal logic of a scene to rules or conventions. Let me now be more precise on what I mean. Conventions are behaviors we abide by without any physical or psychological coercion and "without any direct reaction other than the expression of approval or disapproval on the part of those persons who constitute the environment of the actor."[1] Unlike laws, conventions are not enforced by a specialized agency. Instead, actors themselves buy into and regulate the terms of their submission. Sociologist Max Weber argues, "The existence of a 'convention' may . . . be far more determinative of [one's] conduct than the existence of legal enforcement machinery."[2] What acts or behaviors count as conventions? Conventions arise when the "dignity of oughtness" is conferred on repeated acts, when certain acts and conducts become expected, even required.[3]

When acts become conventions, they structure practices. Howard Becker explains that in the art world, for example, conventions "dictate the material to be used, as when musicians agree to base their music on the notes contained in a set of modes. . . . Conventions suggest the appropriate dimensions of a work, the proper length of a performance, the proper size and shape of a painting or sculpture. . . . Conventions regulate the relations between artist and audience, specifying the rights and obligations of both."[4]

In other words, conventions are implicit, internalized expectations that govern standards of behavior. Conventions make unique attributes of a given society seem natural and self-evident; they go without saying because they come without saying.[5] Conventions instill in participants a real or imagined sense of belonging and provide for participants a set of symbolic tools

TABLE 3.1 Sources of Conventions and Modes of Influence

	SOURCE OF CONVENTION	
MODE OF INFLUENCE	INTERNAL	EXTERNAL
Intentional	Acts and influences intentionally introduced from within the scene that abide by the logic of the scene	Acts and influences from outside the scene that were intentionally transported and translated into the scene via the logic of the scene
Unintentional	Acts and influences that came from within the scene but were unexpected	Acts and influences from outside the scene that unexpectedly became part of the internal logic of the scene

Source: Adapted from Victoria Johnson, *Backstage at the Revolution: How the Royal Paris Opera Survived the End of the Old Regime* (Chicago: University of Chicago Press, 2009).

(e.g., gestures, postures, languages) with which they can distinguish themselves from the outside world. Possessing this internal logic makes an entity a *cultural* entity. They also shape the dispositions of the actors involved and thereby shape the lives of participants outside of the particular world in which they are involved. This attribute makes an entity *social.*

The two chapters in part II explore how conventions arose in the South Bronx DJing scene; how conventions strengthened the boundary around the scene; and how certain conventions made the emerging entity both social and cultural. Some of the conventions came from within the scene—they were informal rules created by actors from within—while some came from outside the scene—they were informal rules incorporated from the social context in which the scene existed.[6] Among those that came from within the scene, some were intentionally introduced, while others arrived unexpectedly. The same is true for those that came from outside the scene (see table 3.1).

Demarcating the source of conventions (internal versus external) and the mode of the influence (intentional versus unintentional) gauges the autonomy of a scene. In its early stages, when it is less autonomous, a scene is easily influenced—especially unintentionally and with little regard for the logic of the scene—by the world in which it is embedded. As it becomes more autonomous and more firmly bounded, more of its conventions are intentionally introduced from within the scene, in accordance with its already established logic.

Flash, Crews, and the Rise of the MC

Herc performed by himself when he started to throw parties, but he quickly enlisted several of his peers in the shows, in part because the participation of others, especially the dancers, made his events more entertaining. Bambaataa also performed with others, perhaps a residual behavior from his participation in group-oriented gang activities. Regardless of the reason, these pioneering South Bronx DJs performed in groups or as crews, so it became expected for others in the scene to do the same. In contrast, DJs in other boroughs, though they might have worked with a team of people, did not have formal performing crews. In the sections that follow, I begin to explore how crews were formed, beginning with Grandmaster Flash's efforts to create his own crew. We see that what became a convention in hip-hop was for Flash an effort to solve a particular problem. In exploring how and why Flash found a crew, I use Troy Smith's data to confirm a story about how another convention—scratching—came about.

Grandmaster Flash's innovative mixing technique did not enhance parties as he had hoped, so he needed to find another way to move the crowd. To reintroduce his quick-mixing technique to the world, he needed a partner, or a crew, so he attempted to convert his friend and breakdance partner, Gene Livingtson, aka Mean Gene, into a DJing partner. "I really wanted him to learn this technique so that we could go out as a team and introduce this new style of DJing all throughout the city," Flash recalled.[7] He tried, repeatedly, to teach his new technique to Gene, but Gene could not master it. Ironically, Flash cultivated in Gene's brother, Theodore, who always hung around with them, a love for and skill in DJing.

Already a lover of music, Theodore would go to Downstairs Records in Manhattan to play pinball and listen to the records being played there.[8] "The guy would be playing records behind the counter. I'd be playing pinball, keeping track of what he'd be playing." He purchased the records he heard, he continues, "so when my brother would be throwing parties on the weekends, they'd have extra records to play."[9] Theodore wanted to become more involved in what Flash and Gene were doing, so he began experimenting with Gene's equipment. As he practiced with the records, he developed a knack for dropping the needle onto the specific part of the record he wished to highlight. It was as if he could see exactly where break beats began and ended in the grooves of the spinning record. Flash noticed this unique and useful skill and wanted to include Theodore in his crew, but Gene, who owned most of the equipment, adamantly refused. "I would try to convince

[him], 'Listen, I just got this feeling . . . I got this feeling that this little kid here can really make us look good,'" recalls Flash. "If we could put this little guy out in the streets along with our crew, he would really help our reputation."[10] Gene was against it, though.

There is an often-told story about how Theodore invented scratching. In an interview with Theodore, Troy Smith confirms the story. One day, Theodore was at home practicing on his brother's equipment with the volume turned all the way up. His mother, who was in another room, grew annoyed after several hours of the loud music, so she banged on the door and demanded that he decrease the volume. To try to hear what his mother was saying, Theodore put his hand on one of the turntables while the record was still spinning. "If you don't turn that music down, you're going to turn it off," she yelled. Unconsciously, he moved his hand back and forth on the record he was holding. The needle, caught between the grooves of the record, made an unfamiliar but interesting noise. Luckily, Theodore was recording the session, so, when his mother left, he played it back. He had never heard a sound quite like it on tape and was intrigued. "I practiced with it and perfected it and used it with different records," he recalled.[11] This was the accidental invention of scratching and an example of how a convention came from within the scene in an unplanned way. When Theodore eventually stepped out to be a DJ, he added the technique to his repertoire. It became a mainstay among South Bronx DJs and persists as part of hip-hop DJing to this day.

Behind Gene's back, Flash began practicing with Theodore and eventually made him part of his crew. Theodore was about thirteen years old when he first performed at 63 Park with Flash, and Gene, still a mediocre DJ, was upstaged by his younger brother. Embarrassed, Gene ended his partnership with Flash. Theodore, though grateful to Flash, left him to avoid further friction with his older brother. Flash was once again a solo performer. It seemed to him self-evident that to survive in the scene he needed a crew. Part of it was because he needed accompaniment. Another part was also that it was now almost taken for granted that DJs would perform with others. (When certain behaviors—belonging to a crew, for example—become expected, when the "dignity of oughtness" becomes conferred on such particular behaviors, it becomes a convention.)

The reaction to his Quick Mix Theory, along with his apprenticeship with Pete DJ Jones, taught Flash that he had to work harder to get the audience to move at his events. Bambaataa and Herc kept the audience moving, but in their cases, audience focus was on the dance floor and the b-boys, not the DJs on stage.[12] Flash did have a crew of dancers, the D Squad, who, according to Cholly Rock, one of the early b-boys, were good dancers, so good that he mimicked their moves. "Mele Mel, Bumpy Face Melvin and my man Fuji . . . Fuji and Mel used to do these moves and they would end up dancing on their toes. Yes, and that is where I got that from and I started dancing on my toes. Fuji and them were nuts and we use to go at it."[13] But the D Squad weren't enough impetus for the audience, who continued to stare at Flash while he played records. Flash's DJing skills were so intriguing that they drew the crowd's attention from the dance floor to the stage and the DJ. Flash knew this meant the entertainment now had to come from onstage. He hoped a good MC could help.

Like other DJs, Flash had a microphone with him when he performed, but in the South Bronx at that point, maybe 1974, it did not constitute an integral part of his performance. Grandmaster Caz, a frequent attendee at these parties, explains how DJs typically used the microphone. He also confirms that those in the crowd were in their early teens and still living at home: "The microphone was just used for making announcements, like when the next party was gonna be, or people's moms would come to the party looking for them, and you have to announce it on the mic. 'So and so, your mother's lookin' for you at the door.' You know, that kind of thing. So different DJs started embellishing what they were sayin'. Instead of just sayin', 'We'll be at the PAL next week, October this and that,' they say, 'You know next week we gonna be at the PAL where we rock well, and we want to see your face in the place,' little things like that."[14] The DJ was often too busy playing records to attend to this task, so a crew member was assigned the responsibility of making announcements over the music. For Herc, this practice was reminiscent of Jamaican DJs (in Jamaica, the MC was called the DJ, while the DJ was called the 'selector') and toasting. Coke La Rock was the person who spoke over the music at Herc's parties.

Flash wished to use the microphone in a different way. He wanted someone with a charismatic voice who could get the audience's attention away from him. He did not particularly like the sound of his voice, and he was busy mixing records, so he needed someone else. At first, he allowed anyone interested to jump on stage and use his microphone to entertain the crowd. But Flash considered most to be"clowns" because they mumbled, had weak voices, or performed nonsensical lyrical routines. "A clown didn't think about rocking the crowd 'cause he didn't understand—I was trying to get the party going, and I needed somebody who could dig it."[15] Then one afternoon, while Flash was playing at 63 Park, a short, bow-legged guy approached the stage. His name was Keith Wiggins, but everyone called him

Cowboy, because he walked as though he had just gotten off a horse. Before Cowboy could get to the microphone, though, another teen named Jamal grabbed it. Cowboy insisted that he go on before Jamal, but Jamal resisted. The struggle over the microphone turned into a fight. After a few minutes, Jamal laid on the ground with a broken jaw, and Cowboy held the microphone in his hand. We might think that Cowboy was destined to become an MC for Grandmaster Flash, but this was not a given. If Jamal had reached the stage before Cowboy and proved to be what Flash was looking for, or if Jamal had won the fight and went on to perform before Cowboy—both conceivable alternatives—the history of hip-hop might have been different. Details like Cowboy's fight to get on the mic are often overlooked, but they are important to historical narratives because they demonstrate that nothing is inherently significant about historical events or historical figures; events and figures *become* significant.

The fight also highlights the performance of masculinity that was prevalent in the scene. Cowboy became Flash's DJ in part because he physically dominated Jamal. To rise to prominence, he would have to engage in other performances of masculinity to dominate other MCs. He and other MCs boasted about their physical strength, the extent of their material possessions (often fabricated), their clothing and sense of style, their lyrical depth, and, most importantly, their sexual prowess. Being a performer in the scene became intertwined with maleness, and because of this, hip-hop became a gendered space.

Onstage, Cowboy provided the kind of accompaniment Flash had in mind. Melle Mel, who was in the crowd that day, remembers: "It just seemed like Cowboy came out of nowhere that day at 63 Park. [He] was on the mic telling people, 'throw your hands in the air and wave'em like you just don't care!'"[16] His elementary rhymes elicited a generous response from the crowd. He also tapped into a rhetorical device common to many forms of popular music, especially in African American and Latin American musical traditions: call and response. Between his crowd-pleasing phrases and his instructions to dance a certain way, Cowboy transformed the atmosphere at Flash's parties to resemble that of Herc's or Bambaataa's. The audience focused their attention away from the DJ and lost themselves in the break beats; they grooved to the music under Cowboy's directives. Cowboy became a key part of Flash's parties, just as b-boys had become central to Herc's and Bambaataa's. Flash was no longer the center of attention, but his music and his mixing technique set the mood of the party. While Flash solidified the need for DJs to perform with a crew, he challenged the crew's established make-up. Prior

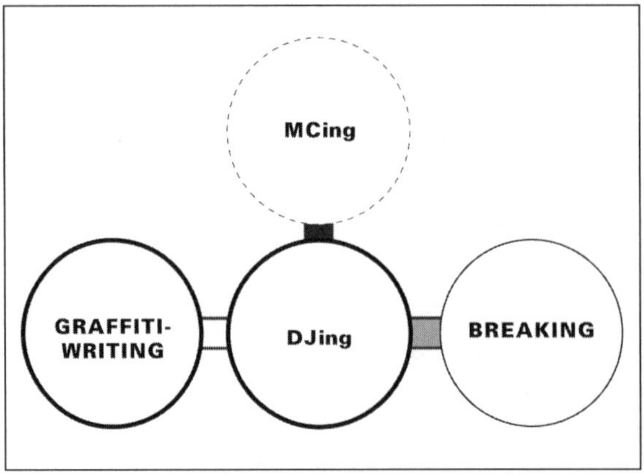

FIGURE 3.1
The Inclusion of MCing.

crews had consisted of DJs, b-boys, and MCs; Flash's included only DJs and MCs (he had gotten rid of the D Squad), and the MC took on a more significant role at his parties. This exemplifies the way a new convention was intentionally introduced from within the scene.

Centralizing the role of the MC had important ramifications, for it changed the very nature of South Bronx parties. Part of Herc's cool was his ability to entice a segment of the audience to "break" on their peers as he played the breaks of a record. Herc was always the main attraction, but his crew of breakdancers was almost as important. Likewise, people attended a Bambaataa party to see Beaver, of the Zulu Kings, one of the first b-boys to gain local fame and respect. By giving the MC an essential part to play in his performances, Flash made the audience to pay less attention to b-boys. Bom 5, a former b-boy, recollects, "When I started dancing more, you could see everyone would stop and pay attention to the MCs. You start losing your circles. People walking away from you when the MCs rocked."[17] B-boy historian Joseph Schloss argues that part of the reason for the declining presence of b-boys was that the rise of the MC caused the tempo of the music to slow down, making it less conducive to dancing and more conducive to MCing.[18] Cholly Rock agrees: "There are a lot of people who associated Hip Hop and certain records that are not Hip Hop records at all, that are Disco records, but because [hip-hop put] more emphasis on the D.J. and his cutting skills and on the emcee and his rapping skills, they became more focused on certain records that were not B-boy records."[19]

The visual representation of the scene now looks different. Breaking, which increased in popularity (see previous figure for comparison), moves farther away from DJing. Graffiti-writing moves even farther and decreases in popularity, mostly because of New York's city-wide campaign to eliminate graffiti from public places.[20] MCing, formerly the least popular of the activities, now has the strongest connection with DJing. DJing maintains its position at the center of the scene.

The 3 MCs

Nathaniel Glover, known as Kid Creole, and his younger brother Melvin Glover, aka Melle Mel, both former b-boys, also became MCs for Flash. Together, Cowboy, Kid Creole, and Melle Mel called themselves "the 3 MCs." With their enthusiastic delivery and rhyme schemes, they set a new standard for how MCs should perform with DJs. "When we first started rhyming," Creole explains, "Flash would have guys on the microphone who'd just get on there and say his name, haphazardly, no real talent being displayed." But Creole's brother, Melle Mel, changed the way MCs rhymed at parties. Creole continues, "My brother . . . I don't know, somehow or another he got in his head that he was going to try to make up his own rhymes, and that's what he did. And when he did that, it spurred me to do it. We used to go back and forth, where we used to like take a rhyme and split it up, you know, that kind of thing."[21] At first, their rhyming consisted of lines with simple poetics:

> One, two, this is for you, you, and you,
> Three, four, cuts galore is what we have in store.

One MC would deliver the first line, and the other would take the second.[22] Over time, they put together lines that were more expressive:

> He tried to rock the spot, with a cheap cheap rhyme,
> The rhyme was a joke,
> The sucker went broke,
> And he died and went to heaven in a little row boat.

The 3 MCs would often shout out to members of the audience, something Herc's MCs, Coke La Rock and Clark Kent, were already doing, but their new rhymes advanced the poetics of MCing. Just as important, these rhymes introduced a common vernacular that shaped the way participants expressed themselves. Audience members now had more words and phrases to describe what they were experiencing at the parties.[23]

The verbal dexterity of the 3 MCs set a new standard in the scene. To return to the framework on the sources of conventions and the modes of influence (see table 3.1 above), MCing was intentionally introduced into the scene and it came from within the scene and, in some ways, from the social context in which the scene was embedded. Importantly, MCing also served as another site of difference, another way the South Bronx scene differentiated itself from those in other boroughs. Hip-hop historians Jim Fricke and Charlie Ahearn elaborate:

> With the emergence first of Cowboy and soon after [of] Melle Mel and Kid Creole[,] the Bronx street scene was developing a distinctive style of MCing. But a smoother style of rapping DJ presided over the turntables in the clubs of Harlem and the [adult clubs in the] Bronx. The style of DJs like DJ Hollywood and Eddie Cheeba was closely tied to the mellow vocalizing of the radio DJs like Jacko Henderson. To a certain extent, these DJs existed in a parallel universe to "street" DJs like Herc, Flash, and Bambaataa, but the two schools were aware of one another and [eventually] influenced each other.[24]

Where did Kid Creole and Melle Mel get the idea to trade off lines? Where did their style of MCing come from? There are two popular answers to this question. Creole's response is: "My sister Linda used to write poetry, so that's how we were introduced to it in general . . . [and] my brother inspired me a lot. There was no real outside force that made us write rhymes, because nobody was writing rhymes. So it was self-motivation."[25] Many historians of hip-hop provide a different explanation, however. They argue that rhyming among DJs in the South Bronx grew out of the oral tradition in black culture. As mentioned in the introductory chapter, some scholars reach as far back as the griots and bards in West Africa for influences on MCs in the South Bronx. The former explanation draws on the influence of present circumstances, while the latter draws upon the past. Which more accurately represents the genesis of MCing? To answer this question, we cannot simply look to the past. Nor is it helpful to view rhyming solely as an original invention, as Kid Creole contends. Instead, MC rhyming must be viewed as a combination of influences from the past, creativity in the present, and projection into the future. Social theorists Mustafa Emirbayer and Ann Mische refer to these three components the "chordal triad of agency."[26]

It is quite possible that rhyming in hip-hop was inspired by from performers' familiarity with the oral traditions of the past. They may or may not have had access to West African griots and bards, but surely they were exposed to more contemporary African American oral traditions represented in the work of Gil Scott Heron, Martin Luther King's speeches and Muhammad Ali's taunting. Coke La Rock, one of Herc's MCs, speaks of some of these influences: "I did listen to the Last Poets. . . . I used to hear stuff like Signified Monkey and [Rudy Ray Moore, and Pigmeat Markham] . . . but we were not really allowed to listen to that stuff because that was what your parents played. . . . That was like the nasty records, the Wildman Steve and them type things. But what really got me with the rap thing was the Richard Pryor records. We used to say this little thing for my man Timmy Tim. Timmy Tim used to do this thing with the monkey routine Richard Pryor had in his show, called 'little tiny feet.'"[27]

It is also conceivable that, for Flash's MCs, the challenge they faced in the present—finding ways to enhance their party performances and outshine the MCs who performed with other DJs—contributed to the emergence of their style of speaking over the music. At this point, Herc's MCs were the most popular. Commenting on how they got started, Coke La Rock says, "It's hard for me to describe it because . . . it was never in the plan. To me it was just me talking on the mic. I always had vibe, I didn't write anything down. It wasn't like on that stage where you came prepared like that. . . . I couldn't see that that's what everybody really grabbed a grip of."[28] Flash's MCs saw what Herc's crewmembers were doing and, in some ways, emulated them. Creole explains: "Tim and Clark Kent would say it to the beat[,] even though it wasn't that rhythmic. It was like 'A taste of the pace with the bass in ya face.' Because it was done in that pattern, we wrote rhymes that were to that pattern."[29] But the 3 MCs advanced this style mostly because they wanted to outdo Herc's MCs. "When we started writing rhymes, we put sentences together," Creole continues.[30] So the will to outperform the competition played a significant role in creating their MCing style.

Finally, we must consider their projecting into the future. As the 3 MCs began performing, they must have believed that rhyming words over music was a legitimate way to entertain the crowd that came to Flash's parties; Flash certainly did. They hoped to set a new standard for MCs to follow, but it's unlikely they envisioned that their style of rhyming over music would turn into what we know today as rapping.

Past cultural traditions, present circumstances, and projections into the future all influenced the beginnings of MCing, but, as Emirbayer and Mische assert, "in any given case, one or another of these three aspects might well predominate."[31] From what we know about how this style of rhyming came about, it appears that the MCs relied more on evaluating their present situation (thinking about how to enhance their performances with Flash) and establishing a new trend for other MCs to follow than on recalling past oral performances in African American culture, although the latter did matter.

That is, developing their rhyming skills was more the result of their will to outdo Herc's MCs and set a new standard for other MCs than a wish to be a part of the black oral tradition. Here, I aim to distinguish between disposition and inspiration. Many authors view the verbal performances of Kid Creole and his peers as having been inspired or motivated by the verbal style of black public figures such as the Last Poets, Gil Scott Heron, Nikki Giovanni, Sonia Sanchez, Daddy-O, or Muhammad Ali. In fact, as William Jelani Cobb writes, "critics and writers generally [recognize] the influence of the Last Poets more than hip-hop artists [do] themselves."[32] Cobb finds their lack of recognition ironic. I find it instructive. Black cultural traditions did not matter as inspiration or motivation. Instead, they mattered because they were part of the dispositions or, as Bourdieu would put it, the *habitus* of those involved in creating hip-hop.[33] These verbal expressions of the past were part of their "systems of schemes of perception, appreciation, and action," which allowed them to perform "without any explicit definition of ends or rational calculation of means."[34] These dispositions, however, should not be mistaken for inspiration.

The Black Door and Security

During this time—summer 1975—DJs performed mostly in parks, so they called the parties "park jams." The parks that littered the city, many of them the product of Robert Moses's urban planning, were not open green spaces with grass and trees. The "parks'" were "asphalt playgrounds surrounded by chain-link fences"—often featuring basketball courts.[35] Performers set up their equipment on one corner atop foldable tables and coffee tables they borrowed from their parents' living room, and they positioned their speakers to project the sound to the rest of the park. Many times, electricity came from plugging extension cords into the electrical panels of streetlight posts. They stacked their equipment and used jury-rigged wiring to connect their systems. Electric fans blew air on the equipment to prevent overheating. People from the neighborhood, both young and old, came out to enjoy the parties. Few tenants complained, since even at high volumes the music was peaceful compared to the sounds of violence that had dominated their neighborhoods just a few years earlier. Even the police, for the most part, allowed the DJs to carry on; they stepped in only when the parties continued too late into the night.

Because winters in New York City did not allow for the same open and all-welcoming "park jams" that characterized summers, performers had to

FIGURE 3.2 Park Jam in the Bronx. (© Henry Chalfants; used with permission)

move indoors. The indoor venues were significant because not every crew was guaranteed a spot. Often, the ability to play inside depended on your success in outdoor performances. "The whole shit was from summer to winter," Melle Mel explains. "You did the parties in the summer to get the rep to do the fall and winter. You couldn't do indoor parties in the summer unless you were Kool Herc, 'cus no one would come inside."[36] Winter parties were held at high school gyms, recreation centers, community centers, the Police Athletic League (PAL), or bars, discos, and clubs. Which venue DJs performed in also mattered; popular venues enhanced a performer's reputation. Herc's parties began at the community center at 1520 Sedgwick Avenue but later moved to clubs like Twilight Zone and Hevalo (later renamed the Executive Play House). Bambaataa had the Bronx River Center, which was the Zulu Nation headquarters. Grandmaster Flash and his crew first became associated with an indoor venue called the Black Door after Flash met Ray Chandler. It came to be legendary and was also crucial to the development of yet another convention: security crews.

Chandler narrates how he met Flash:

> It all started one very cold winter night when we were walking along Boston Road in the Bronx and I seen a whole lot of young kids, like a

> posse situation, in a school yard—PS 163 by 169th. At first I thought it was a fight or something. Then I see one guy with the turntables, and some other guys were saying something over microphones. I had a chance to talk to the young man on the records, and he introduced himself to me as Grandmaster Flash. I asked him, "Why you out on the street in this cold weather?" They said they didn't really have a place to go.[37]

Chandler was fixing up a building to turn it into a social club for adults, but he changed his mind after meeting Flash that night. Flash convinced him to use the building for DJing parties instead. Although Chandler might have been motivated by good will, he agreed to it because he also saw the financial viability of parties. He charged a dollar per person, and Flash and the 3 MCs consistently sold out the 100-person capacity venue. With Flash's rising star at the helm, the Black Door (so named because of the color of its entrance) quickly became one of the main spots for South Bronx DJing. Chandler was able to take in hundreds of dollars a night, even a few thousand on some occasions.[38] The popularity of the venue strengthened Flash's reputation. He was not quite at the level of Herc, but he was on his way. His MCs' reputations also improved with every party. They became permanently linked to the scene and surpassed breakdancers as the DJ's main accompaniment. As a result, every crew needed an accompanying MC who spoke over the music, not simply to motivate the crowd to dance, but to give a performance that combined rhythmic delivery and clever rhyming. MCing became a thriving social activity of its own.

The Black Door soon became so popular that Ray Chandler needed to hire security guards to help control the overflowing crowd. "Getting in the Black Door was a little job, 'cause you'd have to go through security, and they were real selective," says one attendee. "And the thing about it was, it would get crowded quickly, 'cause any party Flash played would draw a crowd. . . . You'd have to wait outside, unless you had clout."[39] Security was needed not only to manage the crowds at the door; it was also necessary to keep the peace inside. Even with the decline of gangs and the advent of the DJing scene, the South Bronx was not free of violence. "To be a DJ in those days," one teen recounts, "you had to have [security] really big because it was rough. Economy was tough, so for you to bring out a system to a park or to a center was a big thing in the '70s."[40] Having security did not always deter former gang members from preying on participants in the DJ scene, however. Two accounts of the danger that surrounded the party scene bear this out:

GRANDMASTER CAZ: A lot of guys would get stuck [i.e., held] up for their shit. A van would come in, and they just packed it in. All those people who'd be there with the DJ? They were just young guys. What would they do?[41]

CHARLIE CHASE: A lot of bad things did happen. Not at every party—it's not fair to say that something always happened. . . . I mean, you have to understand; you're in a park—the bodega is right down the corner, man. You go pick up your Colt 45, which at the time was hot. Or Olde English 800. People have too many to drink, they have a little bit of disagreement, or they're actually battling—the b-boys never really started any trouble, it was just the other knuckleheads that were with them that started the problem.[42]

Indoor parties were similarly volatile. Because the parties were open to everyone, there was no telling who came to the events and what intentions they brought. "As far as being peaceful, people definitely came to party," says one MC. "But you might get stuck up in the bathroom and shit like that. We were playing for murderers, stick-up kids and all that. Overall if you didn't know what was going on, you would think it was just a nice lil' party."[43] Some of the tough guys would, upon arrival at a party, insist that the MCs mention their names over the loudspeakers. It was a way for them to make their presence known. "Niggas would be high on angel dust and come in the club with a gun and make the MC say their name on the mic," recalls Melle Mel.[44] This occurred so frequently that "shouting out" people became a staple among MCs. "They would grab you by the neck, 'yo man say so and so in the house.' That's how the phrase 'in the house' started."[45]

At times, the violent environment led to life-threatening experiences for the participants and their audience. In an interview with Coke La Rock, Troy L. Smith asked about one such incident when Kool Herc was stabbed as he tried to break up a fight:

TROY L. SMITH: So now how did you feel the night Herc got stabbed?

COKE LA ROCK: Tore me up. I almost lost my mind that night. I am going to tell you, Troy, it was a hell of a coincidence because that night before it happened I had to use the bathroom. My apartment was like four blocks away from the club, the Executive Play House. So I ran home and used the bathroom because it wasn't one of those big nights. When I left my house to get back to the club a

> couple of blocks away I started to see the ambulance and police cars. When I got there they had already taken Herc to the hospital. On the low, I asked around who did it, who was involved? The word on the streets was it was some friends of the club. One of my people said they caught one of the dudes and they are now a victim. I told him I wasn't satisfied; take me to him and I am going to put one in his head to make sure. Cats were like, "Let that go; they think they got it right. Go to the hospital and check on Herc because he was stabbed badly." And that was what made me go to the hospital. When I got there I flipped out cause it hurt the hell out of me to see my man hurt like that. It brought me to tears because I had lost one of my other good friends when I was 19. Herc's father was there and he seen that I was bugging, because I got quiet and I was crying. I knew after that I was going to go on the warpath. Herc's father told Herc, "Tell Coke to wait for you before he does anything." Herc called me in the room before they took him into the operating room. He said, "Coke, I know one of them, wait for me." I was like, "Yo, why are you telling me this?" Herc said it again, "Wait for me." I said, "Alright." He said, "Promise me that." Then when I leave out of Herc's room his father says, "Coke, let me hold your gun till tomorrow." Then I started crying again. I said, "No, Mr. Campbell, don't take my gun." He said, "I have to, you are not in your right state of mind. I know you are hurting." I gave him my gun and the next day he gave it back to me. Then I went on the hunt, that's how I felt about it, Troy.[46]

I was deeply moved, almost to tears, by Coke's emotional reaction to what had happened to Herc. After reading the interview transcription, I called Troy to relay my reaction. During our conversation, he admitted that as he listened to Coke La Rock, he, too, got teary-eyed. Such a passage illustrates the particular ability of oral histories to crystallize the impact of historical moments, in this case, the emotional toll that violence took on the lives of early participants in hip-hop. This passage presents another example of the deep association among the participants, to evoke Charles Cooley once again. The DJing scene, for its participants, became a primary group. "In the primary group," as sociologist Lewis Coser explains, "the immature and self-centered person is slowly attuned to the needs and desires of others and becomes fitted to the give-and-take of mature social life. The primary group fosters the ability to put oneself in the position of others, drawing the individual out of egoistic isolation by building into him that sensitivity to the clues of others without which social life would be impossible."[47] In such a manner, the emerging DJing scene brought young people into intimate contact with one another and sustained them at a time when the rest of their social-material environment was in disarray. It fostered a group bond, a spirit of fellowship, among participants. This dynamic helped to make the DJing scene a cultural entity.

To help curb violence at parties, some of the perpetrators became peacemakers. Former gang members, some of whom had initially terrorized the partiers, began to serve as security for DJs and MCs. Already possessing an organizational structure from gang life, they formed security crews.[48] At the Black Door, some former members of the Black Spades (then renamed the "Casanovas"), who initially brought trouble, became the security crew. The first time they came to the Black Door, they tried to get in without paying, but Ray Chandler refused. "There was a group of about sixty young guys outside, and they called themselves the Casanovas. Their slogan was 'Casanovas All Over!'" When they got to the door, they demanded to be let in. "'We're the Casanovas, and we're not going to pay any money to come in. We come to all the parties free.' I found that to be a little funny because I knew that wasn't going to happen."[49] Chandler agreed to allow them in only if they would also look out for trouble. "Every time Flash gave a party, the Casanovas did security for him. It was either beat 'em or join 'em," remarked Grandwizard Theodore.[50] According to Caz, "They just changed their name; they never changed their game! People would be mortally afraid of these guys."[51] Since they served a practical need, the Casanovas became part of the scene. Now DJs needed more than a good record collection, good mixing skills, and good MCs. To be respected, they also needed a great security crew, a neccesity that demonstrates how violence in the external world influenced the inner workings of the South Bronx DJing scene.

Peanut was one of the leaders of the Casanovas. Although he was a physically small, he was the authoritative voice in the crew and kept the members in line. One night, after a spirited argument in the park, someone slipped into the back entrance of the Black Door and shot him to death. The incident sent a wave of terror through the Bronx, as all members of the Casanova crew, filled with anger, searched for the perpetrator. "[It] was one of the most dangerous times in this business 'cause my job was to keep the peace," Chandler reflects. "They were hunting for this guy. Police were looking for this guy. Homicide detectives were looking for this guy. . . . Holy war was going to break out."[52] Members of the Casanova crew were determined to retaliate, which would certainly have provoked a chain of killings. Fortunately, the shooter was arrested and convicted, preventing further violence. But the incident had added to the Casanovas' notoriety. Their public image, along with the popularity of the the Black Door, added to Flash's reptutation.[53]

Flash's rise illuminates the way a new entrant in the field was able to pay homage to an existing convention while simultaneously challenging it. When Flash started DJing, he imitated the way other DJs played music. Like his predecessors, he sought to highlight the break beats. In fact, the idea behind his Quick Mix Theory was to shift smoothly between the break beats of two records, thereby prolonging them. When his innovative technique failed to move the crowd, he added the MCs, which challenged the place of b-boys at the parties. Not only did his MCs help him get the crowd moving, but they also became another source of Flash's symbolic capital. Likewise, the Black Door's rise to prominence exemplifies the way a venue became a source of symbolic capital for performers. In addition to the pragmatic purpose they served, security crews, especially Flash's, also became a way to gain recognition. These micro details show that a wide range of participants contributed to the development of an internal logic in the South Bronx DJing scene.

DJ AJ and Love Bug Starski

Born on the Lower East Side of Manhattan, Aaron Gerald O'Bryant (aka AJ) was orphaned before the age of thirteen. After a short stint in Jacksonville, Florida, where he was expelled from school for throwing another student through a first-floor window, he returned to the Bronx to live with his grandmother at 149th Street and Jackson Avenue, in the heart of gang activities. AJ Aaron was prone to violence, perhaps a result of distress over his parents' death, so his grandmother enrolled him in Lower East Side Preparatory High School, a school for at-risk youth; he later transferred to Harlem Preparatory School.[54] AJ did not last at either of the schools—he dropped out, joined a gang, and started selling marijuana. His monetary gains from dealing drugs made him well-known in the Bronx; as a result, AJ also caught the attention of the police. He was aware of the party and DJ scenes in the Bronx, Brooklyn, and Manhattan. He noticed Herc's popularity in particular. "You know how people in the Bronx are: 'Yo, there is this dude named Herc, this dude is crazy.' 'Well, where is he at?' 'He is at the park on Cedric Avenue,'" AJ recalls the first time he saw Herc. He expands: "I had the drug money; so things were kind of comfortable back then for me. So the next thing is I am sitting there watching this dude like whoa! He would draw a crazy crowd and there were a lot of dust smokers, so things were like whoa, 'This guy Herc is crazy.'"[55] The lively atmosphere and the crowd that Herc drew hooked AJ. While he also watched Pete "DJ" Jones and Grandmaster Flowers play in Brooklyn and Manhattan, he preferred the South Bronx DJs, and over time became an important figure in the scene. AJ's story shows how the emerging scene was able to accommodate people who entered with different dispositions. It is easy to see how DJing appeared intriguing to someone like Flash, who had a lifelong fascination with records. But what about someone like AJ, a hustler who initially had little interest in music? How did he become a part of the scene? And how did he add to its development?

AJ became part of South Bronx DJing as a party promoter. With money from the drug trade, he hired DJs and threw his own parties. For his first event, AJ tried to bring together the two most famous DJs in the Bronx, representatives of two different DJing scenes: Kool Herc and Pete "DJ" Jones. It would be a battle for supremacy. After AJ contacted both DJs, secured a location, and advertised, Herc backed out of the event, so it became a solo performance for Jones. The show went over well with the audience, but without Herc it earned less money than AJ and Jones had hoped for. All the same, it became the start of AJ's career as a party promoter. More money flowed into his coffers from his involvement in both selling weed and promoting parties. As his increasing wealth brought fame, it continued to attract more attention from the police, who began to keep closer tabs on him.

From his contact with Pete "DJ" Jones, AJ met and befriended Love Bug Starski, a DJ and MC who worked with Jones.[56] Starski, born Kevin Smith, was one of the few hip-hop practitioners during the early 1970s who performed as well on the turntables as he did on the microphone. He was also rare in that he was able to move back and forth seamlessly between the DJing scene in the South Bronx and DJing scenes elsewhere. He entered the DJing world by carrying Jones's equipment and records. He was paid meagerly for his services, but he learned a great deal from Jones. Shortly after their meeting, AJ promoted and sponsored Starski's solo ventures in the South Bronx. As the police got closer to exposing AJ's illegal activity, Starski suggested a safer pursuit: he offered to teach him how to DJ. AJ recalls their conversation:

> I said, "DJ?" He said, "Yeah." I said, "I don't want to be no DJ." He said, "You are a drug dealer and you are popular right now; if you start DJing you are going to be bigger. It is going to be better than hustling, plus it is legal." I said, "Well, how are we going to start?" He said, "If you got five or ten thousand, we can go and buy some

> turntables and equipment." I said, "What about all that equipment I seen you playing with?" He said, "That's not mine; that is Pete DJ Jones's stuff." So I was like, wow, and I thought about it. The next thing you know I am going down to Sam Ash [a chain that sells musical instruments and audio equipment].[57]

AJ purchased a new sound system and became a Starski's student. AJ the promoter became DJ AJ ("A" from his first name, Aaron, and "J" from the name of his child's mother, Jane).[58]

As mentioned earlier, conventions become more recognizable when new actors enter a scene because, by paying homage to their predecessors, they transform a set of behaviors into the realm of "oughtness." This is especially noticeable for someone like AJ. Because his predilections were not naturally congruent with the DJing scene, AJ had to work to become a DJ. More than simply learning how to operate a turntable and play records, he had to learn which records to play, which particular segments to play, how to move from one segment to another, and how to communicate with the audience through music. AJ began learning these conventions in the summer of 1977 when he took his system to a park. It was his first major test as a DJ. "They were coming to see him [Starski], not me," AJ admits. "But the thing is, I started getting the hang of it. To be honest, the [people from my] neighborhood [were] coming to see me[,] but the people that were coming from across town were coming to see Starski." Over time, AJ determined which records to play, when, and in what sequence. And, with Starski as his MC, he was able to hold the audiences' attention. "The game got tighter, and when the cold came we moved into this center around the corner." This move was a sign that they were establishing themselves in the scene. "It was called Moore House Center, and it held about 200 people. So we went up in there[,] and we started selling that out." As his name traveled through the streets as a popular DJ, AJ's reputation as a drug dealer waned. Once a detested member of the community, he was now rewarded for providing entertainment for youth. Even the police were happy to see this transformation. "The police were awarding me. Man, the guys that owned the stores close by the park would bring me beer or whatever I wanted because, by me bringing the music out, it made money for them."[59]

It is often said that the rise of hip-hop provided a nurturing space for many Bronx youth who lived in an unsafe social world.[60] AJ's story provides evidence of this assertion, for there is little doubt that without his joining the burgeoning DJing scene, he would have veered further into illegal drug activity and probably ended up in jail during his teens. As the South Bronx recovered from rampant gang activity, amid various other social ills, the rise of this new entity changed the lives of young people: they slowly built their identity and sense of self-worth around what the DJs were doing. Bambaataa deserves special credit for insisting on the positive social value of DJing. Through his Zulu Nation, he recruited and mentored many youth who turned away from illegal activities to be part of his crew. BOM 5, a graffiti writer and breakdancer, speaks of his introduction to the Zulu Nation:

> Bambaataa was giving out fliers—he was giving a party at Bronx River. I got the flier and my cousin was like, "Oh that's some trap! That's some bullshit." He [Bambaataa] wanted to squash all this beef with the gangs. "It's going to be a party. Everybody's welcome. Leave your gang colors home. It's all about Peace, Love, Unity. Come learn about your brothers." I wish I still had that flier; my cousin ripped it up. "I don't trust them Black Spades! That's a set up!" But I went to the Center. It was free for everyone. My other cousin came with me and we just went in. I met Bambaataa. They shook your hand. It was funny. My cousin says, "See, looks like things are changing." I didn't see no colors in there, no vests on. Before, when you went by Bronx River, you'd see the gangs lined up, leaning up against the fence. Masses. You knew it was a gang. Thank God for Bambaataa realizing there was too much violence going on. Bam was like my mentor.[61]

The stories of AJ and BOM 5 are not unique, since many other participants in the scene also had a past with gangs or were involved in illegal activities. The example of AJ and others like him—becoming part of the scene, understanding and contributing to its conventions, and buying into its worth—made them think differently and, in many cases, leave behind illegal activity. In this sense, the DJing scene exerted influence on the participants and changed the way they spent their days; it shaped their behavior even in aspects of their lives not directly related to DJing or to other scene participants. This attribute made DJing a social entity. In addition, the scene became increasingly meaningful for its participants; it began to give significance to their lives, so much so that they willingly abided by its demands and structured their lives around it. To put it differently, the scene became powerful enough to impose a particular vision of the world onto its members. It "establish[ed] meaning and a consensus about meaning, and in particular about the identity and unity of the group, which creat[ed] the reality of the unity and the identity of the group."[62]

Because the influence of the DJing scene cut across many sectors of participants' lives, the burgeoning entity became especially important to them. Though centered on parties, the scene served many other purposes as well, and it mattered to different people for different reasons. For many, it was a way to make money legally. It was what Robin D. G. Kelley calls "play-labor"—when the "pursuit of leisure, pleasure, and creative expression [become] labor [and a way to] survive economic crisis or a means to upward mobility."[63] When parties moved from outdoor and public places, such as parks, community centers, and high-school gymnasiums to nightlife spots like bars and clubs, performers began to engage in lucrative negotiations with club owners.[64] Here, according to Coke La Rock, was the new math: "The same money we started making off playing music was the same money cats I knew were getting that were coming off 116th and 126th Street in Harlem. When cats would come up after scrambling all day, he might have ten or twenty thousand on him. Our first party together, Herc and I made $8,000. That's when I knew right then through the law of average [*sic*] if I leave the drugs alone and get into this here I could settle for at least $5,000 a week. Compared to going to jail in the process of that other hustle."[65]

In addition to getting paid for playing in clubs, many Bronx DJs and MCs earned money from making and selling audio tapes of their performances, just as DJ Hollywood was doing in Harlem. By 1975, it had become common practice for crews to record their shows, just to listen to and evaluate their performances. Soon, though, the tapes became a commodity; people demanded them so they could play them at home and on their boom boxes. "Back then," Coke La Rock remembers, "I made eight-tracks and sold them to hustlers for $50. $50 a pop, because I only sold them to hustlers. I put your name on it, your car, I will even put your mother on it if you want! Whatever you wanted Coke La Rock to say on it I would say."[66] The tapes also served to introduce the unique DJing style to those who lived outside the South Bronx. It was from tapes that Rahiem, for example, first learned about Flash. "I had heard Flash, and at that time, they were the 3 MCs: Melle Mel, Kid Creole, and Cowboy. I heard them on tapes only. I had never seen them, and when I listened to Flash's cuts on tape, I didn't have a clue as to the mechanics behind what was going on."[67] Figure 3.3 depicts the inclusion of tapes in the scene.

Having an impact on so many different aspects of the lives of the participants—being a source of (legal) money, creating a positive sense of self, and promoting a positive group image—made the scene more durable. Andrew Abbott attests that "an entity's causal influence may reflect

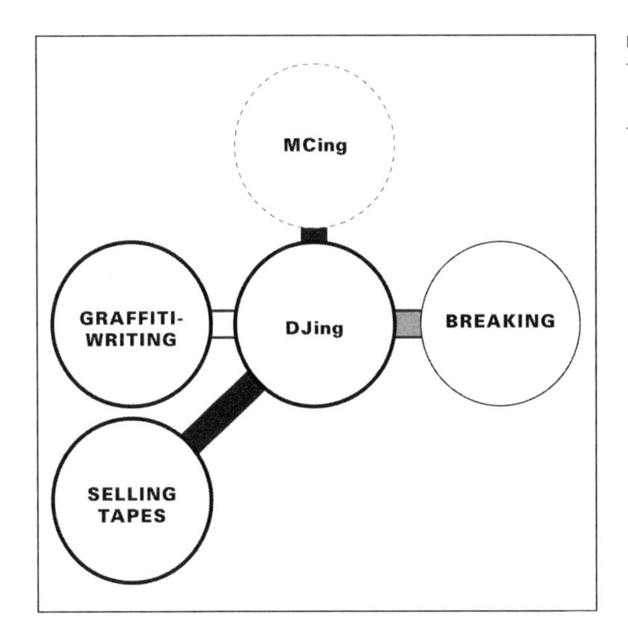

FIGURE 3.3
The Inclusion of the Making and Selling of Tapes.

vast extensions along certain particular dimensions. That is, while it might seem that compactness would allow an entity to reproduce and defend itself against rendition out of existence by other entities, what produces causal authority may well be connections across long reaches of the social world."[68] If the South Bronx DJing scene had served only as entertainment for its participants, it is unlikely that it would have been as resilient. However, because it reached into several aspects of their lives, it gained traction and became deeply rooted among the youth.

Battling

Competition arose quickly among the various South Bronx DJing crews. Perhaps this attribute came from the competitive and territorial nature of gang culture infused into DJing culture by former gang members. Or perhaps it was an offshoot of b-boy and b-girl dance battles that occurred as early DJs spun break beats.[69] Whether they emerged from internal or external sources, clashes among crews became common. The explicit motivation, or "manifest function," of these battles was to vie for the admiration and following of the audience. For a DJ, to win a battle was to win over the fans of his competitor. However, battles served many implicit or "latent" functions as well.[70] First, they were the sites where participants defined and redefined the rules of the field and of the symbolic capital at stake in the field. Second, these battles were occasions for the consecration of figures considered important members of the community. During contests, the celebrated figures cashed in their accumulated social-cultural capital while protégés earned respect and moved up the ranks. Third, the audience asserted its role most loudly expressed, during these battles. Battles were also moments of "collective effervescence."[71] That is, the battles lifted people out of themselves, out of their ordinary thoughts and imaginings. The actors brought their very best to these shows, and the audience, in turn, was at its most exuberant. The audience also determined which skills and techniques would be accepted, as well as which individuals would be inducted into the ranks of celebrated figures. Performing this task united the audience, since it made them more than mere recipients of performance.[72]

Some battles were planned and advertised, while others happened on the spur of the moment. The format, or what Erving Goffman would call "ceremonial rules," was simple.[73] One DJ would play for about an hour; another DJ would play for the next hour. They would switch back and forth as long as the party lasted. The crowd served as the judge, and the deciding factor was this: whoever was most effective at getting the crowd into a frenzy, or, to put it in the language of the scene, "whoever got the crowd to lose their goddamn minds" or "whoever rocked the shit out of the crowd" won. The night did not necessarily end with a formal declaration of a winner and a loser. Everyone had his or her own verdict; at times there was consensus, at other times there was not, and the debate over who won continued into the coming days and weeks. During interviews in which actors recount battles, especially in Troy's interviews, the fondness with which participants tell their stories conveys how exhilarating these events were for them. Their accounts make it clear that these events were sites of intense emotional energy, the "glue" of the scene's solidarity, and thus played a large role in the South Bronx DJing scene's becoming a cultural entity.[74]

Herc was able to maintain his status as the most respected DJ in the South Bronx because, for a while, no one could defeat him in battle. In one impromptu encounter with Bambaataa, he took advantage of his clout, as well as his booming sound system, to disgrace his competitor. (At the time, the sound system was among a DJ's most important tools. This would soon change, however.) Here is what happened, according to Jazzy Jay, one of Bambaataa's followers:

> Herc was late setting up and Bam continued to play longer than he should have. Once Herc was set up, he got on the microphone and said, "Bambaataa, could you please turn your system down?" Bam's

> crew was pumped and told Bam not to do it. So Herc said louder, this time with a little echoing effect, "Yo, Bambaataa, turn your system down-down-down." Bam's crew started cursing Herc until [he] put up the full weight of his system and said, "Bambaataa-baataa -baataa (with the echo increased), TURN YOUR SYSTEM DOWN!" And you couldn't even hear Bam's set at all. The Zulu crew tried to turn up the juice but it was no use. Everybody just looked at them like, "You should've listened to Kool Herc."[75]

In addition to having an excellent sound system, Herc also seemed to know just the right records to play at his battles, although he was known to soak the labels off his records so that no one could see what he played. Moreover, he often teased younger DJs who came to his events to listen in on his playlist. If, for example, Flash went to a Herc party simply to take note of the records he played, Herc would call him out on the microphone. "Herc would say, 'Flash, in order to be a qualified disc jockey . . . you must have highs.' Then he would crank up the highs and they would sizzle through the crowd. Then he would say, 'And most of all, Flash, you must have bass.' And when Herc's bass came in, the whole place would be shaking. Flash would get so embarrassed he would leave."[76]

Just as Herc won battles to stay on top of the scene, newer DJs had to win battles to climb up the ladder. DJ AJ—along with his mentor, Lovebug Starski, and his new MC, Kenny Gee—had been successful in selling out the community centers near his home, further south in the Bronx near St. Mary's Park. However, to move up to other parts of the Bronx, he had to battle. Ray Chandler came to one of his shows, was impressed, and asked AJ to battle Flash and his crew at the Dixie Club on Freeman Street—Flash's territory. AJ, understandably intimidated, declined the offer. He did not want to battle Flash, particularly in the latter's territory, where he would be playing in front of Flash's audience. "I told Love Bug that was not a good idea at that time, because we are just moving up. We were just rising to the top. Why should we battle Flash?" Although he was making decent money from DJing, AJ dared not compare himself to the newest star of the South Bronx DJing scene. "Flash was a DJ, I am a record player. I play records, Flash is a DJ." But his mentor urged him on. "Love Bug was like, 'Yo, the way shit is going now that's right in front of us anyway. So, for us to excel together, we have to take that date.' He was like, 'I am going to hold you down anyway. All you have to do is everything I taught you. We might not win but we are not going to get embarrassed.'"[77] AJ reluctantly agreed.

About 500 people packed the Dixie Club that night. Not surprisingly, most were there to support Flash. Even before the battle started, the rowdy cheers were enough to scare AJ. Flash basked in the glory of his reputation and the adulation of his home crowd. To ensure victory, he had borrowed an Infinity Machine, a top-notch sound system superior to AJ's, just for the battle. Disco Bee, a member of Flash's crew, warmed up the crowd, and AJ followed with the first round of the battle. He started his set with "Groove to Get Down" by T-Connection, "Catch a Groove" by Juice, and "Funky Granny" by Kool & the Gang, records that were funky but still new to the crowd. As he switched from one record to the next, the crowd grooved with him, impressed with his skills. The audience had come for Flash, but in fact their loyalty was more to the funky beats than to any one person, and AJ played to their desires. The height of his performance occurred when Starski jumped on stage to rhyme with his DJ. The crowd, well aware of Starski's skills, lost their minds. It was a great showing for the rookie DJ. AJ won over many of the fans, which upset and worried Flash. Would this be the beginning of his downfall? When Flash got on stage, he gave it his absolute best. His performance was just as impressive, so it was difficult to decide who had won the battle. The ambiguity worked in AJ's favor because he was the newcomer. And significantly, as Starski had hoped, he did not embarrass himself. The prize for his respectable performance? An invitation from Ray Chandler to be the opening act for Flash and the 3 MCs at the Black Door. Not only did this put AJ in the limelight, it also associated him with one of the premier venues of the time. Unlike Flash, however, AJ's years of promoting experience meant he would not limit himself to the Black Door.[78]

One of the most memorable battles, circa 1976, was a showdown between Kool Herc and Pete DJ Jones. This was the battle that AJ, as a promoter, wanted to put on. It represented a clash between the younger South Bronx DJs and the older DJs. Pete Jones, originally from Durham, North Carolina, was a teacher by day and a DJ at night. As discussed earlier, Jones was one of the most popular DJs in the older clubs. The battleground was the Executive Playhouse on East Mount Eden and Jerome Avenues. Because Herc played there regularly, he was familiar with the venue. He did not view DJ Jones as a competitor because Jones did not play the right records, and Herc knew the crowd would not appreciate Jones's song-centered DJing skills. In fact, Herc agreed to participate in the battle so he could, as he put it, "see how the other side of the spectrum sounds."[79] Unbeknownst to Herc, Jones had pertinent information that would make the battle more difficult than Herc anticipated. A week before the date, Herc's breakdancers the Nigger Twins retaliated against Herc for mistreating them in a dispute and gave Jones a list of the songs Herc intended to play and the order in which he would play them.

Jones made use of the information. "I figured if I went first and played what he was gonna play, it would look like, to the crowd, he wasn't doing anything different. That was the edge I had over him that night."[80] Jones did exactly that: he played all of Herc's set list. Realizing what Jones was up to and determined not to be embarrassed, Herc dug deeper into his record crates and responded well to Jones's performance; after all, he was playing in front of a crowd that favored him, not Jones. When it was Jones's turn again, he turned to his own records. They were funk and R & B records, but not the ones most appreciated by the crowd, which did not respond particularly well. Because Jones played the entire record, the audience had to wait for the breaks—the parts of the song best for dancing. This annoyed them, so the cheers died down. DJ AJ, an audience member that night, describes Jones's showing: "The Executive Playhouse was not Pete's kind of crowd. It wasn't that he was a lazy dude, it just wasn't his crowd. It wasn't Nell Gynn's or Nemo's [places where Jones regularly played], it wasn't downtown, and so he wasn't comfortable."[81] Desperate, Jones called on a couple of his protégés to get on the turntable and rescue him from embarrassment. First Love Bug Starski, who now performed alongside DJ AJ, and then Jones' secret weapon, Grandmaster Flash, took the stage. Love Bug performed admirably, but according to those in the audience that night, Flash took it to a whole other level. "Flash tore Herc's ass up that night," remarks E-Z Mike. Mark Skillz, another attendee, adds: "That was the first time I ever saw Flash play. The people were amazed. You see, Flash was a deejay, he was doing all that quick-mixing and spinning around and stuff—the Bronx lost its mind that night because we had never seen anything like that."[82] DJ AJ explains why and how the great Herc was defeated:

> Flash did his thing in front of Kool Herc's audience, and after that show, Flash snatched up all their following. It was so amazing—I mean he did it so fast that you didn't even believe it. It was like, "How could a DJ do that? I gotta go pay to see Flash again to see if he could do that same quick-mixing he did that night." It took maybe two or three weeks, but Flash snatched up all that clientele. Maybe people was a little tired of just hearing break beats; they wanted to find something new. And I think they found something new in Grandmaster Flash.[83]

Flash's techniques symbolically overpowered Herc's massive sound system and tough break beats. Flash thereby broadened people's outlook with regard to what a DJ could do; he transformed the space of possibilities. In addition, Herc's defeat signified not only his first major loss in a battle, it also represented an important change in the conventions of the scene. It altered the significance placed on the size of one's speakers—speakers were no longer the most important aspect of a DJ's presence. Although a DJs' mixing skills had always mattered, now these skills were of paramount importance. This change, which is most observable in a battle, is what Pierre Bourdieu would call a shift in the principle of hierarchization.[84] Significantly, this battle marked the beginning of Herc's decline in the South Bronx DJing scene. Although he retained the respect of his fellow DJs, he was no longer authoritative. Flash became the central figure. After the battle, his crew moved from the Black Door to the much bigger Dixie Club.

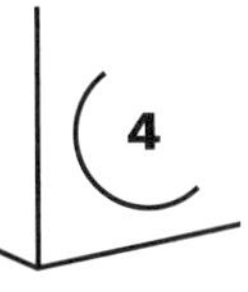

4 Crews and Outside Influences

This section of the book argues that the creation of conventions allows an emerging entity to endure over time; it also illustrates that well-bounded entities create an affinity among their participants and exert influence on the individuals involved in making the entities. The previous chapter showed how individual attributes of the DJing styles of Herc, Bambaataa, and Flash became permanent features of South Bronx DJing, how new entrants simultaneously challenged and abided by the ways of the scene, and how conventions emerged. This chapter considers further empirical evidence to demonstrate how new actors became part of the scene. It provides more examples of how crews came together by exploring the rise of the L Brothers, the Funky 4, and Caz and Wiz. These crews were by no means the only ones active in the Bronx, but they were the most popular, especially by 1976. This chapter provides detailed accounts of how they formed. Doing so offers another look at the skills and dispositions that different actors brought to the making of hip-hop. More importantly, the stories of these crews reveal the reification of already established rules of the game and the introduction of new ones. For example, the number of members in each crew, the required skills and responsibilities of each crew member, the style of their performance, the venue in which a crew performed, and a crew's attire all came to have great significance for the internal logic of the emerging entity. Crucially, competition among crews drove the hip-hop scene to new heights because it spurred creativity in the performers. And for audience members, there was nothing more thrilling than watching their neighborhood crews take on other groups.

This chapter also examines developments in the South Bronx that shaped early hip-hop conventions, especially performance routines and fashion. It pays particular attention to the citywide blackout of the summer of 1977. And it addresses how the term "hip-hop" came to identify the scene, making clear that some conventions were a combination of both internal and external influences. Finally, the chapter illustrates how older conventions changed as new ones took shape; as Howard Becker acknowledges, conventions are "complexly interdependent," and a change in one, or the rise of a new convention, affects the others.[1] The closing pages of this chapter describe how changes in the scene's internal structure affected b-boying and graffiti-writing, two of the three original components of hip-hop.

Crews

THE FUNKY 4

Keith Williams, as a teen living around Gun Hill Road, was involved in the Bronx's popular activities—graffiti-writing and breakdancing. As a graffiti writer, albeit not a very well-known one, he used three names: BREAKOUT, CRIP, and T. Following a friend's suggestion, he did away with the latter two names and had "Breakout" written on the side of his pants; it became his b-boy name when he went to jams. "I used to go to Bambaataa's parties and listen to 'Bongo Rock' and go bananas," he recalled.[2] Around 1976, he started visiting Downtown Records to buy some of the music he heard the DJs spin and then began playing the records at his house and inviting neighborhood friends, including Kevin Smith (who went by KK Rockwell), to come and listen. KK, who lived a block away from Breakout, was allowed out of the house only because his mother trusted the slightly older Breakout to look after him. After attending a few of Breakout's gatherings, KK began imitating the rhyming style of the 3 MCs. "Breakout would be like, 'Yo, I got some fresh beats. Let's go up to my crib.' He'd play his new records and I'd practice my new rhymes over them."[3]

Like many other teens living in the area, Breakout and KK dreamed of forming their own crew. They wanted the fame, the money, and the attention from women that came with being able to rock parties in their neighborhood. At the time, there were no big-name DJs from their area. Flash had the South Bronx; Bambaataa was on the East Side, and Herc had the western section. Cholly Rock, who, like Breakout and KK, was from the northern part of the borough, explains:

> You have to understand, the mindset and culture of the Northeast Bronx, where we were from, was more middle class and conservative. There weren't many DJs playing B-Boy music—usually only in Edenwald Houses, at their community center parties, or at house parties. In the house parties, we brought our records with us. We would "ask" the DJ to play this or that record, like "Just Begun" or "Apache". Then we would clear the floor and "Go Off" either to the delight—or usually the disgust—of the other partygoers.[4]

Breakout was among other crews that eventually sprung from those neighborhoods—including Kaos and the Together Brothers—but they would become by far the most popular. Breakout recounts how they began: "I took my mother's record player and another record player and went right here to this schoolyard with my man Mark Fisher, and we played one record, stopped, and dropped the needle on the next one, with no mixer."[5] Baron Chappell and Angelo King (Tony Tone), through random and serendipitous connections, joined Breakout and KK to form the Funky 4.

At one of his parties, Breakout met Baron, who was born in Harlem and lived on 129th Street between Madison and Park Avenues. When Baron was fourteen, his family moved to the South Bronx, a block from where Herc lived. Baron went to school in Manhattan and spent most of his leisure time there, so he did not know Herc well and was less familiar with South Bronx happenings than Breakout was, but he did notice the DJing scene. "My older brother used to hang out with Herc and go to his parties. In order for me to go, I had to help him with his equipment. So I used to roll around with Herc, but if I was late, I had to pay to get in."[6] After seeing Herc, Baron decided that he, too, wanted to be a DJ. If nothing else, being a DJ would guarantee him easy access into the parties. Baron's brother, Kimoni, who was in a karate class with Breakout, took him to one of Breakout's schoolyard parties. It was there that Baron and Breakout met. They clicked right away and started DJing together while KK Rockwell MCed. Tony Tone, the fourth member of the Funky 4, went to Adlai Stevenson High School with Breakout. Tone was a DJ with a crew called Unity Productions, not a particularly good or well-known group—considered a "toy" crew. Breakout impressed Tone with his skills on the turntable, so Tone began to hang around him more frequently. Breakout and Baron were the DJs, KK Rockwell was the MC, and Tony Tone played a managerial role. Breakout's brother Jazzy Dee, who had just finished his first year in college, saw their potential and bought them better equipment with his student loan reimbursement. For their first party, they billed themselves as "Baron and Breakout and the Voice of KK."

Every so often, David Parker, known as Busy Bee Starski, joined their line-up. Parker, who lived on West Farms Road, a few blocks from Melle Mel, Kid Creole, and Cowboy, was called "Busy Bee" because he was known to jump from one group to the next. The "Starski" part of his name came from his peers who thought his rhyming style was similar to that of Love Bug Starski. Before joining Breakout, Baron, and KK, Busy Bee played with Disco King Mario, one of the former Spades turned DJs, most known for his sound system. Busy Bee explained that he left Mario for Breakout because

Breakout had his own system and would travel, instead of throwing parties only in his neighborhood.

Busy Bee performed with Breakout's crew for the first time at a party held at Evander Childs High School, in a battle against Afrika Bambaataa. "Afrika Bambaataa was on one side of the gym, and we was on the other," DJ Baron recalls. "The place was jam-packed. We were going back and forth, and all of a sudden, you couldn't hear us no more, 'cause Bam borrowed this amp from Mario and blew us out of the water, just drowns us out totally. We lost the battle, but we made our money, 'cause it was our party."[7] The next day, Breakout and his crew bought a BGW power amp and built a new system. The called it "the Mighty Mighty Sasquatch." It was rare to find such a sound system in the Bronx, although they were popular in Brooklyn and Queens. Tony Tone, who oversaw their system, explains: "I was their hook-up man. We had fifteen-inch speakers made out of fifty-five-gallon steel drums. They laid on the floor, and they had six-inch legs that shot 'em up. The speakers faced down so that you could get a bass reflect, and it would shoot out—you could hear it for at least ten blocks."[8] The Sasquatch instantly boosted their reputation on the scene. Having a great sound system did not produce as much symbolic capital as it once did, but it was still essential for throwing a good party. The love they got for their system was for its appearance as much as for its sound. "We had unique equipment—we had garbage can speakers," Breakout adds. "Everybody knows about those garbage can speakers. . . . It made a lot of noise, but it was just the uniqueness of a garbage can as a speaker."[9] The rare shape of "the Mighty Mighty Sasquatch" brought a lot of attention to Breakout and his crew in the circuits of block parties and high school jams, but they had a while to go before getting gigs at bars and clubs.

One of the ways they sought to improve their crew was by bringing on more MCs. In addition to KK, and when Busy Bee was not around, they needed someone else on stage to move the crowd into a frenzy. For this purpose, Sharon Green, who went by Sha-Rock, the first significant female MC in the hip-hop scene, was added to the group. Keith Keith, a good friend of KK who also MCed and had been around the crew from the beginning, came on board as well. These three, Keith Keith, Sha-Rock, and KK Rockwell, performed with Breakout more than with Baron, so Baron brought on one more MC (Rahiem) to work with him. Below, Rahiem provides an eloquent and fond account, with exquisite details, of how he became part of the group. In his story, we again see how DJs drowned out their opponents who had inferior sound systems.

FIGURE 4.1 The crowd at an Indoor Jam. (© Joe Conzo; used with permission)

When I went to the community center where the auditions were, it was actually a battle between Brothers' Disco (Breakout and Baron) and a group called the Little Brothers from Co-op City—DJ Aaron and DJ Leo. The Little Brothers were on when I walked into the party; angel dust permeated the air; the walls were sweating because the place was jammed packed. The Little Brothers set up Peavey columns, and it seemed like they were rockin' the joint. . . . Everybody was enjoying the music that they were playing. Sha-Rock and KK were on the stage standing around, and Breakout got on the tables. His sound system was massive. I had never seen a sound system like this before, and the only ones equal at the time were Infinity Machine from Queens, Disco Twins also from Queens, Kool Herc, and Disco King Mario. I remember Breakout's tweeters were on two ropes spanning the width of the room, held up by two horns on tripods on either side of the room. Breakout was listening to the headphones, cueing up a record. . . . He picked up the mic and said, "Little Brothers, the highs in your eyes." He turned up the music and all you heard were the tweeters. The volume of those alone interfered with the Little Brothers' system. Then Breakout said, "Feel

> the horns," and it sounded like a thirty-piece marching band was in the spot. After that, he said, "Feel the bass," and then it was over. . . . Then, when Baron got on, he handed me a mic. I said some stuff, and they didn't want me to put the mic down. From that night on, I was down.[10]

Together, Keith Keith, Sha-Rock, KK Rockwell, Rahiem, and Breakout became "DJ Breakout and The Funky 4 MCs." (DJ Baron was the backup DJ because he played more disco music. Having spent more time in Harlem than in the Bronx, he perhaps did not appreciate the funkier music as much as his fellow group members did.) These young people, all of whom were under 18, had only a few months earlier been playing around with makeshift microphones and speakers. Now they were invested in the same enterprise as former gang members and former drug dealers. In some odd way, the new DJing scene held relevance for teenagers with starkly different social realities. As I argued earlier, the elasticity of the scene, its ability to include a wide array of life experiences, made it more durable.

THE L BROTHERS

Mean Gene's partnership with Grandmaster Flash did not last, but because of it, his brother Grandwizard Theodore became a well-known DJ. Here is one recollection of Theodore's debut at the park:

> The first time I saw Flash was in Arthur Park; [it] was the same day I also saw Theodore for the first time. I had got word that Flash was appearing at the park, which was only four blocks from my house. . . . He put together his sound system, and he's playing and he's got the crowd, man. He got the crowd and it's building and building, and dusk is coming. . . . All of a sudden, Theodore is setting up with his people like maybe a hundred yards away, in another section of the park. I already got a dose of what Flash can do, but Theodore was a kid I never even knew he existed. He just came out of nowhere, and this kid blew me away. . . . And what amazed me about Theodore was that he picks up the needles without having to spin back, and catches the beat, time after time after time after time. . . . Continuously! And he's rocking this thing, he's just ripping this party up. . . . That was the first time I saw Theodore, he just stayed there until two, three in the morning.[11]

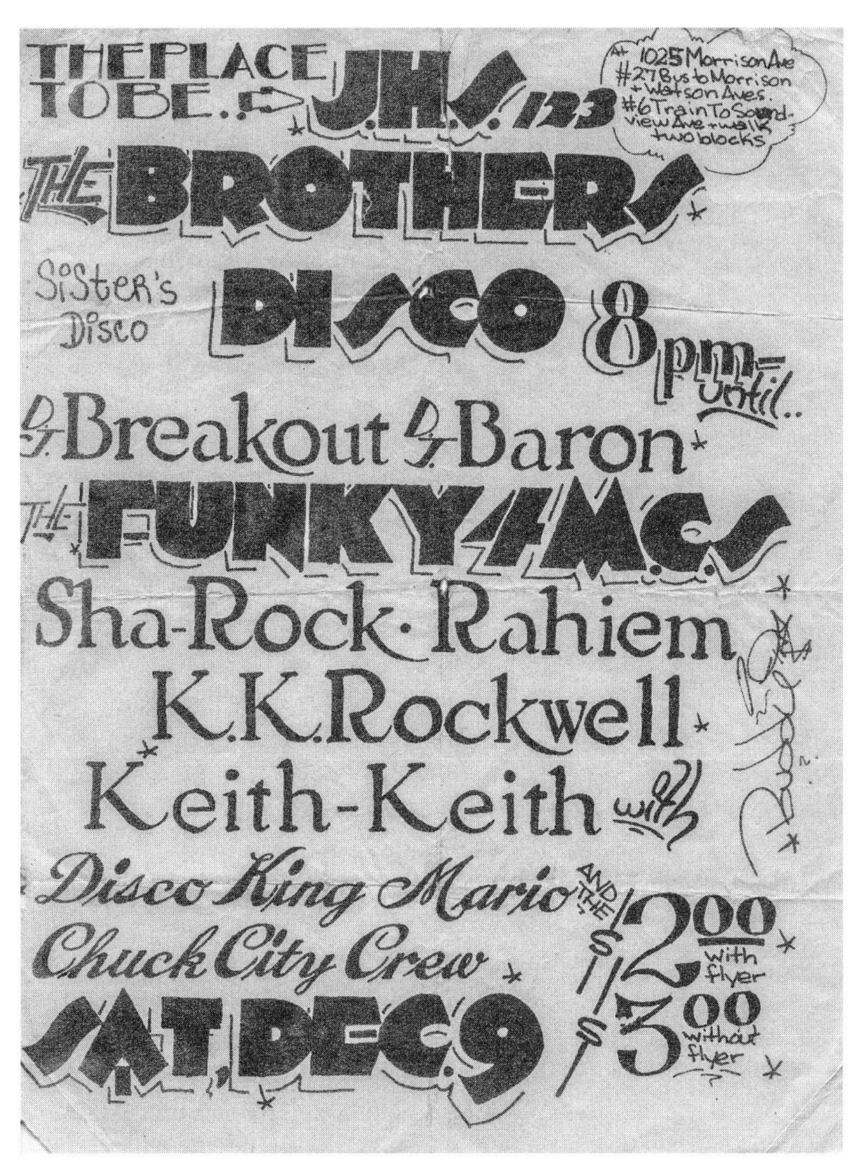

FIGURE 4.2 Flier advertising a Breakout and Baron performance, the L Brothers.

Cordie-O, the other brother in the Livingston family, also interested in DJing, joined Gene and Theodore to form the L Brothers (L for Livingston). Theodore notes: "People already knew who we were; they just had to get used to the name L Brothers. Once they saw me and Cordie-O DJ, people realized that we were ahead of our time. We were ready like overnight."[12] But they could not continue without an MC, so they allowed Kevie Kev (whom Theodore had known since third grade when they were in the same class) to rock the mic during one of their block parties. He gave a respectable performance, so the L Brothers invited Kev for a formal audition. Kev arrived at the house with his brother Master Rob, who by Kev's own admission authored the rhymes that Kev used. The crew liked the lines that Rob wrote and the way Kev performed them, so they admitted them both. (Master Rob, who also went by Robbie Rob, was the one who gave the name *Busy Bee Starski* to David Parker.) Rob was, at the time, performing with Bambaataa and Busy Bee, but he cut ties with them and joined the up-and-coming L Brothers. The crew was now made up of two sets of siblings: the Livingston brothers, and Rob and Kevin Ferguson.

Busy Bee, famous for jumping from one crew to the next, left Breakout and the Funky 4 and joined the L Brothers. He recalls how he got down with the latter crew: "I was there [at Johnson's restaurant] one night getting some chicken, and Gene was in there. Gene says, 'Yo Starski, why you be going across town rocking and all that and we right here?' Then he says, 'I am not down with Flash anymore. I got Kevie Kev and Robbie Rob, and my brothers Cordie-O and Theodore[,] and we call ourselves the L Brothers.' So I am like, 'Where am I going to fit in, I am not anyone's brother.' He said, 'Well shit, you be our brother, you live right down the block.'"[13]

Based on this "fictive kinship," Busy Bee became a member of the the L Brothers.[14] The "L" now stood for "Love," not Livingston. They were the "Love Brothers," and they quickly moved up the ranks because, according to Whipper Whip, a fan of the crew, "It was the same formula as with Flash." He explains further, "Busy was the type of guy to rock the party, to rock the crowd [like Cowboy]. Master Rob was a great rhymer; he had a nice tone in his voice, and he was real smooth [like Melle Mel]. And Kevie Kev rocked the echo, like Creole. They really tore up the Bronx; the L Brothers' parties were big parties. Just like Flash's parties were huge, the L Brother parties were real huge."[15] The L Brothers imitated and reinforced the 3 MCs' standard for how MCs should participate in South Bronx jams. What is more, they played in different parts of the city. "L Brothers spread like a disease," Busy Bee explains. "We'd arrive with station wagons. . . . Gene would show up and say to someone, 'We'll be here playing a little music. We'll give you $30, if we can plug into your house for three hours.'"[16] Once they had permission, they would run their long extension cord from their system to the house, invite local vendors to set up for business, and put on a show.

Their parties increased their symbolic capital, but to gain more respect from their peers and rise up in the social rankings, they had to battle, so they went after the crew they emulated, Grandmaster Flash and the 3 MCs. Win or lose, being able to go toe to toe with them would add to their reputation. For Flash and his crew, battling and defeating this new crew was important, if they were to maintain their supremacy. The event was held at a high school. The L Brothers set up on one side of the gym; Flash and the 3 MCs set up on the other, with a door dividing the two sides. The object of the battle was to see which group could attract the biggest audience to its side of the gymnasium. Flash arrived with a U-Haul truck full of rented equipment, while the L Brothers made do with their usual system. Bambaataa, who was in attendance that night—the event was being held on his turf—noticed Flash's rented equipment and determined that he was competing unfairly. The unwritten rule was that crews had to play with their own equipment. They could borrow from other crews, but renting professional equipment was out of line. To penalize Flash, Bambaataa sent for his own crate of records and coached Theodore on what records to play and when. Because the audience was familiar with Bambaataa's music, they gravitated toward Theodore's side of the gym. Flash pulled out all his tricks, but the audience kept trickling over to the L Brothers. His MCs gave it their all, but they could not keep the crowd's attention. Flash's skills mattered, and so did the talent of his MCs and the quality of his speakers, but in this battle, playing Bambaataa's music won the audience over. Utterly baffled, Flash gave up and walked to the other side of the gym to see what was going on. When he saw that Bambaataa was behind Theodore, he broke into laughter. It made sense. Theodore was a good DJ, but everyone knew that he was not quite on Flash's level. Flash embraced Bambaataa, the legend who, only a few years earlier, had inspired him to get into the game. Then he got on the microphone and, with his arm around Theodore, exclaimed, "Yo! This here's my son, Grandwizard Theodore."[17] Grateful for a superb night, and for witnessing three generations of South Bronx DJs, the crowd cheered exuberantly.

The Funky 4 and the L Brothers abided by and further entrenched the need for crews. By imitating the 3 MCs, they affirmed that there was an identifiable manner of being that defined the DJing scene. But they did not merely copy what they saw; they molded existing practices to fit their style and vision. Caz & Wiz, considered in the next section, did much of the same, but they pushed the boundaries of the scene more than the previous two crews did.

CAZ & WIZ

Curtis Fisher had a knack for self-expression and a gift for words, so he wrote poetry. And like the youth in his neighborhood who wrote their names all over the city, he drew and painted. However, he was a student at a Catholic school, so he was deterred from fully partaking in the graffiti culture. "It's not anything that I thought would come into play later on," Fisher remarks about his appreciation for language. "But when hip-hop came along, that just opened up a whole new world of expression for everything."[18] While some turned to this new scene as a way of getting away from gangs and other illegal activity, he used it as an outlet for his creativity, and it brought him into contact with people with whom, perhaps, he would not otherwise have associated. After hearing Herc jam in the parks, he became a b-boy, along with Luis Cedeño. Cedeño brought a different history to the scene.[19] A former graffiti writer, a delinquent, and an ex-gang member, Cedeño's entrance into hip-hop was an attempt to escape his troubled life. He simply needed something else to do if he was to stay out of the criminal justice system. Fisher and Cedeño became fast friends when they both joined the Casanova Dance Crew (not to be confused with Flash's security crew). Fisher called himself Casanova Fly (Caz); Cedeño became Disco Wiz, the first Latino DJ in the scene.

They soon moved up from being b-boys to being DJs—DJ Casanova Fly and the Magnificent Disco Wiz. A two-man DJ crew (Casanova would also play the part of the MC) was unconventional at the time—around 1976—but they rose to a respectable stature. They had different DJing styles. Wiz played like Herc. He loved the funky break beats the b-boys longed for. "My thing was always the beats. . . . The b-boys used to be fidgeting on the sidelines, saying, 'Wiz, when you getting' on? Wiz, when you getting' on?'"[20] Caz, by contrast, played with the eclectic style of Bambaataa; nothing was off limits to him. "I would play whatever I felt like playin'. . . . I'm gonna open your eyes to some stuff, you know what I mean?"[21] Caz was also able to mix records with the speed of Flash, so he inherited the title of "grandmaster": Grandmaster Caz. Each, in his own way, bolstered the style of his predecessor.

Their DJing and MCing skills made them well known, but a large part of Caz and Wiz's popularity came from a unique performance gimmick they introduced. By that time, it was common for crews to record their performances and sell the tapes. Caz and Wiz did the same, but on someone's recommendation, they decided to have the recordings transferred to acetate disc. Wiz recalls how it came about: "So one time this guy came up to us, this tech-head in the lunchroom, and said, 'You know what? You can take

FIGURE 4.3
Flier advertising Caz, Wiz, and Bambaataa.

that downtown to this recording place and put that on wax.' We looked at each other like, 'This guy was from another planet.' We said, 'Word?' He said 'Yeah.' So we went and checked it out. We did the homework; and we confirmed it."[22] They went home and created a few pause tapes—compilations of various samples and scratches manually pieced together—got their tapes put on an acetate record, and started performing with it. In the Bronx, it became known as "the Plate." "That tape made us famous," Caz recalls. "DJs used to invite us to their parties and say, 'Yo, bring the Plate.' 'Cause we had a secret—we had something that nobody had and everybody wanted."[23] Caz and Wiz made full use of this novelty, even during battles. "We combined our routine with our plate," Wiz explains. "When it was time for our set[,]. . . you had your two lights over your turntables, and you had me and him behind the set. We would put the plate on, turn off the lights, walk away from the set, leave the whole thing unmanned, and the plate would just play. We would stand over on the side with our arms crossed, in the b-boy stance, and the plate would play for itself. And the opposing DJs would lose their minds when we did that. It was like a KO punch."[24]

The crowd loved it, because Caz and Wiz were able to defeat their opponents without lifting a finger, literally. It worked wonders for numerous parties, but its effect eventually wore off. Once everyone saw "the Plate," it was no longer impressive. The DJing scene was so performance driven that it made little sense for people to gather around to listen to a record playing without human intervention. In a way, this was the first time hip-hop music was put on a record, but it did not mean much without the backing of a record company. Since no other crew repeated this technique, it did not receive the "dignity of oughtness" and did not become a convention.[25]

Outside Influences

The preceding discussion details the way various conventions arising in the emerging South Bronx DJing scene in the mid-1970s structured the scene's internal logic and contributed to the specification and durability of the entity's boundaries. These conventions, which came from within the DJing world, can easily be traced to one particular actor or crew. For example, it is clear that Theodore added scratching to the DJ's skill set and that the rhyming style of Flash's 3 MCs set a standard that other MCs emulated. The following sections explore external influences—the way the social context in which the scene existed shaped its inner workings. Because these sources came from outside the scene, their genesis is elusive and not easily attributable to one person or crew. Some of these influences revised the scene according to its existing internal logic, while others transformed it with little regard to its rules.

FASHION

Dressing nicely already had been a way to gain a name in South Bronx neighborhoods before the emergence of the DJing scene. Gang members, hustlers, and anyone else who could afford expensive, good-looking gear held a special position in the social rankings. Van Silk, a party promoter of the time, recalls, "All the hustler types that went to [Club] 371 shopped at AJ Lester's on 125th Street. You had to be making money then to shop there." If hustlers did not buy clothes there, they had them tailor-made. "Ron Isley and that old R & B group Black Ivory, they shopped at AJ Lester's too. Brothers used to go there and buy sharkskin suits and gator shoes and Al Packer sweaters."[26] Those who dressed in this type of clothing were said to be "looking fly." For partygoers in Harlem, looking fly was a must. Men wore dress shoes, suit jackets, and slacks, while women wore dresses.

In the South Bronx DJing scene, however, looking fly was not important initially. At first, b-boy attire was not considered fashionable by others. It included "sweatshirts with individual names, bell-bottom jeans, which were always rolled up on the outside instead of being hemmed, Pro Keds tennis shoes, and white sailor's caps with the brims ironed to stick straight out."[27] But in time, the social significance of dressing up increased at South Bronx parties. Performers and audience members brought into events the fashion sensibilities of the outside world. This incorporation occurred subject to already existing internal rules of the scene, however. One could not become a celebrated member of the DJing scene simply by "being fly"; dressing nicely had to be combined with existing ways of gaining a name.

Fashion sensibilities became part of South Bronx parties because they were part of the dispositions of various actors, especially former hustlers like Coke La Rock and DJ AJ. Before he became an MC with Herc, La Rock was an avid attendee of parties in Harlem. He was able to afford the expensive clothing and accessories popular with the Harlem crowd with whom he socialized because he sold marijuana and placed winning bets on basketball games. Below, in his interview with Troy, he provides a colorful and humorous account of how he developed his fashion sense:

> I was seventeen years old when I started hanging out at the Sand Club down on 34th Street between 7th and 8th Avenue. At that time it was a club and a restaurant and a bar all in one. You had to be twenty-one to get in, but I got through and it was the first club I really loved. And during this time, on the Fourth of July, all the fellas that were balling or getting a little paper would go out to Coney Island and you chilled by The Himilayer ride, dancing and showing your wears off. I lived fly, and I loved lizards, so I stayed in the reptile house. Cats were wearing Penny loafers; I was wearing reptiles. I couldn't even go in the zoo because the animals acted up. And I was G money man. I kept a G and better on me. I walked around with sixteen, seventeen hundred a day on me. That was a normal thing with Coke La Rock.[28]

When he became Herc's right-hand man, La Rock continued to dress as he had. His sense of fashion, the product of a different social world, came with him into the DJing world and became part of his reputation as an MC.

Likewise, DJ AJ's sense of fashion, also rooted in the hustling world, became part of his identity as a DJ. He, too, shopped at AJ Lester's, which often had the initials "A.J." printed on its clothing. "I was getting that money to be able to shop there and, you know, I was killing it going back to the Bronx with that fly gear." He believes his fashion sense added to his popularity. "I wasn't the best DJ nigga. But I made the people dance. . . . It was real simple, and the thing was I was fly! I had diamonds and gold on. I was accepted. Flash was like a regular dressing cat. He didn't have any jewelry."[29] Another relatively new performer, Busy Bee, also contributed fashion sense. Before he played with Disco King Mario, DJ Breakout, or the L Brothers, Busy Bee was a member of the Casanova Gang. The Cooley High Fly Guys, the Casanova Gang subgroup to which Busy Bee belonged, was known and admired for dressing well. When Busy Bee became a sought-after figure in the DJing world, his fashion sense bolstered his reputation. Bambaataa also made a mark in the scene with his fashion, and as one might expect, he brought a completely different style. "Well, a lot of groups started following us because when a lot of groups was out there, there was more dressing looking like the Temptations, you know, with the suits being cool. And I said no, we want to come from another angle. So I started looking at the groups like Sly and the Family Stone, Parliament Funkadelic, I said that's the way we gotta go."[30] The Funky 4 MCs, in their own way, also added to the fashion sensibilities with their look-alike white sweaters that had their names printed on them in black.

As the attire of the performers changed, so did the style of the audience. For the ladies, "shrimp earrings were in fashion then," says Sheri Sher, who frequented these parties. "If you had a pair of big gold shrimp earrings, you were considered a fly girl. Oh, and don't have on the Lee jean suit, heels, and the tight hair-do to go along with the shrimp earrings—all eyes would definitely be on you." In her view, the guys had it easy, because they did not have to do much to look fly. "For guys, if you had the big gold medallion around your neck, a brim hat, and a quarter field coat with big fake fur around the collar, you were a fly guy. You could have worn the same jeans all year long; all girls would see is that big-ass medallion around your neck and the quarter field coat."[31]

Audience attire changed in part because those who came to represent for a particular DJing crew were expected to wear whatever the crew wore on stage. Sher recalls: "Of course, the crowd was full of all types of crews representing in sweatshirts bearing their crew's name on the back in iron-on letters. The females wore tight-fitting Sergio Valente or Jordache jeans while the fellas had the Lee bell-bottoms with the permanent crease ironed down the middle. In those days, to be down with a crew, you had to be at all the jams where your DJ crew was playing and be ready for whatever might go down on any given night."[32]

Beginning with the DJs and MCs and trickling down to the audience, a sense of fashion embedded in social worlds outside the DJing scene became incorporated into the growing cultural entity. As anthropologist John Borneman would describe it, these particular ways of dressing became symbols of belonging in the South Bronx DJing world.[33]

ROUTINES

When the 3 MCs started rhyming simultaneously, as opposed to taking turns one after the other, their rhythmic style was something new to the scene. No one, up to that point, had seen performers throw words back and forth at each other. Additionally, they changed the way MCs performed with their DJs. They spurred what would become known as "routines"—choreographed dance steps and crowd-pleasing moves that were popular with singing groups. (Think of the coordinated dance steps of a group like the Temptations.) With the advent of multiple MCs performing on stage at the same time as the DJ, parties fundamentally changed. They were no longer composed of a DJ's spontaneous selection of songs and occasional talk over the music. Likewise, audience members were no longer attending dance parties; they now were attending mini-concerts where they could also dance. Routines ushered in this crucial shift in hip-hop's development. As one member of the scene explains, "Routines were very important when you put on a show. Even though you performed in the streets, if you did not have your steps, choreography, and routines together, you would look whack. People actually expected to see a free performance as if it was show time at the Apollo."[34]

It is not completely known how the dance steps became part of the DJing scene, but we know that they did not appear out of the blue, given the context in which the scene developed. Just a few years earlier, the Bronx had been one of the urban neighborhoods from which doo-wop arose. Doo-wop consisted of three or more singers harmonizing and performing choreographed dance steps. In high schools in the Bronx, such as Morris High School, talent shows often featured such singing groups.[35] It would be tempting to argue that these groups directly affected the MCs, but such an assertion would be uncritical speculation. Here, again, I want to draw a distinction between disposition and inspiration. Because the dance steps of these groups grew out of the imaginations of teens involved in DJing and MCing, and because doo-wop groups were something they saw regularly, it is reasonable to expect that, when multiple MCs got on stage to perform together (especially when, at least in numbers, the MCs resembled the doo-wop group), they drew from what was familiar. Mel, Cowboy, and Kid Creole did not develop routines in intentional imitation of the dance groups. That style of performance was simply part of their disposition, part of their cultural toolkit. When they needed something to impress the audience at their events and to improve their stage presence in order to remain the best crew in the Bronx, they reached for it.[36]

Within the Funky 4, Rahiem's experience created a more direct connection between the doo-wop singing groups and their performance style. "I originally was a singer, and I was in a group with Christopher Williams. We used to sing in the hallways of Truman High School on a daily basis and we had a nice following."[37] He also was a big fan of another guy named Rahiem—from whom he got his name—and of his group called G.Q. "They used to do block parties all around the Bronx, and their bass player Sabu was from my block. I would stand at the ropes and just stare into Rahiem's mouth and suck up every bit of technique that I could."[38] Rahiem of the Funky 4 went from singing to MCing because he noticed that MCs received more attention from the ladies than did singers. "There was this guy who called himself Jazzy Joe, his name was Joe Goodwin. He was from the valley, and he would walk around the halls saying these little nursery rhymes. Every chick in the school was sweating Joe and asking him to rhyme. That was my inspiration. I knew that I could write better rhymes, so I challenged him to a battle one day and took him out. That got me a pretty good reputation at school. I started MCing around '77."[39] When Rahiem joined the Funky 4, he brought with him all the techniques the singing groups used, including choreography. With his routines, the Funky 4 became a force to reckon with. "They used to look at us like they were hypnotized," recalls Funky 4 MC Keith Keith. "That's where we got the name Hypnotizing Funky 4 MCs. The crowd was shocked and amazed. . . . We were blazing them with the harmonizing and slamming them with the dance steps."[40] When Herc and Bambaataa were at the helm, b-boys were the main attraction. When Flash became the star, DJing skills captured the audience's attention. Now, it was the MCs' performance styles that people came to see.

With the addition of fashion and routines, our visual representation of the scene changes once again. DJing is still at the center, graffiti-writing and breaking are not as strongly connected, and the importance of MCing continues to grow.

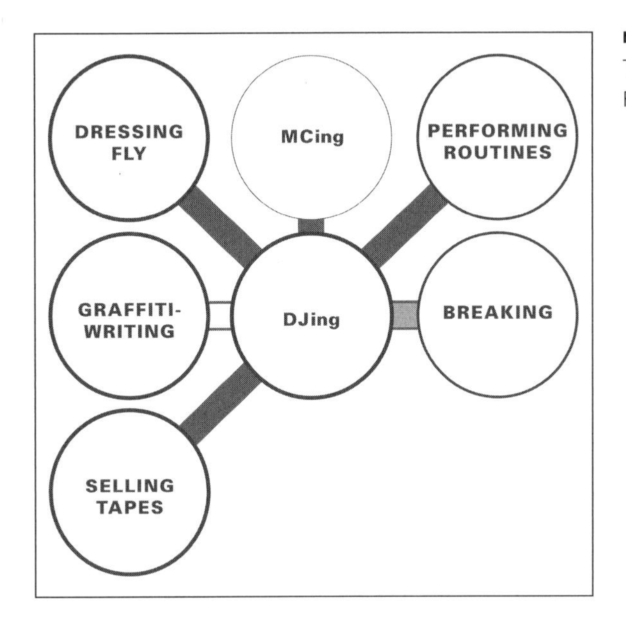

FIGURE 4.4
The Inclusion of Fashion and Routines.

JULY 13TH, 1977

In the preceding pages, I have described the way outside influences transformed the scene through its internal logic. This was not the only way that the external world affected the scene, however. Sometimes outside influences were so strong that they imposed themselves without regard to the scene's rules.

On one hot and humid summer night in 1977, DJ Disco Wiz and Grandmaster Caz were playing for a crowd at a park on Valentine Avenue and 183rd Street. "We were in the middle of a frenzied battle," Wiz recalls. "In those days, we used to plug our stuff into a lamp post, and many a time we blew the lamp post out." Wiz played first that night, offering the crowd the funkiest break beats. Then it was Caz's turn. "I throw on one record over here, boom, the crowd is going nuts, 'cause they know I'm going to get into my thing. I take the other record. I know this is gonna kill 'em. So, boom. Time comes, boom! It was the back of 'Indiscreet,' by D.C. LaRue. I bring in the record. 'Love, looove, loooovvvve . . . ' It just slows to a stop."[41] The system turns off. "And then the streetlights started going out one at a time, all the way up the block, like, 'poof, poof, poof, poof.' We looked at each other. I go, 'Oh Shit,' 'cause we're plugged into one of the street lights, and I thought we blew out the whole street. The whole neighborhood went dark."[42] Caz and Wiz could not believe it. They had blown out a street lamp before, but never had all the lights on an entire block gone off. As they would soon learn, it was not their fault, though. It was July 13th, the night of the 1977 blackout.

The chairman of Commonwealth Edison called it "an act of God" when, at 8:30 p.m., the first of four lightning bolts struck and knocked out the two transmission lines that carried power from the Indian Point Nuclear generating station to New York City. Between 9:34 and 9:40 p.m., all of New York City and part of Westchester County lost electricity. Mayor Abe Beame was giving a campaign speech at the Co-op City Traditional Synagogue when the lights went out. Thinking a fuse had blown, he joked, "This is what you get for not paying your bills."[43] A pilot flying a plane full of strawberries was approaching JFK Airport when the airport disappeared under him. He frantically radioed the control towers and asked what to do about landing. He was told to head to Philadelphia and eat the strawberries. All airports in the city shut down soon after. At Shea Stadium, the New York Mets were down 2 to 1 against the Chicago Cubs, in the bottom of the 6th inning, with Lenny Randle at bat, when the lights went out. The cast of experimental theater revue *Oh Calcutta!* was nude on stage at the time. Without lights, they could not find their way back to their dressing room and had to borrow clothes from the audience when they ended the show. The rest of the city was in chaos. Journalist Peter Goldman writes:

> Nothing worked except telephones, transistor radios and a certain gritty New York resilience in the face of disaster. Subways ran dead. Elevators hung high in their shafts. Water pumps failed, and with them sinks, tubs and toilets. Streetlights and stop lights went out. Traffic thinned and slowed to a wary crawl. Refrigerators and air coolers quit. Commuter lines stalled. Stores, banks, businesses and stock exchange closed. Theaters went dark. Office towers stood nearly empty. Hospitals switched to back-up generators when they worked and flashlight medicine when they did not. Produce wilted and frozen food melted in stores. The stranded flaked out on hotel lobby floors. The mayor held his first crisis councils by candlelight.[44]

This was the second time in twelve years that New York City had experienced such calamity. The blackout of 1965 had struck on a chilly afternoon in November, and most people had stayed indoors. "There was very little civil disturbance, and something like a Battle of Britain camaraderie prevailed in New York."[45] The reaction to the 1977 blackout was different, though; it brought mayhem.[46] After a moment of disbelief, people rushed to get what they could out of stores.[47] In downtown Manhattan, patrons of some restaurants and bars attempted to leave without paying their tabs. Looting, arson, and violence were rampant in many neighborhoods, especially on commercial streets. According to *Newsweek* "[m] ore than 2,000 stores were pillaged and guestimates of property losses ran as high as $1 billion—enough to qualify the stricken areas for Federal disaster aid. A mile and a half of Brooklyn's Broadway was put to the torch. Protective metal grills were torn off storefronts with crowbars, battered down with cars, and dragged down by brute [force]. Teen-agers first, then grade-schoolers and grownups rifled shops and markets for clothes, appliances, furniture, television sets, groceries—even 50 Pontiacs from a Bronx dealership."[48]

Geographer Ernest Wohlenberg argues that neighborhoods with higher concentrations of poverty saw a larger number of lootings and damage to businesses than did other areas.[49] Second only to Brooklyn, the Bronx—especially Southwest Bronx (the High Bridge, Morris Heights, Morrisania, and Tremont districts)—saw more than 460 lootings, causing more than $15 million in damage. DJ Disco Wiz and Grandmaster Caz were playing a few blocks north of Morris Heights that night.

As Disco Wiz recalls, the first sign of pandemonium was the crashing of the gates of the bodega across the street. People screamed "blackout!" and ran in all directions. Others shouted "Hit the stores!" and rushed to the ones still open. Wiz and Caz guarded their equipment as the crowd scattered, to avoid becoming victims of the moment. Those who attempted to come for the equipment faced the barrels of their guns and were directed to go elsewhere. After ensuring the safety of their equipment, Wiz stayed with the system while Caz ran around the corner to the Sound Room, an electronics store that sold DJing equipment. He crawled through the window and helped himself to a Clubman Two mixer.[50]

As bad as the South Bronx socioeconomic environment was prior to the blackout, it grew worse afterward. Many store owners whose shops had been looted did not return to the neighborhood, and few insurance companies would risk covering merchants opening new businesses. Arson continued as landlords torched their buildings for insurance money.[51] A *Time* article from 1977 argues that addiction to drugs drove others to set buildings ablaze:

> Unable to afford the tools to remove valuable brass plumbing, sinks, bathtubs and refrigerators in abandoned buildings, junkies pour inflammable liquid around the rooms, set a blaze and wait for firemen to chop up the floors, exposing the loot. Then the "mango hunters," as New York cops call them for their practice of reaping a harvest of stolen goods, move in, drag out the fire-resistant fixtures and sell them—a bathtub is worth $25 on the open market, a wash basin $15. Some areas of New York are being burned, systematically, block by block. As frightened residents move out, slumlords make no move to protect their all but empty—and insured—buildings, and the torchers move in.[52]

When President Jimmy Carter arrived in the South Bronx for an impromptu visit in October 1977, the area was in ruins. After driving along Grand Concourse, Washington Avenue, Third Avenue, and Boston Road, he remarked: "It was a very sobering trip for me to see the devastation that has taken place in the South Bronx in the last five years."[53]

Even within this mayhem, the blackout managed to positively impact the South Bronx DJing scene by increasing the numbers of aspiring DJs and MCs. It is plausible that many participants of the scene joined in the looting, as the blackout afforded more teens the opportunity to help themselves to equipment they otherwise could not afford.[54] DJ Disco Wiz believes this to be the case. "You know what? Before that blackout, you had about maybe five legitimate crews of DJs. After the blackout, you had a DJ on every block. . . . That blackout made a big spark in the hip-hop revolution." Caz agrees. "Everybody was a DJ. Everybody stole turntables and stuff. Every electronic store imaginable got hit for stuff. Every record store. Everything. That sprung a whole new set of DJs."[55] Would the scene have died out if the blackout had not occurred? Probably not. But there is little doubt that this unexpected event contributed to the growth of hip-hop by providing many with the opportunity, albeit through unfortunate means, to participate.

For better or worse, the blackout trumped all the internal rules. It allowed anyone to be a DJ without having to pay his dues as a b-boy, like Breakout; as an avid record collector, like Flash and Bambaataa; as a promoter, like DJ AJ; or as a devoted party-goer, like Baron. The sudden access to DJing equipment made performing in the scene more accessible and thus helped the scene to blossom. On any given corner of the South Bronx, at any given time, people would set up turntables to DJ in the spirit of Herc, Bambaataa, Flash, AJ, and Breakout. And as their style of playing music became more widely accepted, more people became invested in the scene, and the boundary around the scene strengthened. The 1977 blackout was traumatic for New York City, especially for poor neighborhoods like the South Bronx, but for hip-hop's development, it turned out to be a good thing.

On the Term "Hip-Hop"

A nebulous "thing" comes into focus when it is named. Pierre Bourdieu argues: "By structuring the perception which social agents have of this world, the act of naming helps to establish the structure of this world, and do so all the more significantly the more widely it is recognized."[56] In other words, naming prompts others to accept the existence of something. The more the name is recognized, the more established the "thing" becomes. For emerging social and cultural entities, naming is just as crucial. Yet little has been written about how hip-hop received its name.

The term *hip-hop* is believed to have started with Keith Cowboy, the first member of Flash's 3 MCs. "Without a doubt," claims Melle Mel, who goes on to explain. "This kid named Kokomo was going to the army and Cowboy was messin' with him, teasing him, with the marching Hip-hop rhythm Hip/Hop/Hip/Hop; and he just took it on from there and kept goin' with it. It just took on a life of its own."[57] In separate interviews with Troy Smith, two other people have corroborated this account. Neicy, Cowboy's sister, also confirmed it when Troy relayed Mel's explanation. "Yep , Yep that's it. . . . And then he started goin' further into the 'Hip Hip-hop bop bop ya don't stop,' he even had us goin' along with him. We didn't know what he was sayin,' but we went right along."[58] That segment, "Hip Hip-hop bop bop ya don't stop," became part of Cowboy's stage performance—and eventually that of many other MCs who emulated his style. Love Bug Starski, for example, was known to frequently use the phrase "hip-hop" in his repertoire.

In an interview with Kid Creole, Troy Smith asked how the term came about, and got the following story as a response:

> A friend of ours named Billy was about to go to the Army, I think this was '75. We had a party at the Black Door over on Boston Road and 170th Street. That was one of the first places that my brother, myself and Cowboy, played as the 3 MCs, along with Flash. This was Billy's last weekend before shipping out, and Cowboy was on the mic playin' around doing that Army cadence: Hip/Hop/Hip/Hop. But he was doin' it to music and people was diggin' on it. So we never thought much of it.[59]

As more MCs used the phrase in their rhyming, it became one of the expressions that marked the DJing scene. But despite its ubiquity, the participants did not use the term to identify themselves or their scene. It was those outside the scene who, rather arbitrarily, latched onto the term *hip-hop* to describe the South Bronx DJing scene. "Disco was king at the time, and the Disco crowd referred to us as those 'hip-hoppers,'" explains Kid Creole.[60] As scholars of social and collective identity suggest, social categorization by outsiders is just as important in the process of identification as is internal formation.[61] For outsiders, the term *hip-hop* was a simple way to characterize the scene that had emerged; it was their way of distinguishing it from other things that existed, but, Creole adds, "they used it as a derogatory term."[62] The older crowd who partied outside the South Bronx looked down on this DJing scene composed of young people. Nonetheless, they recognized that its participants had created their own social scene, and the older crowd referred to it as "hip-hop." It is unclear when the participants themselves embraced the name, but it is reasonable to assume that it would have been after 1975, when the scene had established itself enough to be recognizable to outsiders. According to Cheryl Keyes, Bambaataa was the first to use the term to describe the DJing world in the Bronx.[63] These empirical details reveal two important things about hip-hop's development to this point. First, it is clear that, by the late 1970s, perhaps around 1977, the proto-boundaries established around 1973 were now well-defined. Second, one of the most important conventions of the scene, the most enduring of them all—the name—originated from outside the scene.

New Scenes

Conventions in a given social world do not exist in isolation. A change in one affects all the others. At times, a new convention can even push another right out of existence. The remaining pages of this chapter explore how newer conventions affected b-boying and graffiti-writing, two original components of hip-hop.

GRAFFITI

From early on, the South Bronx DJing scene was entangled with the graffiti scene because many audience members at the parties, and some who were onstage DJing or MCing, participated in the graffiti movement as well. The very act of taking on a nickname as a performer was something that, at least in the beginning, came from the graffiti convention of writing with a pseudonym. After this initial overlap, however, the two worlds progressed in different directions with little regard for one another, even though graffiti writers still came to South Bronx parties. By 1977, none of the premier DJs or MCs were active as graffiti writers. As the DJing scene became more centered around performance, graffiti simply did not matter much. This is not to say that graffiti-writing went out of fashion among the youth: it was, after all, a more established social scene than DJing. However, from the mid-1970s on, graffiti-writing continued on its own evolutionary path. The scene moved into New York City's subway system as writers covered the insides and outsides of trains with their work. Writers like IZ THE WIZ prided themselves on watching their work run throughout the city.[64]

As graffiti artists moved the locus of their writing from walls to trains, they faced considerable opposition from public officials. To try to contain and eventually end the spread of graffiti, New York City politicians, beginning in spring 1972, declared war on graffiti artists, a war supported by City Council President Sanford Garelik and MTA Chairman William T. Ronan. Mayor John Lindsay passed legislation that severely punished those who engaged in what Garelik called "the worst form of pollution to the eye."[65] The graffiti writers fought back, developing creative ways to evade the city's efforts. Indeed, the allure of tagging the trains increased, since graffiti artists knew they had the attention of politicians. The writers were eventually defeated, however. Nonetheless, a victory for the city officials did not mean the end of graffiti. Members of the art world in Manhattan became interested in it, especially those who had supported Pop Art during the 1960s. Hugo Martínez was among the first to take graffiti into art galleries when he organized the United Graffiti Artists, a union of elite writers. Although his organization eventually died out, other graffiti artists capitalized on the new craze. None is more famous than Brooklyn-born, Haitian-American Jean-Michel Basquiat, who, within one year, went from living in the streets to selling his paintings in art galleries.[66]

Other graffiti writers, displaced from tagging trains, used their artistic talent to make unique fliers advertising parties and battles and thereby began to participate in the DJing world. Just as they had competed over tags on the trains before, they competed over fliers now. This time the stakes were different. The rivalry focused not only on how much work they could produce or how aesthetically complex their fliers were. It also included how successful the fliers were at bringing an audience to parties.

The most famous of the flier makers was Buddy Esquire. Esquire had been born in the Bronx and raised in the Monroe Housing Projects in Soundview. He began high school at Clinton but graduated from Stevenson High School, where Tony Tone of the Funky 4 was a classmate. Esquire started tagging in 1972, inspired by the first generation of New York City graffiti writers. "A friend of mine got me into it," he recalls. "He was writing first and he used to show me so I started to do it also. From there I started going out tagging with him on trains and at the yards."[67] He had the same motivation other writers had: he wanted to get his name out. "It's like an itch," he says, "a drive to want to do it, to want to get better, to want to work hard at it. Sometimes you do it on a couple of pieces of paper, [and other times] you just want to go out and write. When that time came . . . I graduated to the trains and I used to hit the Baychester layup. It was a crazy rush tagging inside and outside of the trains."[68] He used different names for a while, but when he got to the trains, he settled on an abbreviation of his last name: ESQ. Buddy Esquire was an active writer for a few years, but his career came to an abrupt end when, caught hanging with other writers, he was taken to the police precinct and written up. A letter was sent to his parents. "I didn't know when [the letter] was coming to the house but when my mother got it, I knew because that's when *I* got it. Moms and Pops broke on me, they weren't very pleased with the situation. They couldn't find the stash of markers so they hid my comic books."[69] His parents also grounded him for two months and allowed him out of the house only to run errands for them at a local store. He still had the "itch" to write, so he got into a new hobby that put his name out without negative repercussions. He started to paint people's DJ, MC, or crew names on their clothing: "I went to the library and I took out a book on fine painting, where they talked about letters, proportions and lay outs and stuff like that. . . . What made me go to the library was because when people would put paint on jeans and stuff, it was either graffiti or some kind of sloppy-looking handwriting. So I was like figuring let me do it this way and that will make my stuff noticeable. So I started doing it like that. People seen what I was doing and started wanting me to paint for them."[70]

Given his reputation for good work, he was approached to make fliers for parties. The first was for a block party in Summer 1977. "The second one I ever made in my whole life, which was in November of 1978, came about because Tony Tone told me that the crew that he was with[,] which was [with] Breakout at the time[,] needed somebody to make their flier. When I look at it now I feel it's a piece of crap. But I did it for Breakout because they were having a jam at 131."[71] It took off from there. For the next two years, Esquire was the go-to flier-maker for the Funky 4.

In the graffiti subculture, a process emerged for creating fliers. Party promoters, like Van Silk, would drop off the basic information needed on the flier—names of performers, date, time, venue—and the flier makers would get to work. They had complete creative control over the flier's aesthetics. PHASE 2, a predecessor whom Esquire admired, worked closely with Silk. "PHASE actually sat in his mother's living room and did the fliers," recalls Silk. "We'd be so glad to get that master cardboard flier."[72] The master would then be taken to a printing center to make copies, sometimes several thousand of them. "We could tell if we was gonna have a good show or bad show by how they treated the flier—a person folds up a flier and puts it in their pocket, if you don't see no fliers on the floor, you're gonna have a good show," Van Silk explains.[73] The flier became a space of artistic competition in its own right. Besides Buddy Esquire and PHASE 2, other flier makers included Eddie Ed (Esquire's brother), Vega Ray, Straight Man, Danny T., A Reilly. They earned respect for their use of an array of fonts, imaginative drawings, and creative titles. And, in their own way, they added to the larger scene in which they were embedded. In addition to their fashion sense, physical gestures, and dance style, verbal expressions as popularized by the MCs, and unique musical taste, participants in hip-hop now also had their own visual aesthetic. These items, which I call cultural attributes, helped the emerging entity to endure in its first few years. Given the addition of flier makers, our diagram looks like the following.

B-BOYING

With the change in the make-up of crews, DJs and MCs became central to the hip-hop scene, and b-boys no longer mattered at parties. According to Cholly Rock, things changed in 1978: "The first generation of B boys, I'm talking about the original Zulu Kings, the Twins, Clark Kent, all that crew and all of us . . . we were done by 1978."[74] B-boying, like graffiti-writing, developed a scene of its own. Interestingly, this coincided with a shift in the racial make-up of b-boys. When b-boys were central to the South Bronx party scene, and were part and parcel of the performances of Herc and Bambaataa, it was mostly African American teens who were breaking. Crazy Legs, one of the most famous of all breakers, explains, "A lot of people used to call it, you know, morenos means black, so they be like, 'Yo that's that moreno style.' And that's the original style of b-boying."[75] But when b-boying lost its symbolic relevance in the hip-hop scene, it stopped being "a black thing"; when it became an activity in its own right, it became a Puerto Rican entity. Another b-boy Jo Jo comments, "I know for a fact that when I went to some parks, it was rare to see a Puerto Rican dancer breaking. When you did, it was like 'Oh shit, check out the Puerto Rican breaking,' you know."[76] Did b-boying become a Puerto Rican activity because it no longer mattered quite as much to the hip-hop scene? Or did African Americans stop b-boying because it was no longer central to their world? I explore these questions in the next chapter, where I address the racialization of the scene.

Among the new breed of b-boys were Batch and the Salsoul Crew, the first all-Latino crew of breakers. Then came TBB (the Bronx Boys) and the Crazy Commander Crew, featuring Spy, "the man with a thousand moves"—both

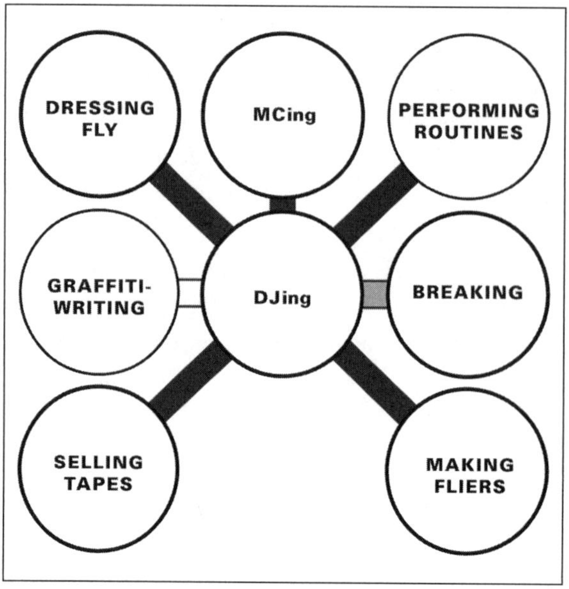

FIGURE 4.5
The Inclusion of Fliers.

groups made up primarily of Latinos. These groups introduced acrobatic moves to b-boying. Spy, then a karate instructor, is credited with bringing breaking to the floor and adding moves such as the leg swipes in the air made famous by Crazy Legs, who admired Spy. Trac 2, Jimmy Dee, and Jo Jo were known for traveling around the city to battle other b-boys and for maintaining fly attire, something unusual for b-boys at this point.[77] In 1977, some of these notable b-boys joined together to continue rocking (another term for breaking) and to protest the assertion that "breaking was played out."[78] They adopted the name "Rock Steady."

This chapter and the preceding one show how several actors became part of hip-hop, how DJing crews formed, and how crews waged battles. Further, they explain the invention of the scratch, the development of MCing, the importance of security crews, the role of performance tapes, the significance of youth fashion, the introduction of performance routines, the influence of the 1977 New York City blackout, the source of the term "hip-hop," the rise of flier makers, and the emergence of a new b-boying subculture. These empirical details give us a better sense of hip-hop history in the typically obscured period between 1975 and 1979.

PART III

Symbolic Capital in the New Entity

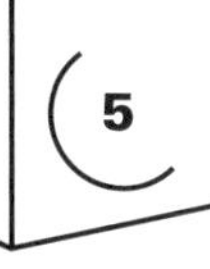

Race, Gender, and the Pursuit of Recognition

Part I of this book explored the beginnings of a new entity—the development of random sites of difference and the way they lined up to create proto-boundaries. Part II examined the ways in which these boundaries became stronger when an internal logic, in the form of conventions, developed within the scene; it also described how the entity took on cultural and social attributes. Part III explains the durability of the boundaries around hip-hop by exploring how actors gained and used symbolic capital and how participants used the rules of the game to gain fame in the hip-hop world.

Hip-hop performers earned a name based on their role at parties. At the start, the scene was an amalgamation of DJing, b-boying, and graffiti-writing (see figure 2.3). Because DJing was the central activity, DJs earned more symbolic capital than anyone else. When b-boys began to make their mark as personalities in their own right and shifted the crowd's attention from the DJs on stage to the dancers on the floor, b-boying became a viable way to earn a name. DJs remained essential and were well-known because they were responsible for the music at the parties. Graffiti-writing, by contrast, was not connected to DJing as strongly as b-boying was, so it was not a way to become popular in the music scene. It was all about how the b-boys responded to the music the DJs played, until Grandmaster Flash introduced his innovative mixing techniques. This turned partygoers' attention from the dance floor back to the stage and the DJ. At Flash's events, few paid attention to the b-boys on the floor, so they faded into the background and eventually disappeared from hip-hop events all together. Then the MCs appeared, beginning with Flash's 3 MCs. They became the DJ's accompanists, and, because their activity was so closely connected with DJing—still hip-hop's central activity—MCing became a source of social status (see figure 3.1). Thereafter, each successive activity that became part of the scene—flier making, selling tapes, performance routines, and fashion sensibilities—contributed to DJs' performances (see figures 3.3, 4.4, and 4.5). The closer an activity was to DJing, the more symbolic or "functional" capital it offered.[1]

The accumulation of capital in hip-hop did not depend solely on the role an actor played, however. Performers' individual attributes, and their ability to fit those attributes into the logic of the scene, also mattered. Afrika Bambaataa, for example, was immediately admired because his reputation as a high-ranking gang member transferred into the DJing world.[2] Additionally, his parties were popular because he had charisma, in the sense that he was able to amass a following of people.[3] Specifically, he had extraordinary power to move several of his peers from destructive behaviors to social activism. Bambaataa also had an eclectic collection of music and knew how to play exactly what the audience wanted to hear. He became legendary because he was able to convert these aspects of his personal background—his personal capital—into symbolic capital recognized in the DJing scene.[4]

Participants also earned capital for having the right attitudes, skills, and outlooks. The L Brothers and the Funky 4, for example, entered the scene easily because they possessed all the right dispositions: they loved music, they admired DJs, they had the patience to mess around with old record players, they had the know-how to build their own speakers, they liked coming up with rhymes, they enjoyed practicing routines, and they aspired to make hundreds of people move to their beat. Those who did not enter the scene with the right predilections had to go out of their way to build them. For instance, even though DJ AJ regularly attended parties given by Herc and Pete DJ Jones, he did not have the feel for performance that the DJing scene required. He was a hustler, so for him the park jams were simply a place to make money. To become a performer, AJ had to apprentice with Love Bug Starski. Besides learning how to operate a turntable and select records, he had to learn how to think like a DJ and understand that DJing was not just about playing songs, it was also about connecting with the audience through music.

Taking up the right activity and possessing the right attributes made participation in the DJing scene easier for some than for others, but they were not the only things that mattered. Being black and male also made a difference; it was no accident that most of the performers were black men. The remainder of this chapter demonstrates how the emerging entity we call hip-hop fashioned itself to make it difficult for women and non-blacks to become celebrated figures.

Masculinizing Hip-Hop

Early hip-hop jams appealed as much to the young men in the South Bronx as they did to the young women. But most of the performers were young men. Why? Were the young women simply uninterested in performing? Or were they excluded from participating? If so, why and how?

Just as I have pointed to how the social context of the South Bronx—poverty, youth activities, popular music—impacted the shaping of the emerging social entity, it should come as no surprise that the constructions of gender during that time and space also impacted this developing social scene. The participants in hip-hop had available to them two worlds that proposed contrasting logics of gender and sexuality. In their immediate surroundings in the South Bronx, masculinities and femininities mostly adhered to broader American patterns of patriarchy and heteronormativity. Historically, both black and Latino communities have assigned rigid gender roles to (young) men and women, even if each community holds a somewhat different notion of those roles.[5] In one study, Latinos and Latinas reported different levels limitations placed on them regarding curfews and interacting with the opposite sex.[6] Even if there has been more gender-neutral socializing within black communities, they still maintain hierarchies of sexuality in which men are dominant.[7] In Manhattan, disco clubs were sites of gender and sexual logics that differed from the mainstream. In a time when homosexuality was punishable by law, club goers defiantly rejected the normalized understandings of gender and sexuality and subscribed to more fluid notions of each. Gay, lesbian, and bisexual dancers were welcome on the dance floor; they were not relegated to the peripheries or the back rooms. After their stand against the police in 1969 at the Stonewall Inn, sexuality became more central to the social identities of these club goers.[8] Their sexual orientations became a source of their consciousness—they came to view themselves not just as a group in itself but also as a group *for* itself.

The formation of hip-hop was only a few years removed from these developments and a few train stops away, so one might reasonably assume that hip-hop participants were, in some ways, exposed to these alternative constructions of gender and sexuality in Manhattan, especially since they were participants in an activity shared by both scenes—DJing. But if they were, there is little evidence that they embraced any of the more fluid understandings of gender and sexuality. Why were they unmoved? One obvious explanation is their closeness and intimate contact with Latino and African diasporic culture. They lived in the South Bronx, with black and Latino families so they were socialized towards those communities' particular logics of gender and sexuality. Even though they were engaged in the same social activity as Manhattan DJs, they came from different socialization processes. They were more inclined to abide by the logic of gender and sexuality in their neighborhoods also because, as expressed above, they defined their DJing scene against those in Manhattan. In addition to being break-centered rather than song-centered and being in their early and mid-teens and not their twenties, they were also, consciously or not, not as open to different displays and performances of gender and sexuality. The gendering of hip-hop began with the social milieu in which it was created, but it did not end there.

Performers in hip-hop were mostly male also because of the gendered nature of leisure activities. Men, even young men, generally have more time for leisure activities than women because of gendered socialization processes.[9] Economic resources, facilities and programs, and time are all important factors, but perhaps more than anything else, the ethic of care work best explains women's participation in leisure activities.[10] While young men in the South Bronx spent hours tinkering with record players, sorting out records, and listening through them for the perfect break beat, young women most likely spent their "free time" at home with their mothers participating in domestic labor.

Relatedly, leisure activities are themselves not gender neutral. They are grounds on which gender stereotypes and gender inequities are reinforced.[11] Hip-hop drew from several existent social activities in and around the South Bronx, most of which were male-dominated. So, from the beginning, hip-hop was shaped by the predilections of men. DJs had, for the most part, always been men. Although the DJing scene in Manhattan challenged heteronormativity on the dance floor, there were very few well-known female DJs in any of the clubs. Bert Lockett, a butch lesbian who presented herself as male by wearing short hair and a shirt, jacket, and tie, was one of them. "Some of the men didn't know I was a woman," she explains. "They would get very angry if they found out I was a girl. I looked like a fella, and they had a problem with that." From one coworker, especially, she received so much harassment that she eventually quit. "He worked six nights a week, and he was so jealous of my ass he started to tell me what records to play. The audience was saying, 'They need to get rid of him and let *her* play!' In the end, I had to leave that place because he was getting out of hand."[12] Recall gang practices: some organizations, like the Savage Skulls, had female members, but these women were often the friends, girlfriends, or sisters of male gang members. As a result, their contributions were subordinated. Likewise, the graffiti world included females, like EVA 62 and BARBARA 62, but most were on the scene's periphery because they had to rely on their male counterparts to traverse the city. "You always have to go out with the guys," explains LADYPINK, perhaps the most famous of all female New York City graffiti writers. "At that time, New York City was very dangerous at night. [Being] a little 15-year-old, 90 pounds, 5'2, [it] wouldn't be a good idea to go out at night. So I had to go out with a bunch of guys; the night belonged to the men folk."[13]

What is more, the technology—and the knowledge required to operate it—was more accessible to men than to women.[14] Tricia Rose made this observation years ago. "Because [hip-hop] music's approaches to sound reproduction developed informally," she writes, "the primary means for gathering information [was] shared local knowledge."[15] Many of the male DJs and MCs learned how to hook up their turntables to their speakers from an older male neighbor across the street or down the hall. "For social, sexual, and cultural reasons," Rose continues, "young women would be much less likely to be permitted or feel comfortable spending such extended time in a male neighbor's home."[16] The above reasons go some way toward explaining why hip-hop performers, at the very beginning, were males. But these factors still do not fully explain how or why performers continued to be mostly men—for that we must look to the performance of masculinity.

Despite the scene's masculinism, women were not irrelevant to hip-hop's creation.[17] In fact, the involvement of women was important as this new social and cultural entity became defined as masculine. As feminist theorists have argued, the construction of masculinity seldom takes place independently and without interaction with femininity.[18] Masculinity and gender in general are not sets of traits within an individual but a "product of social doings." Doing gender thus "involves making use of discrete, well defined bundles of behavior that can simply be plugged into interactional situations to produce recognizable enactments of masculinity and femininity."[19] The most obvious set of behaviors that made the hip-hop scene recognizably masculine revolved around performances of heterosexuality.[20]

For the mostly male DJs and MCs, performing on the stage gave them an advantage in doing their masculinity. Women made up a small minority of performers in the DJing scene, but there is every reason to believe that the audience at parties was made up of as many women as men. "One of the first things I seen in the hip-hop music was the girls," one male attendee observes. "Mad attention from the girls. If you was a DJ or an MC, you had girls. And at the time, being 14, 15, you needed girls."[21] Some of the male performers were motivated to join the scene primarily by their desire for female attention.

"That's what motivated me to rhyme," Keith Cowboy attests, "'cause Mel was on the mic and he was getting girls. I couldn't just stand on the sidelines."[22] Another MC adds, "At the time, I was just a kid from a small town in Jersey, and I'm seventeen trying to get laid and all that kinda stuff, and I had issues about that stuff. I didn't think I was the best lookin' guy, so the record was a chance to be who I wanted to be. I wanted to be a ladies' man in real life."[23] Male participants thus used their positions as DJs and MCs to enhance their masculine appeal and thereby attract women who were primarily audience members.[24]

If these male actors entered the scene to get women's attention, they structured the scene to keep that attention. With the increasing importance of MCing emerged a particular style of rhyming dedicated to wooing women in the audience. "You have guys that write rhymes for battles, and you have some who write rhymes for the ladies," Grandwizard Theodore explains as he attempts to categorize Kevie Kev, an MC in the L Brothers crew. "Back then[,] I don't think [Kev] was like a battle emcee; he was like he is going to rhyme for the ladies."[25] KK Rockwell of the Funky 4 did the same. One of his signature rhymes was: *I'm KK Rockwell and I rock so well, and I like to make love to all the jazzy females.* Keith Keith used this rhyme: *I'm Keith Keith, but you can call me Keith Caesar, the reason why 'cause I'm the woman pleaser.* Likewise, the motivation to look fly was not simply to look cohesive as a crew but to attract the attention of women in the audience. For this reason, a crew would be more likely to admit a well-dressed male into its lineup than an equally qualified male who was less fashion-conscious.

In many ways, hip-hop became a masculinized space because it helped the male participants onstage to perform their masculinity, especially their heterosexual desires.[26] This was the foundation underlying the masculinization of hip-hop. The result was that hip-hop performers were to be males who exhibited their heterosexuality to females in the audience. There were two important effects of this. First, it was difficult for young women to participate in the scene as performers. Second, the rules of the scene insisted on a hyper-masculine sexuality that forced non-heterosexual participants to hide their sexuality, so we don't know much about the sexual diversity of participants during the early years of hip-hop—histories of hip-hop have often presumed most participants to be heterosexual. In many ways, this mirrors representations of lesbian, gay, bisexual, transgender, and queer figures in other (African) American histories. To use Essex Hemphill's words, "The black homosexual is hard pressed to gain audience among his heterosexual brothers . . . . This is what the race has depended on in being able to erase homosexuality from our recorded history. The 'chosen' history. But these sacred constructions of silence are futile exercises in denial."[27] Even if some participants knew of homosexual behaviors, or more broadly non-heterosexual activities, it was kept quiet. Sadly, the limited information available about non-heterosexual activities among early participants of hip-hop comes from accusations of sexual abuse. The most widely publicized example of such allegations involves Afrika Bambaataa and an accuser named Ron Savage. On March 29, 2016, in a videotaped interview with the *New York Daily News*, Savage accused Bambaataa of molesting him in 1977, when he was around thirteen or fourteen years old.[28] After Savage's allegations, three other men have made similar accusations.[29] Bambaataa and his attorneys have publicly denied all of the allegations. That said, stories such as these can raise broader questions about what is still unknown about sexuality and heteronormativity during hip-hop's early years.

Sha-Rock, Lisa Lee, and the Mercedes Ladies

The masculinization of hip-hop had another important consequence: it shaped how young women participated in the scene as performers. Just ask Sha-Rock, Lisa Lee, and the Mercedes Ladies.

Sha-Rock was an impressive MC who was very comfortable on stage partly because early in her teens she had taken part in theatrical productions sponsored by her neighborhood community center. Her mother and stepfather, both former members of the Black Panther Party, had encouraged Sha-Rock and her siblings in the arts, and on numerous occasions, her mother had written poems for her to recite at Black History Month celebrations.[30] DJ Breakout remembers when Sha-Rock came to audition for the Funky 4 MCs. "Sha-Rock said, 'I can talk, too.' I was like, 'Well no, you can't.' There never was a girl MC."[31] Perhaps it was not just that "there was never a girl MC" but also that MCing was then seen as being a "guy thing." Even Sha-Rock's mother was initially hesitant. "My mom was worried about me being a female out there," Sha recalls, "but once she saw that this wasn't something that would lead me into the wrong direction, she was alright with it."[32]

Across town, in Bambaataa's Zulu Nation, another female MC, Lisa Lee, was a member of the Cosmic Force. She started writing rhymes when she was twelve years old and got on the microphone a year later. At a party held by Disco Mario and Bambaataa at Junior High School 123, she asked if she could perform; to her surprise, they agreed. She and her ten-year-old brother had snuck out of the house to go to that party. Two weeks after her debut on the mic, Lisa Lee's name appeared on a flier for a Bambaataa party. "I remember my brother coming home, running to me, [and] showing me my name on the flier.

And we was in the house jumping around, excited," Lee recalls. They put the flier in the lobby of their apartment building for everyone to see: Lee was the first female MC in her neighborhood. "I never heard a female, but that was just something that I wanted to do. . . . [P]eople kinda looked at me like, 'word'; your name is on a flier. They were shocked." She performed alongside Bambaataa, whose parties were not just for entertainment; they were also about steering youth away from negative influences. Because of her parent's activism, Lisa was sympathetic to Bambaataa's mission. She became one of the leaders of the Zulu Queens, the branch of the organization focused on the well-being of young women. "We had [our weekly] meetings [at Bambaataa's house]. . . . We would just stay with him; spend weekends there. And he took us all in as his family. His moms was okay with it, and, . . . you know, I didn't have a mother, so, you know, it worked for me. Just to have someone there that called me family."[33]

During his interview with Lisa Lee, Troy Smith asked her how Bambaataa was able to get so many people to listen to him. She responded, "I wish I knew what it was about it but some people just have that aura that make people listen." Then she elaborated: "I'm sure everybody wants some peace in their life. And if he's offering that there is away for us to still protect ourselves, you don't have to punk down, but there is a way for us to actually have peace, as a whole, as a group, as an organization, if we come together, and just be cool? Who wouldn't want that? So I think that made people listen. Like, you mean we can actually do this? We can still protect where we from? And enjoy some good times at a party with music? I mean I guess everybody would try to see if it was possible." Bambaataa's message resonated with her. Like him, she had been a member of the Black Spades, and Bambaataa's organization saved her from sinking deeper into life on the streets. "I did get me a Black Spades jacket, but I don't remember wearing it that often. I do remember getting calls in the middle of the night to go and fight or whatever."[34]

At one event, Lisa Lee and Sha-Rock came face to face. "The first time I became aware of Lisa Lee was when we performed at Stevenson High School back in like '78," Sha-Rock recalls. She was there with her crew, and Lisa was with Bambaataa and the rest of his crewmembers. "I was rocking on the mic for a couple of minutes," Sha continues. "When I started to pass the mic to Keith, Lisa Lee began to rock on the mic from across the room." "Sha, she's trying to come at you," DJ Baron whispered to Sha-Rock, hoping the two MCs would battle. "When she finishes, I want you to get at her."[35] They went back and forth for a few rounds, and neither outdid the other. Perhaps because no clear winner emerged, they earned respect from each other, from the other MCs and DJs present, and from the audience. In fact, after that night, the two MCs became good friends. According to Lisa, they often recreated their rapidly alternating performance whenever their crews played together.

While Sha-Rock and Lisa Lee were celebrated figures in the hip-hop scene, we should not read their popularity as a sign that hip-hop embraced women performers as much as they embraced men performers. They were included not just because they were talented in their own right, but also because they belonged to predominantly male crews. Their participation therefore did not threaten the construction of hip-hop as a masculine world.

Sheri of the Mercedes Ladies, an all-female crew, had a different experience of navigating the hip-hop world. She was one of several children in a single-mother household. The family moved frequently, mostly due to evictions. But one place remained constant in Sheri's life: Boston Road, around Morrisania. "[It] was the place to be, especially during the summer months, because you always had different DJ crews playing music on the corner. The block was always rocking. Come on, with Grandmaster Flash and [his MCs], Grand Wizard Theodore and the L Brothers, Kool Herc and the Herculords, DJ Breakout from uptown—and the list goes on—Boston Road was the original home base for hip-hop."[36] Sheri first learned about hip-hop from her friend RD Smiley, who lived on the block. Smiley knew most of the performers because another friend, Tracy Tee, had a brother who was a member of the Boston Road Crew, a security crew loosely affiliated with Flash. The first time Sheri, Tracy Tee, Smiley, and Lil Bit (another of Smiley's friends) went to a party on Boston Road, it was held at Saint Mary's Park and featured Flash, Herc, and DJ AJ. This was in 1976. Over the next few months, Sheri and her friends became regulars. Sheri was a fan of DJ Breakout and the Funky 4 in particular because of Sha-Rock. Sheri and Sha were in the same math class at Evander Childs High School. "I'd always see her in class with a notebook and a pen in her hand—not for class notes, but for writing rhymes. I'd be like 'What's up Sha?' She would lift her head with that little girl smile, and say, 'Just chillin', girl.'"[37]

Sheri and her friends began to skip classes so they could spend more time on Boston Road. Soon the girls made their friendship more formal by becoming a crew—the Mercedes Ladies. They picked the name because "it sound[ed] classy, like the Mercedes Benz."[38] Like another all-female social crew that frequented Funky 4 parties—Sister's Disco—the Mercedes Ladies were a social organization, a collection of fly girls who would show up at jams to party and flirt with the performers. "All eyes were on us as we walked through a jam in the schoolyard at 165th and Boston Road on summer nights," Sheri wistfully remembers. "Of course we had on our full outfits from the yellow sweatshirts with black velvet lettering to the Lee jeans."[39] "We knew we were on the right track when MCs started incorporating our names into their rhymes," Sheri continues. "Everywhere we went," RD Smiley adds, "dudes were shouting our name out on the mic, 'Mercedes Ladies! Mercedes Ladies! Mercedes Ladies!' So we started getting into the best clubs. . . . Wherever we went, we didn't have to pay to get in."[40] The allure of the streets, the music, the dancing, the favors, and the attention from men kept them going back and added to their sense of selfhood. Sheri reflects on how it felt to be a part of the group: "Coming up as a child, I never felt like I fit into anything. I didn't know my purpose, why I was born, and could never find the right answers. [With the Mercedes Ladies], I finally felt I belonged to something in my life that was just for me."[41] This all-female crew provides another example of how hip-hop mattered in the lives of its participants, how it bonded those involved.

Zina and Evelin became part of the crew, and then several more girls joined. At its height, the group had about twenty-three members. With more members, the Mercedes Ladies broadened their aspirations. "We wanted to open up our own club," says Sheri. "What we was really trying to do was to start something in the hood that was never heard of, like have females promoting parties and things."[42] They were certainly popular enough to do so, because their presence at events was already drawing people; but at the time, party promoters were all men. The Mercedes Ladies also wanted the crew to have a more significant mark on the lives of its members. "We tried to be a little more cultured as well as try to have a little more of an idea of what we wanted in life."[43] They became selective about whom to let into the crew by asking new recruits questions about past relationships with boys and behavior at parties. "We tried to think about these questions [ahead of time,] but at times they were random and it was to see if the girl was loose and too much into men. We also questioned the girls about their relationship with drugs. As well as checking to see if she was plain dumb," Smiley explains. "Then we would switch over to [questions like]: what is your favorite drink? How much drinks do you have a day? What type of music do you like? What is the name of your favorite artist? It would be back and forth random questions from the [original four ladies]."[44] After being accepted into the group, new members still had to prove they were worthy to remain members. Smiley continues: "See, the first night we would hang with them would be like probation-type thing. They might get loud after drinking too much [and] the drugs were there, so a lot of them didn't know how to handle themselves. So the whole thing was here, we are going to parties and knowing how popular we were[,] you don't stand around till the very end of the party, you leave. Don't be the first to go to the party, and don't be the last to leave the party. And some people, when they get drunk, they just hang on the bar stool and get all loud. Well, that was how we knocked them out of the crew."[45]

The founding members had complete authority to enforce standards, rules that allowed them to be in control of how the women interacted with men at parties. It was their way of performing a type of femininity that fit within the gender norms of the scene while also resisting complete subordination. To put it differently, the Mercedes Ladies showed up to parties to play their role in the heteronormative exchange, but they did not give in completely to the desires of the men. Eventually, though, the Mercedes Ladies made the transition from being a social crew to being a DJing and MCing crew. When they did, they lost their power over their crew and the power to control their position in the scene. They became subject to the masculinist conventions of the larger DJing scene, which proved to be unfriendly.

Trevor, a Jamaican-born party promoter interested in forming an all-female DJing and MCing crew, saw the Mercedes Ladies as the perfect crew because they already had so much buzz in the streets. He approached the group with his idea, and they agreed. At their first meeting, the women decided who would play what role in the group. Sheri nominated RD Smiley to serve as DJ because she had already started learning how to use her brother's DJ equipment at home. Baby Dee, and later DJ Spank, also became DJs. Sheri Sher, Zina, and Evelyn were the MCs, and Tracy Tee handled day-to-day operations.[46]

Trevor also worked with the L Brothers, so the Mercedes Ladies rapidly became affiliated with that crew, which created a problem. According to the rules of territoriality in the scene, it was odd for Trevor to have a crew from the Boston Road area, Grandmaster Flash's territory, and another crew (the L Brothers) from another section of the Bronx with which Flash competed. Moreover, it was a conflict of interest for the Boston Road Crew, the security crew that worked with Flash, to look out for the Mercedes Ladies if they played alongside the L Brothers. In fact, Donald Bird, a member of the Boston Road Crew, refused to allow his sister, Tracy Tee, to be part of the Mercedes Ladies until Trevor and his business partner West negotiated with the Boston Road Crew. Smiley recalls: "So Trevor and West went down there. West[,] with his long locks[,] went over to Boston Road and sat down in the territory of The Boston Road Crew and they talked and they talked some more. In the end[,] Donald Bird said, 'they are cool kids[;] they just want to make music and being as they came and spoke to us it's all good. . . . Being as we got y'all back, we also got the L Brothers' back.'"[47] Beyond highlighting the persistent territoriality of the scene, a lasting remnant of gang culture, it also points to hip-hop's male-centric culture. Simply put, the Mercedes

FIGURE 5.1
The Mercedes Ladies. (© Mercedes Ladies; used with permission from Rene D. Pearson)

Ladies could not have become a DJing-MCing crew without these men convening to approve their formation. Hip-hop was not masculine because of anything intrinsic in its activities, but because of the conventions that structured the internal logic of the scene.

The Mercedes Ladies practiced and played with the L Brothers and on their equipment. They held their first party at 63 Park in June 1977, and the L Brothers opened for them. In a nearby lobby, the ladies huddled up and said a prayer before hitting the stage. Smiley remembers:

> Everybody got into the prayer group. While we were praying, I told everyone we are going to do good because we would not be in this predicament if it wasn't meant to be. So we turned the corner all together and we went into the park. Trevor was mad, asking where we were at. I was like, "Calm down, we are here." Like I said, the L Brothers were there and Kevie Kev introduced us. I was shocked to see all the people that were there. A lot of our friends were there, as well as our pastor

> from school. Dee started with "Catch a Groove" and "The Bells." I played Anita Ward's "Ring My Bell." At that time, there was no routines. We just wanted to show them that we could do it. We just wanted to show them that women can DJ, and women can get on the mic. Then Sheri would do roll call, "Sheri Sher rock the house, Lil Bit is the Shit, Baby Dee what you got for me. Tracy Tee to the highest degree, RD . . . Smiley."[48]

It was a strong showing for the first-time DJing and MCing crew, and they were rewarded with more performances throughout that summer. Indeed their stock rose high enough that they were able to book indoor gigs when winter came. Their popularity was due as much to their fine performing as to their affiliation with men: a well-respected, all-male crew, and the backing of a male manager. That they were black also mattered, as we shall see in the next section.

The Mercedes Ladies incorporated routines in their shows. Smiley, who at this point stopped DJing and stepped into the role of manager (eventually becoming known as the mother of the group), recalls how they came up with one of their routines: "One night I was hanging out at 371 watching DJ Hollywood and I seen him do this routine where he is saying, 'Let's do it, let's do it. Everybody go ha ha.' So I told Sheri what Hollywood did and I said let's do something different but the same thing in a female voice. So she used to do, 'Lets Do iiiiiiit, Lets Do iiiiiit everybody go ha ha because I am that girl that will rock your world' . . . and she will sing her whole routine and we will be her background singing, 'Wonder Girl!' So that was one routine and we gave most of the routines to her because we put her out front."[49]

As the Mercedes Ladies continued to ascend the ranks in the scene, Trevor got arrested for selling marijuana, and the New York City Police Department confiscated all his DJing equipment, which the ladies had been using for performances.[50] When the Mercedes Ladies lost their manager, they also lost their relationship with the L Brothers, whose equipment they relied on for practice sessions. With no equipment for practicing or performances, the ladies had to play their gigs on whatever machines were available, and they had to manage themselves, which ended up posing a bigger challenge. Because the networks of party promoters and club owners were entirely male, these young women were at a disadvantage. They had neither the social capital nor the "muscle" (physical strength or weapons) to navigate the scene, so they needed a male manager.

On one occasion, Ray Chandler invited them to play at Hotel Diplomat. They were auditioning in hopes of being included on Chandler's roster of A-list performers, which included Flash, DJ AJ, and Lovebug Starski. Flash performed before them that night, and then Lovebug took the stage. As Smiley remembers, "When we got on, the girls checked their mics. There was no juice, no sound. Baby Dee was scratching away, and there was nothing, no sound. I asked her what was going on. She said she wasn't getting anything. The knobs start falling off, [and] the mics started falling off the mic stands and breaking in the girls' hands. So I am like, what's going on here?"[51] Smiley believes they were sabotaged that night, because Lovebug was in the audience laughing. When they finally got the system working and got the crowd yelling their name, Chandler cut their performance short. At the end of the night, the ladies who performed were paid $30 each, but Smiley, as manager, received only $20. These amounts were a pittance compared to the several hundred dollars each of their male counterparts received. "They didn't want us to play in Harlem. It's as simple as that. See, I thought we were cool because we did PAL with Ray Chandler. I thought we were going to get down with Flash, and me and the girls were all cool with that. I was excited. So when we did the Hotel Diplomat and that situation happened, it was over. Because after that night he never returned our calls, and we put two and two together. We just figured they didn't want us in that circle."[52]

On another occasion, they recalled, a new manager who claimed to be a millionaire invited them to play at a skating rink on Long Island. Because the group did not have many other options, they agreed to perform, although they knew it was not the right event for them. The audience members, unfamiliar with the hip-hop scene, were not into their music and booed them. The manager paid them a measly $7.26 each. In response to this unfair treatment, Smiley wrote the following rhyme:

> We got paid 7 and a quarter and a penny to our names,
> trying to put Mercedes in the hall of fame,
> but that's alright we just begun,
> and all we want to do is have some fun.
> Some people might say that we're the wack,
> but we took the chill,
> and now we're back,
> to rectify, to bonafide,
> to the boogie y'all, to the boogie y'all!

These stories about early hip-hop's female participants reveal how hip-hop came to be a masculinized space that excluded women performers; remnants of this masculinism persist in today's hip-hop world. As hip-hop came to serve a social function for men, as it enabled them to perform their masculinity—especially in their pursuits of heterosexual desire—hip-hop stages became spaces reserved for men. Some women were able to perform but only with the explicit or implicit endorsement of men. The Mercedes Ladies, the only all-female crew during hip-hop's early days, were unsuccessful especially after they lost the support of prominent male actors.

If gendering helped some to succeed, did racializing help others, and if so, how? The next section focuses on this question.

How Hip-Hop Became Black

According to sociologist of music William G. Roy, cultural objects, like genres of music, reflect boundaries between social groups.[53] That is, social groups generally come to identify with specific cultural objects and cultural forms, like music. They adopt an *aesthetic identity*, which aids them in distinguishing themselves from other groups. This of course does not mean that, for example, all black Americans appreciate soul music or all white people like country music. "But," Roy argues, "people recognize that they are members of groups that are associated with particular genres. Individual blacks may not savor jazz, but they often take pride in it."[54] Today, hip-hop is viewed as a black cultural art form. Despite the fact that white and non-black youth of color consume hip-hop music as much as black youth do, hip-hop is part of the aesthetic identity of young African Americans. Why is this? The answer can be found in understanding the broader processes through which hip-hop was racially constructed.

During the 1960s and 1970s, the neighborhoods of the South Bronx were composed mostly of black and Puerto Rican residents—76 percent in 1960. Thus one would imagine that Puerto Rican youth were involved in the creation of hip-hop along with blacks. Indeed they were, although their numbers were small. Some historians discount Puerto Ricans in their accounts of how hip-hop was created simply because the scene had few Puerto Rican DJs and MCs.[55] Other scholars argue that, while few Puerto Ricans took the stage, their role in hip-hop's formation was central, and thus hip-hop ought to be viewed as both a black and Puerto Rican social entity. Scholars in this latter camp usually make their argument on three grounds: the involvement of Puerto Rican b-boys, the dedicated attendance of Puerto Rican youth at South Bronx parties, and Puerto Rican music played at the jams.[56]

Although it was Puerto Ricans who carried on the tradition of b-boying, as discussed above, their involvement as b-boys came precisely when b-boying became less significant for the hip-hop scene. Moreover, given that blacks and Puerto Ricans were predominant in the neighborhoods where hip-hop formed and grew, and given that performances took place in public parks, high schools, and community centers, it is likely that the audience at jams included as many Puerto Ricans as blacks. In fact, Busy Bee recalls an event with Master Rob where the presence of Puerto Ricans was quite apparent. While he was on stage performing, Master Rob noticed the large number of Puerto Ricans. He said: "'Bee, look at all the Puerto Ricans in here yo. You got to give them a shout.' I didn't know what to say at that moment. . . . I was like, 'What the hell am I going to say for some Puerto Ricans?' I said, 'Shit you say something.' He grabs the mic and says, 'Puerto Rico Ho . . . Puerto Rico Hey.'" Indeed, hip-hop audiences comprised as many Puerto Ricans as blacks, but, as we have seen, performers had more power to shape the scene than did audience members. Even with the high visibility of Puerto Ricans at parties, the scene was still, for the most part, viewed as "a black thing."

With regard to the music played at parties, it is true that DJs played predominantly songs by African American musicians, but musicologist Ned Sublette explains that funk music, the foundation of hip-hop, derived some of its characteristics from Afro Cuban and Latin bands.

> [In the 1970s,] conga drums had become one of the signature sounds of African American musical nationalism. . . . Along with the one-chord groove tune that the conga helped define, the instrument was an important part of the sound of another of America's great cultural achievements: funk. When I asked Bobby Byrd [James Brown's music director in the glory days] . . . he told me, "It was the syncopation of the instruments—everybody playing a different part. Okay, now we winded up with a seven piece band, but everybody had a different part to play." That's exactly what Latin bands did, and exactly what American bands, until that time, did not do. Funk polyrhythmicized the R & B combo the way the mambo had earlier polyrhythmicized the jazz band.[57]

The hybrid nature of music at the events notwithstanding, hip-hop was seen as belonging primarily to blacks. How did hip-hop acquire and retain its racial classification despite the significant participation of Puerto Ricans and the diverse music DJs and MCs performed? Hip-hop became racially constructed as black because of, rather than in spite of, the participation of Puerto Ricans, especially as MCs and DJs.[58] Even as Puerto Ricans and blacks identified with their respective ethnic groups and saw themselves in opposition to the other, there was a good amount of cultural and social overlap between blackness and Puerto-Ricanness in New York City during the 1970s. The story of the talented and popular DJ Charlie Chase—who happens to have been Puerto Rican—bears this out.

Chasing Flash

Carlos Mendes, who went by the English nickname Charlie, was born in Spanish Harlem to Puerto Rican parents who had emigrated from Mayaguez. He did not live in Harlem long, though. "I grew up in Williamsburg in [Brooklyn] from the age of two to nine. I moved to the Bronx, on Brook Avenue and 141st Street, . . . from ten to about thirteen."[59] Then, his family moved back to Brooklyn before returning to the Bronx for good. "We went to 180th and Arthur, and from there it was Grand Concourse and 183rd, then Valentine and 183rd, then back to 180th."[60] His family was part of the 613,000 Puerto Ricans in the Bronx who, in 1960, made up 80 percent of the Latino population in New York City.[61] Most of the neighborhoods he lived in were those in which Puerto Ricans and blacks shared the space, the poverty, and the neglect from city and state policy makers.[62] In fact, several scholars argue that there are more shared experiences between Puerto Ricans and blacks than between Puerto Ricans and other Latino groups.[63] According to one scholar, "Their histories of unemployment and underemployment, police brutality, negative portrayals in academic literature and media, housing and employment discrimination, residential displacement and racial violence have not only been similar but also linked. Puerto Ricans have come to be considered a native minority that shares the bottom socioeconomic structure with African Americans."[64] The two groups have made an "alliance of survival."[65]

Not surprisingly, the shared experiences that made them allies also led to cultural intermingling between Puerto Ricans and blacks.[66] In music alone, the merger of their cultural traditions is most evident in the creation of boogaloo. Journalist and music historian Aurora Flores describes the merger in the documentary *Latin Music USA* as intimacy resulting in procreation: "Mambo that was so popular gets married to R & B and they have a baby named boogaloo."[67] This melding occurred when the "Nuyorican" children and grandchildren of Puerto Rican immigrants fused the sounds of traditional Afro-Latin rhythms, which they heard from their parents, with the popular music of their time, in which African Americans figured prominently. The success of records like Joe Cuba's "Bang Bang" or Pete Rodriguez's "I Like it Like That" made boogaloo the sound of the 1970s for Latinos, especially Puerto Ricans.[68]

Charlie's neighborhood in the South Bronx reflected this intimate relationship between blacks and Puerto Ricans.[69] At home, however, he was raised on the sounds of his parents' beloved island. His mother was an avid music collector. "She was the one who bought all the Latin records. . . . She bought Tito Puente, she was into Trios, el Trio Los Condes."[70] His father and grandfather were musicians who played Latin music. At first, Charlie resisted following his family's musical path. "My father actually tried to teach me to play guitar first and I just flat-out said, 'no.' I tried it and I just said 'no' and walked away from it." It was not until high school that he was willing to play. "I had a friend called James Sullivan, who was a bass player, who encouraged me, you know. . . . [W]e became really good friends and he inspired me, and then I just decided to pick up the bass guitar and just start learning from there."[71] As a musician, he had diverse tastes. In addition to playing in his high school band at Alfred Eastman High, he also played Spanish ballad, meringue, salsa, rock, funk, and Latin rock with different bands.[72] "The first band I had gotten into was a Spanish rock band, we'd play Santana music. All we'd do was cover songs, Santana cover songs, that's all we played. Everything Santana. And as I got better with my bass playing, . . . I got into the funk bands that was in the projects."[73] He made his first dollar as a professional musician at age fourteen when he played with a Spanish ballad band in Brooklyn.

Living in the Bronx, Charlie could not escape the hip-hop scene. He became aware of it through his friends Tony and Rueben, with whom he played in a salsa band. "They had just started learning how to DJ. . . . I went to their house one day, and I saw them DJing, and I was amazed. . . . Seeing the mechanics, watching everything happening, I was like, 'Oh, I wanna do this.' Because I knew a lot about music and timing, it was easy for me."[74] He began practicing DJing with Tony and Rueben, more often with disco than funk records, because that is what they played. But he did not particularly like disco music. "It was cool, but it was too corny. I mean, it's just something about [it] I wasn't feeling."[75] He did not realize it, but his natural aversion to disco music satisfied a prerequisite for participating in the hip-hop scene. What is more, his broad musical palate, reminiscent of Bambaataa's, would serve him well. Nonetheless, in 1977 Charlie had never been to a hip-hop jam and thus was unaware of the social status DJs acquired.

When Charlie eventually made it to a jam, it was one given by the Monterey Crew, a little-known group of which he was aware only because it included the younger brother of one of his band mates. The jam took place in a community center. The DJs and MCs played at one end, and a door divided the jam from the other end, where Charlie happened to be playing ping-pong. "So I'm hearing this music, and I'm like, 'What's this?' You know, I put the paddle down and I got up to see what's going on." The space was dark and packed with people around his age. The only visible lights were those the DJs pointed at the turntables. "And you could see these shadows off the ceiling moving around quickly. And I'm like, 'What's this going on?'" Intrigued, he made his way through the crowd, bumping shoulders with people attempting their best dance moves. They stared at him, puzzled. Why was he not dancing? Charlie stared back, mesmerized. "Who was responsible for stirring the audience into such hysteria?" he wondered. When he got close enough, he saw that the DJ was switching between the same two records on turntables in order to prolong the break beat. "And then this one guy, he isn't really even rhyming, he's just blurting out stuff. Maybe every now and then he'll say a little rhyme, one line rhyme, and that's it." What astonished him was the way the audience responded to the music. "The crowd was totally into the vibe, people are dancing, they're just enjoying it like it's a thing that's supposed to happen, it's the norm. They weren't amazed like I was," he recalls. By 1977, moving to the music in those particular ways *was* a thing. "That just blew me away."[76]

After the event, Charlie purchased more records with break beats and practiced the DJing style he had observed at the jam. He still played with Tony and Rueben, now a disco DJing duo called Tom and Jerry. "They were good, but they sometimes dragged things out, and the crowd would die." When it did, they would put Charlie on the turntables to save them because he was already better than they were. "They'd go, 'Ok, it's dead. Stick Charlie in there.' I'd play my hip-hop records, [the break beats] everybody likes[,] the floor [would] get packed, and I'd get bumped off the turntables."[77] Sometimes Grandmaster Caz was in the audience for Charlie's time on stage. Impressed with the rookie DJ, Caz would jump on stage with him and lend his MCing skills.

Although the venues in which Charlie played and the duo with whom he performed were on the fringes of the hip-hop scene, his name began to travel. However, he was seen as an outsider treading on foreign land, partly because he was still not well-versed in the conventions of the game, but mostly because he was Puerto Rican. The more he moved into the center of the scene, the more resistance he faced, most of which focused on his race. "What the fuck are you doing here, Puerto Rican? Why you fronting like you're black?" audience members both black and Puerto Rican would ask.[78]

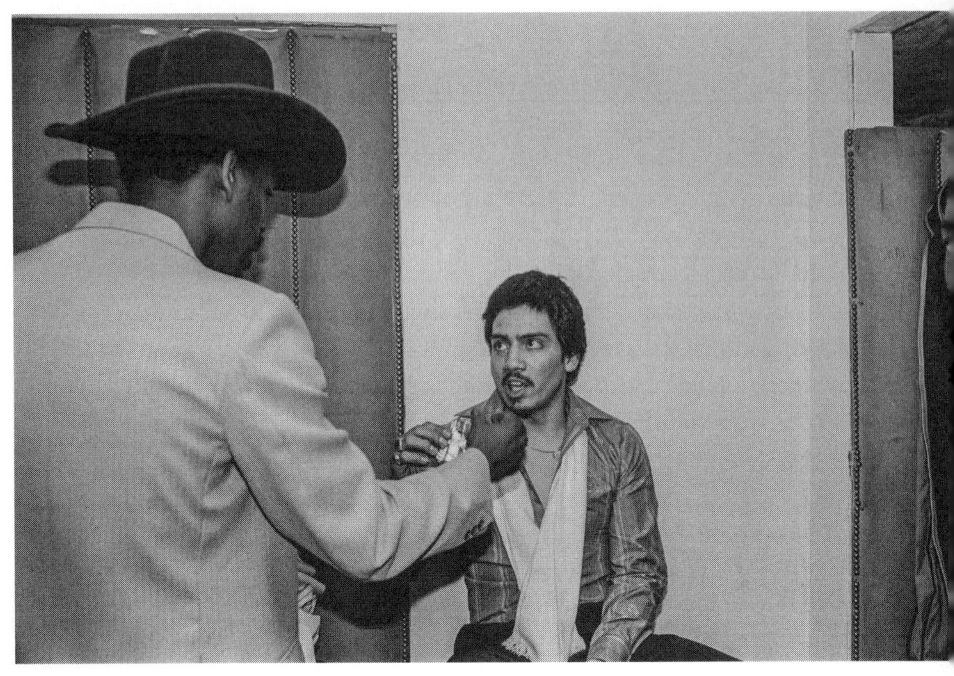

FIGURE 5.2 DJ Charlie Chase and Grandmaster Caz.
(© Joe Conzo; used with permission)

These questions made it clear to him that DJing and MCing were for blacks only. Moreover, it was not just those inside the hip-hop scene who perceived things this way. According to Chase, questions regarding his participation also came from older Puerto Ricans who were baffled about his involvement with "cosas de morenos" (blacks' things)—a presumption that hip-hop was not theirs.

Hip-hop was racialized according to the activity that offered the most symbolic capital. It was considered black because, from the start, DJing was the most lucrative source of fame and most DJs were black. When b-boys mattered, they too were mostly black. Puerto Ricans took up b-boying later when, in the hip-hop world, b-boying was going out of fashion. Similarly, Charlie Chase entered the game as DJs were slowly declining in significance. Like Puerto Rican b-boys who succeeded, Chase was able to thrive in part because DJing was losing its position to MCs as the most lucrative source of symbolic capital. Thus, hip-hop remained a black thing because MCing, the new face of the scene, was dominated by blacks.

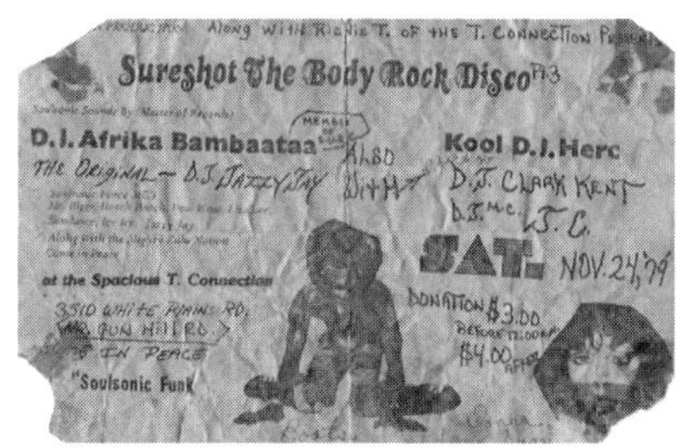

FIGURE 5.3 Samples of fliers advertising various crews.

After about a year with Tom and Jerry, Charlie decided to put together his own crew. He asked Cisco to be his MC (Cisco also made the group's fliers) and later added another MC named RC. As a newcomer to the scene, Charlie knew he had a long way to go. He had to learn the ways of being in the scene, a kind of dues paying: "I started from zero, you know. I didn't know nothing about hip-hop and the next thing you know I threw myself head-first into this, and I started increasing my collection of records. I started playing in the streets [and making the tapes], because that was where you got your notoriety. So I was making the tapes, I was playing in the street jams, and I'm getting popular and everybody's listening, knows about me, here and there, and we're getting the little parties, in the little social clubs, and [in] little local bars, you know."[79] At some point, he had to get a DJing name, so he kept his first name and added "Chase." "'Chase' came because I'm like, damn, you need a good name, man, and Flash was on top and I was down here. So I was chasing that nigga. I wanted to be up where he was. So I said, 'Let's go with Charlie Chase.'"[80]

The Birth of the Cold Crush Brothers

Whatever resistance Charlie faced at the beginning of his days as a DJ was trivial in comparison to what he encountered as he ventured deeper into the scene.[81] After he connected with a well-known hip-hop figure and expanded his crew, his reputation shot up, but so did antagonism toward him, especially for being a Puerto Rican DJ.

At one of Charlie's gigs, Tony Tone, then the DJ and sound manager for DJ Breakout and the Funky 4 and a classmate of RC, met Charlie Chase. "I was telling RC—a young kid who lived in my building—that I was thinking about putting my own group together, and he says, 'There's this Puerto Rican guy named Charlie Chase and he's good. I'll introduce you to him.' I told Charlie who I was, but Charlie didn't seem like he was impressed."[82] This response was indicative of Charlie's lack of familiarity with the scene. Tony then took Charlie to a Funky 4 event before Charlie realized who he was. "That was my first time I was ever taken to a real, honest-to-goodness hip-hop party," recalls Charlie. "That was when I got the real look, feel, and intensity of a sound system, 'cause Breakout had a sound system that could punch a hole in the wall, man. The bass was incredible."[83]

Shortly after their meeting, Tony Tone and Charlie joined forces to start a new crew. Tony came up with the name: Cold Crush. "One night I was dreamin' of something, and then I woke up and I was thinking 'Cold

FIGURE 5.4 Members of the Cold Crush Brothers (left to right): Almighty Kay Gee, Jerry Dee Lewis (JDL), Easy AD, and Grandmaster Caz. (© Joe Conzo; used with permission)

Crush.' Cold Crush, when I thought up the name, meant anybody steps in our way, they get crushed, cold crushed, no remorse."[84] With Charlie's love for and understanding of music and quickly improving DJing skills along with Tony's knowledge and connections in the scene, they made a good team.

To continue to groom his new DJ, Tone introduced Charlie to Downstairs Records, where most DJs went to shop for break beats to add to their collections, and to Elroy, a sixteen-year-old employee who knew about all the hottest music. "When Tony took me to this store, it was a hip-hop break-beat store, which I never knew existed. He took me to this store, and you've got break beats hanging all over the place. Of all types. Break beats I never heard, break beats that I knew about that I didn't know they were considered to be break beats. Like, rock 'n' roll records and stuff like that. You know?" He became a regular at the place. "Every time I got paid, I'd go in there and I'd buy records. You know? My check, I'd put some away for the rent and the rest went [to records]. I didn't even care if I didn't eat. I bought 'Wild Magnolias,' 'Let's Dance' by Pleasure[,] . . . 'Black Betty.' I really started getting crazy with the break beats at that store."[85] Charlie built up his record collection and his knowledge of the scene, thereby aligning his musical sensibilities with those of other hip-hop DJs. He noticed the way they accentuated certain parts of the record and recognized the way these sections ignited the audience. As he became familiar with the music of the scene, he started playing alongside better-known crews at venues more frequented by the hip-hop audience. And at his parties, the Puerto Ricans in the audience moved to the fore.

Charlie was, by 1977, now part of the inner circle of the scene. For his reputation to grow, he needed to battle and win, and this happened in the most unexpected way. "I think the thing that really made people take notice of me was one day, I'm playing at the PAL, and Flash appeared." Still the most popular DJ in the scene, Flash was intimidating to young DJs like Chase. "He walks in. We got the sound system cranking. The place is packed." There were about 600 people at the PAL that night. "The party's going, and Flash just walks on stage. He's like Don Corleone, you know? It's funny. But somebody convinced him to get on the turntables. The record that was playin' was 'Let's Dance.'"[86] Flash attempted to cut the record, but he was unfamiliar with that particular turntable. "Back then, everybody always had a different type of turntable," Charlie explains, "and it needed a little getting used to. You know, you had to have the right touch to make it work." Flash tried to manipulate the record that was playing, but he had no luck. "He's trying to do it, [but] he couldn't do it. He couldn't do it for the life of him. [It] kept skipping on him and . . . he got up and he walked away." The record continued to spin. Charlie knew exactly what Flash had been trying to do, so he gave it a try. "I walked over, picked up the headphones, and I did it, continuously back and forth. I wasn't trying to show him up or anything. I was just doing it because I could do it." The crowd went nuts, not just because of the way he was cutting the record, but also because Charlie Chase just did something that Grandmaster Flash could not do. "So you know how the rumor machine goes. . . . By the end of that summer, [the rumor was that] I had taken on Flash in a battle. And it wasn't really all that. But that was when people started taking notice of me."[87] The audience demonstrated its power once again, even though what people perceived was not actually what happened. Chase was now a budding star, so the reputation of this crew, the Cold Crush Brothers, increased. The crew soon added two new MCs, Easy AD and Donald D, because even with a talented DJ, it was by now more

FIGURE 5.5 Tony Tone and his mother. (© Joe Conzo; used with permission)

important to have good MCs. With their routines, MCs were becoming the main source of entertainment at jams.

DJ Grandmaster Caz, who performed with DJ Disco Wiz, was now known more for his MCing skills than his DJing talents. Alongside him were Whipper Whip and Dota Rock. These two wrote and rhymed together and were called Salt N Pepper. (Whipper Whip is black and Puerto Rican. He was rarely criticized or harassed because many assumed, from his manner of speaking and style of dress, that he was black.)[88] Together, Caz, Whip, Rock, and JDL (more on him in the next chapter) formed the Mighty Force. Dota Rock was friends with Charlie Chase, so he and Whipper Whip left Caz and Wiz to MC with Charlie, the new rising star. They brought with them another MC, Mister T (also known as Mister T-Bone). Because they wanted to be permanent members of the Cold Crush Brothers, they asked Charlie to get rid of his other MCs, Easy AD and Donald D, but Charlie refused. As a result, Whipper Whip and Dota Rock left to become part of the restructured L Brothers, now called the Fantastic Five. The Cold Crush Brothers then added the talented and respected Grandmaster Caz to their crew, boosting themselves even further in the rankings. Anchored by Charlie and Caz and managed by Tony Tone, the Cold Crush Brothers were now among the top crews in the scene.

How was Charlie able to gain so much symbolic capital, even though he faced opposition for being Puerto Rican? First, he was a man, which was an advantage for navigating the hip-hop world. Second, he was a talented DJ. Because he played musical instruments (he was the best musician among all the DJs of the time), he understood the musicianship of DJing better than anyone in the scene. Third, he aligned himself with people who had already gained respect in the hip-hop world. His relationship with Tony Tone, especially, granted him access to popular venues, alongside respected performers, and in front of appropriate crowds. Moreover, with Grandmaster Caz in his lineup, he had one of the most talented MCs in the scene. Fourth, Chase was able to enhance his status as a DJ because, as MCing became the central activity in the scene, the exclusivity around DJing decreased. While DJing retained its significance, MCing was increasingly more important. As a result, DJing was no longer restricted to blacks alone. In fact, Charlie jokes that the MCs' use of microphone stands blocked him from the view of the audience and allowed him to play undisturbed. Often, audience members who did not know he was Puerto Rican would walk up to him after a performance and comment, "You're so good! I never would have thought you were Puerto Rican."[89] These interactions demonstrate that both participants in hip-hop and observers of the scene viewed it as a "black thing."

Chase also had a cultural claim to hip-hop, a "black thing," even though he was a Puerto Rican. In a sense, his entrée into hip-hop supports what I have discussed about the relationship between the two groups in New York City. For one thing, it shows that, despite their shared experiences, alliances, and cultural intermingling, boundaries did persist between the two groups, and each guarded its sense of racial and ethnic distinctness.[90] Because hip-hop was considered black, tensions rose when Puerto Ricans became too involved in it. Blacks in the scene did not want too many Puerto Ricans taking up key roles. For this reason, it was unthinkable for there to have been an all-Puerto Rican DJing and MCing crew. It was possible for hip-hop to be considered black and for it to include Puerto Rican attributes because blackness in New York City during the 1970s overlapped with Puerto Ricanness.

FIGURE 5.6 Overlap of Black and Puerto Rican Life in the South Bronx during the 1970s.

The diagram below illustrates my argument. Hip-hop is placed in the center of black life in New York City because it was racialized as black. However, the scene included aspects of Puerto Rican culture and thus existed on the periphery of Puerto Rican spaces in New York City, because black culture itself included aspects of Puerto Rican culture.[91]

6 MCs Take the Stage

When we think of hip-hop today, it is the MCs (or the rappers), such as Jay-Z or Nicki Minaj, who come to mind. DJs and producers, such as DJ Drama, Timbaland, and Swizz Beats, are also popular, but, by and large, the MCs are the "main characters" of hip-hop. As we know by this point in the present book's narrative, this has not always been the case. During the first decade of hip-hop, DJs were the dominant figures, but somewhere along the way, MCs began to chip away at the power of DJs.[1] By 1978, all crews had MCs—not just one or two, but three or four. With the development of routines, MCs became the main source of entertainment while DJs were relegated to the background. This chapter shows how this internal shift unfolded.

Additionally, this chapter presents the story of the most famous crew from the late 1970s, the Sugar Hill Gang. In 1979, the Gang released the now-iconic "Rapper's Delight" and, almost overnight, became the most popular group in the hip-hop scene. They surpassed everyone, including Grandmaster Flash and his MCs. As their popularity grew beyond the South Bronx to every corner of the city and across the country, their fame surpassed that of DJs in the Bronx and Manhattan. Even today, their name is recognized more readily by hip-hop fans than the names of any of the performers discussed earlier in this book. "Rapper's Delight" moved the relatively obscure DJing and MCing scenes of New York into the mainstream of U.S. popular culture. *Rolling Stone Magazine* regards it as one of the 500 greatest songs in the history of popular music, and VH1 ranks the song number two on its list of 100 Greatest Hip-hop Songs.[2] The importance of "Rapper's Delight" cannot be overstated. What is peculiar about the Sugar Hill Gang is that they did not have a DJ, did not perform with any routines, and did not play in parks, discos, or clubs in the South Bronx. They were not even a product of the Bronx. Moreover, they had not battled other crews, and their name had never appeared on fliers. So, how did this happen? How did the Sugar Hill Gang emerge seemingly from nowhere to dominate the scene? And how did they almost single-handedly bring hip-hop to national attention?

Exploring the significance of the MC and the rise of the Sugar Hill Gang provide insight into the ever-evolving internal dynamics of hip-hop. This chapter examines changes in the sources of symbolic capital and the effects of these changes on the social and cultural entity being formed. When MCs became central figures, MCing became the easiest way to gain a name, hip-hop moved closer to already-established social worlds, such as the DJing world outside the Bronx. In addition, the hip-hop world became more easily influenced by social norms outside of it and thus became less autonomous.[3] This is why a group like the Sugar Hill Gang was able to enter the scene. If hip-hop had continued to be insular, that is, if it had continued to operate mainly under the conventions that came from within, it is unlikely that the Sugar Hill Gang could have left a significant a mark on the scene. These crucial shifts in hip-hop's inner workings illustrate how the scene continued to evolve, how boundaries around it became redrawn, and how its durability changed over time.

Rhymes Galore

When MCs such as Flash's 3 MCs, Love Bug Starski, and Busy Bee started performing alongside DJs, they also began to compete with both the DJs and other MCs for audience attention. Even if the music DJs played was what energized the crowd, the MCs' showmanship provided the visual and dramatic appeal of the events. MC performance was what the audience came for. Battles no longer focused on the power of the sound system or the DJs' mixing and cutting skills. Instead, they were competitions between MC groups, battles waged through rhyming and routines. The DJs simply provided the background music.

Not only did MCs' roles at parties change, but the number of MCs in crews also increased, beginning with Flash's MCs. "Mel got his best friend interested, Scorpio, who was then known as Mr. Ness. Mr. Ness was more like a fly guy," Flash recalls. Fashion sense mattered for the crew's reputation, so Mr. Ness's style made him a particularly attractive candidate. "How can I say it? Women used to be just going nuts over him. He was the cool, silky smooth, fly type of guy. Incorporatin' him into the style made more of an impact visually."[4] With Mr. Ness, the 3 MCs became the Furious Four. As a result of a battle, both Flash's group and Breakout's added one more MC to their lineup, setting a new standard for the scene. The following section explores this battle to illustrate how MCs challenged the centrality of DJs in the scene. The heightened prominence of MCs turned out to be one of the most significant internal changes that explains how hip-hop became what it is today.

Furious 5 and Funky 4 + 1

By the late 1970s, Flash and his MCs, still the premier crew in the Bronx, began to gain popularity outside the borough. "They had a following pretty much throughout the tri-state [New York, New Jersey, Connecticut] area at that time," according to Funky 4 MC Rahiem, "whereas our following was isolated to mostly the North Bronx . . . and Far Rockaway."[5] Rahiem and his crew wanted to challenge Flash's MCs and thereby enhance their own reputation and, perhaps, broaden their appeal beyond the Bronx. "I thought we had a legitimate shot to take these guys," surmised Rahiem. Flash's MCs obliged because they believed they were unbeatable, and a victory would cement their reign. In response to Rahiem, one Furious Four MC proclaimed: "It don't make no sense in y'all keep talking about this Funky 4, know what I'm saying, so we will kill them now and get this over with."[6]

Ray Chandler, the Furious Four manager whose only concern was making money, did not want the battle because, as Funky 4 MC KK Rockwell recalls, "[The Funky 4] didn't have enough clientele yet. Most of the people that came would be the Furious clientele, so [the challenging crew] wasn't bringing anything to the table."[7] However, Chandler's opposition did not stop the battle from taking place—the scene's internal conventions overshadowed financial concerns. "Furious Four knew that we were making noise and they wanted to kill that noise," Rockwell adds. "They wanted to show everybody that they were the best, that's how Furious Four was talking."[8] So behind Chandler's back, Flash's crew organized and advertised the event with a flier that read: "Friday, May 1, 1979; Brothers' Disco (DJ Breakout, DJ Baron and The Funky 4 MCs) vs. Grandmaster Flash and the Furious Four MCs; PAL, 183rd Street and Webster Avenue; $4 for Males, $3 for Females." Rahiem remembers how excited he and his crew were for the opportunity to take down the best group in the Bronx. "I was feeling myself. I was looking forward to the battle. We had done all of this rehearsing, practicing singing routines while dancing, and doing tricks with the mic stands and all that."[9]

The night came, and the anticipation of battle grew so intense that, at one point, a member of the Casanova Crew (Flash's security) slapped DJ Breakout's girlfriend, and things got heated. Tony Tone, the technician and back-up DJ for Brothers' Disco, remembers: "The tension was thick. We were just trying to make it through the night 'cause we knew at any point something could happen with the Casanovas."[10] For protection, Tone invited the Soundview Crew to help them out. "They [pulled] me to the side and they say, 'Yo, we got your back.' They had snuck two .45s in."[11] At another point,

Jazzy D, Funky 4's manager, got into an altercation with another member of the Casanova Crew. KK Rockwell recounts what happened:

> Jazzy D wound up getting in a fight with some of the Casanovas . . . because Ray Chandler was like, "Well, that's my crew, and I deserve some of this money from this party[.]" Jazzy was like, "No, you don't." Ray had already told his [security] crew, "If they act funny with the money, make trouble." So that's what they did. They started the trouble. So they broke up the little issue on stage, and they took Jazzy downstairs in this room and Ray Chandler was like, "Well Jazzy, get in the ring with him, you and him fight."[12]

Jazzy D refused to fight, though. Apparently, the Casanovas pulled out guns, but Tony Tone was able to broker a peace between them. Jazzy D gave Ray Chandler a few hundred dollars, and the event continued.[13]

The battle began with Flash's Furious Four performing first, so the Funky 4 went into the audience to see what the group had to show. "Well, they pulled all of the stops," Rahiem remembers. "They sung. They danced. Flash cut and danced, and did some new tricks that we had never seen before; then he whipped out the beat-box, and they sang [more] songs."[14] "I think we did three sets apiece," Kid Creole (of the Furious Four) recalls of the performance. "We came on[,] we changed clothes on them[;] we made up new routines. We did a chair routine off of 'Get Up, Get Into It,' where we sat down on chairs, crossed our legs all together."[15] When Flash pulled out a manually operated drum machine, which he called the beat box, the crowd lost its mind.[16] It was absolute pandemonium. "If you saw them first, you'd be like, 'the battle is over,'" Rahiem adds. "And I think other members of my group had the same feeling at the time. They were intimidated by the way that the Furious Four hit the stage."[17] As a result, Rahiem recalls, the Funky 4's performance was poor. In his view, some crew members performed as if they had already lost. After they finished, Rahiem jumped on stage and performed by himself. "I waited until the other MCs were finished, and then I went on after them and did my thing. I was like, 'There's no way that I'm going to be slighted because one person doesn't wanna do what we worked so hard to get here for.'"[18]

Other Funky 4 members give a different account of the event, according to interview transcripts from both Troy Smith and the MoPOP. Here is KK Rockwell's version of what took place: "They [Flash and the Furious Four] did everything they had. They did the beatbox, all the dance routines. Everything we knew they was going to do, they did. But we sat and we watched them. We was like okay, you finished now? Now was our time."[19] As Rockwell recalls, it was Rahiem who seemed intimidated. In fact, he refused to perform at all. His excuse was that his throat hurt:

> So all through the night, Rahiem kept complainin' about his voice. "Yo, something's wrong with my voice. Oh, oh, my voice . . . oh, oh, my voice." So, I didn't really pay too much attention to it. But then, when it was time for us to go on, he said, "Yo, I don't want to do it." We all looked at each other like, "What do you mean, you don't want to do it?" He just said, "I don't feel good; I don't want to do it." So we were just standing on the wall just looking at each other and we didn't get on, that's how disgusted we were. Then, out of nowhere, Rahiem gets on the mic and starts rapping. So me and Keith are really looking at him. Sha was looking at him too, everybody was looking at him, Breakout, Baron. We was like, "You supposed to be sick," ya know what I'm saying?[20]

We may never know which of these accounts is most factually accurate, but as I argued in the opening chapter, that is beside the point. The credibility of oral histories "consists in the fact that wrong statements are still psychologically 'true' and that this truth may be equally as important as factually reliable accounts."[21] Thus while it is important, for the sake of historical accuracy, to know how the Funky 4 MCs performed that night, it is equally important to understand why Rahiem remembers the event so differently from his peers. One explanation for this discrepancy is that Rahiem's version of the events can easily serve to justify why he subsequently left the Funky 4 to join the Furious Four.

Impressed with Rahiem's performance, members of the Furious Four courted Rahiem and invited him to join their group. "I don't know what happened with Rahiem," DJ Baron (the Funky 4 DJ) explains. "I guess he was feeling the Furious Four MCs; he felt they were a little better. And then it was a money thing, where we couldn't pay the MCs the way we wanted to pay them—we were still building the system."[22] KK Rockwell adds that Rahiem had been a fan of the Furious Four for quite some time. "Even before that night[,] Rahiem used to sing Furious Four's routines around us. And I used to always say, 'why are you always doing that? They the enemy.' When I asked him why he is always singing that, he said, 'I just like it.' "[23]

With an additional MC, Flash's crew became the Furious 5. Adding one more MC to their line-up pushed the DJ, even one as talented as Flash, further back on stage. Their shows relied less on the skills of the DJ and more on the performance of the MCs, particularly because of Rahiem's expertise in creating routines. Losing Rahiem was a devastating blow for The Funky 4. With Rahiem gone, Sha-Rock, perhaps their most talented MC, decided to leave as well. "Rahiem was like my brother," she recalls. "After [he] left the group I was like, 'Well, if he's leaving, I'm gonna leave, too,' you know? I didn't leave to go to another group; I just left just 'cause he did. I just took a break."[24] Her departure meant that the Funky 4 needed to restructure if they were going to survive in the scene. Because hip-hop events focused now on routines, it would be impossible for DJ Breakout and DJ Baron to perform with only Keith Keith and KK Rockwell. They had to find new MCs, so DJ Baron went on the hunt: "I had an emergency interview[,] and I interviewed Special K. [He] came to my house, and I don't know what was wrong with him, but, at the time, he didn't sound too good. I said, 'Yo, you have to practice more, K.' I said, 'You are okay, but you have to practice more.'"[25] (Special K did "practice more" and went on to become part of a dynamic Harlem hip-hop group called Treacherous Three.) On KK Rockwell's suggestion, Baron and his crew interviewed Lil' Rodney Cee—who, along with Jazzy Jeff, was a member of a lesser-known group called the Magnificent 7—to audition for the Funky 4. Rodney accepted Rockwell's invitation and brought along Jeff for the try-out. Before the audition, Rodney and Jeff made a pact to join the Funky 4, but only if they both got selected. When they arrived, Rockwell kicked off the session before passing on the microphone to the two newcomers. Baron was impressed with one but not the other. "I heard Rodney do his thing, and he was off the hook. [He was] just what I was looking for. He had flow. Jeff was a little weak to me. . . . but he came along with the package."[26]

On July 11, 1979, at a park jam celebrating DJ Breakout's birthday, Rodney and Jeff made their debut with the group. The crowd was ecstatic for the return of the Funky 4 and wholeheartedly embraced the new lineup. Sha-Rock was in the audience that night. "They was all upset at me because I had left," she recalls.[27] Although the performance went well, it was obvious that they missed and desperately needed Sha-Rock. So, from Sha's recollection, "Jazzy Dee says, 'Sha-Rock, I want you to get on the mic. The crowd wants to see ya.' So I got on there, and the crowd started just going crazy. So they said, 'Okay, Sha this is good for us. Just go ahead and come back.'"[28] She did, so they changed their name to the Funky 4 + 1, pronounced "Funky 4 Plus One More." Following the example set by the Furious Five, they now had five MCs.

Galaxy 2000

Arthur Armstrong, originally from Louisiana, moved to the Bronx (165th Street and Washington Avenue) when he was 29 years old. He held several odd jobs before finding his way into music. "I got into music by accident," he says. He used to hang out with the Pazant Brothers, a band that made mostly instrumental funk tracks. "So by me hanging out with these guys, and they had some friends over in Teaneck or Englewood, New Jersey, they asked me to help with this little young band. . . . One thing leads to another when working with bands and, basically, that's how I really got started dealing with the music."[29]

Armstrong became a part of hip-hop in a similar way to Ray Chandler. In 1979, he decided to rent a venue on University Avenue (between 175th and 176th Streets) and open a club that featured live funk and R & B bands. He wanted his place to be like Harlem's Top Club or the Baby Grand Bar Café. When he arrived at the location, another young man was there, interested in booking the place for a party. He introduced himself as DJ Kool Herc. During their conversation, Herc told Armstrong about the popularity of hip-hop jams among Bronx youth. "I had never heard of rap music. Herc explained to me that it was a new music, and there was a large clientele. The kids love it; it was their music, and he was the primary mover behind it, the inventor. I think his exact words were that he was 'The Muhammad Ali of rap at the time.' I will never forget that."[30] By the end of their conversation, Herc had convinced Armstrong to abandon his original plan and rent the place for hip-hop events instead. "Well, I was impressed by these young guys; it seemed like they were trying to do something, you know what I mean. That was what I was impressed by. It wasn't the music that I particularly would listen to by myself, but it wasn't bad."[31] He named his new spot Galaxy 2000, "the Galaxy" for short, and Herc became his house DJ.

Armstrong's entry into the scene raises the question of how outsiders viewed it. Was it as bounded a cultural phenomenon to them as it was to those intimately involved? This question gauges hip-hop's "entitivity." That is, at which point was the scene viewed as a well-bounded and easily recognizable social and cultural entity? Armstrong's entry can help determine this.

Before throwing the first Galaxy jam, Armstrong had to learn how the hip-hop world operated. He met with Herc and spoke to several other participants in order to understand the "dos" and "don'ts." "The kids start[ed] filling me in on who was who. Who could draw [people]; Who had the power."[32] He learned about the downside as well: he could not book shows anywhere he pleased. "Rap at that time was very territorial. . . . It wasn't like, say, jazz or whatever. So, in other words, you didn't bring [certain people] into certain areas and stuff like that. You didn't go into Bambaataa's territory without talking to him and booking him. You didn't go to the North Bronx without booking the Funky 4 and talking to their management."[33] Armstrong did not want this territoriality at his place because it was bad for business, so he made the Galaxy a neutral ground for crews. Anyone was welcome. The performers loved playing there in part because of the neutrality but also because it was lucrative. In one night, they could potentially earn about $700.

Despite his attempt to avoid territoriality, Armstrong realized that he still needed a good security crew, just in case shows got out of hand. "Put it like this . . . how can I put it? You just [had] to hope nothing [bad] happen[ed]."[34] Even though most of the MCs and DJs who played at his place brought security, he wanted his own crew, because it was not unusual for people to come to the Galaxy with guns and knives. At first he hired some men he knew, who were likely unfamiliar with the conventions of hip-hop. "Then I had an incident one night, and I realized I didn't have the right *kind* of security, so I hired the 9 Crew." Like Flash's Casanova Crew, they were composed of former gang members who were participants in the scene. "They were from the South Bronx, 169th Street, so they named themselves [The 9 Crew], as in 69. And that solved my problem."[35] Another key to keeping his place peaceful, he learned, was to get to know his patrons: "Like Bambaataa and some of his guys, you let in free but not all of them. They knew you, and you knew them, and they gave me X amount of respect. I had guys on security, but Zulu and other guys would help in security also . . . like the Casanovas with Tiny, Cletus, Football, all of those guys you know. If they were in the house, I didn't worry about security that much. If anybody did something stupid, they would be on their case. So, for the most part, most of them had unwritten rules."[36]

If partygoers abided by the unwritten rules, they would check their guns and knives at the door and thus would not be searched. He carefully watched those who misbehaved. DJ AJ, for example, gave him trouble on one occasion, so when AJ returned to the club for another event, he had to follow the house rules. "AJ and his boys had to be searched because they lost their gun privileges. And that is how it was dealt with."[37] Despite this, Armstrong could not keep violence out of his club. On one fateful night, his establishment became the setting for the worst episode of violence the hip-hop scene had, up to then, experienced. Because this night was pivotal for their reputation, members of the L Brothers spoke of it in interviews with both Troy and the MoPOP.

The L Brothers were booked to play at the Galaxy that night while Herc went to their territory on the East Side to play. "It was the L Brothers' first show out of our area," Busy Bee remembers.[38] According to Kevie Kev, going out of the territory was a huge risk. "I'll never forget that night, I cross my heart. I called all my cousins; they called all their girls to come to this party. It's over on the West Side. West Side was always considered more down and dirty than the South Side."[39] They arrived to a packed place; there were about 500 people already inside. With the entrance fee at $5 a head, it was going to be a lucrative night. "And happy as a motherfuck," exclaims Busy Bee, "music was rocking! We're doing routines, Mean Gene and some females were at the door collecting the money. Everyone came up the stairs, got searched, paid, then came inside."[40] But the night took a disastrous turn.

Trevor, the former L Brothers promoter, was in the audience that night and saw some suspicious activities outside, so he said to Kevie Kev, "Yo! They getting ready to stick it up." His suspicions were confirmed when, shortly afterward, seven men wearing ski masks ran into the club waving guns. Arthur Armstrong was at the door. "Basically, around two, three o'clock in the morning a bunch of guys bust through the doors with shotguns and pistols and slammed me on the floor. I had a few other people at the door but I can't remember their names. But I know Darnell [Breakout's brother, also known as Jazzy Dee], who managed the Funky 4, was there."[41] "I hear a POW!" Busy Bee recounts, "'Don't nobody move! Everybody freeze!' Girls started hollering and screaming and falling down."[42] Grandmaster Caz, an attendee that night, stood next to Mean Gene, who held the money. "I was divin' over shit upstairs."[43] Busy Bee jumped into a box of pickles. Master Rob jumped over the bar and got his leg stuck as the bar fell on him. Some people jumped out of windows on the first floor; others hid under tables. The perpetrators started shooting as they headed to the bar for the cash, and the security crew shot back. "One of the crooks never made it; he got it. That was a message to his two pals. When people were trying to leave, they couldn't cause his body was blocking the bottom of the stairs. His legs was shaking," Busy Bee explains. [44] Kevie Kev adds: "He died on the steps, and that song, 'And the Beat Goes on,' by the Whispers, was playing." In the end, one person died, several were seriously injured, and many more were traumatized. Armstrong was forced to close the Galaxy. Although violence was not new to the hip-hop scene, it rarely had led to death. When news of the event hit the streets, it damaged the reputation of the L Brothers—no one came to their parties out of fear of more violence.

Arthur Armstrong opened another club on Jerome Avenue, the Ecstasy Garage—so named because the venue was in fact a former car garage. After a couple of months, he moved to a bigger location on Macomb Street, but he kept the name. "The one on Macomb was a better place, it was bigger, and it had a big bar area where you could probably put two hundred people. Then you walked through a door to the back part, it would hold like five or six hundred people in the back."[45] Armstrong had no trouble bringing his clientele to the Ecstasy Garage, despite what had occurred at the Galaxy, because it was one of the few clubs that catered exclusively to the hip-hop scene.

In the introductory chapter, I asked, "When, if ever, does a set of relations actually count as a 'thing,' a substance, or an entity?" There is no single right answer to this question when considering a given case. But in the context of the present narrative it is plausible that by the time Arthur Armstrong entered the scene, hip-hop was a well-established, well-demarcated entity. Those involved in the scene, as well as outsiders, were able to distinguish hip-hop from other entities because the symbolic boundary around it was, at this point, fairly stable, as a result of the scene's internal logic. Hip-hop had conventions that structured participants' ways of being. Moreover, an understanding existed among participants regarding how to accumulate and expend symbolic capital. Hundreds of actors were deeply invested in hip-hop, and they not only influenced the way the entity was shaped but were in turn influenced by it. Hip-hop became recognizable in the neighborhoods of the Bronx, and it also came to exist, as it were, within the participants themselves. It became a cultural entity and created in them a tendency, a predisposition, an organized inclination—in a word, an "attitude."[46] Hip-hop intimately bonded young people from various walks of life, including hustlers, former gang members, Catholic-school students, and art enthusiasts, ranging in age from about thirteen to about twenty. It instilled in them a common musical taste, from the breakbeats that DJs spun; a common bodily comportment, from the moves of b-boys who once dominated hip-hop parties; a common vernacular, from the rhymes of MCs; a common sense of fashion, from the fly attire of wealthy, flamboyant performers; and a common visual aesthetic, from the artistic tastes of flier makers. Furthermore, hip-hop developed social attributes. It became a significant structuring force not only when its participants were taking part in hip-hop related events, but also in aspects of their lives not directly related to hip-hop. For instance, being immersed in hip-hop motived DJ AJ to quit selling drugs; it inspired Bom 5 and Lisa Lee to participate in the Zulu Nation and serve their community; and it drove Buddy Esquire to explore his artistic talents beyond graffiti-writing.

DJs Fall Back at Disco Fever

Despite hip-hop's status as a clearly demarcated cultural entity with well-established conventions and a stable symbolic boundary, the scene was constantly changing. One the most significant transformations was a shift in the lineups of DJing and MCing crews. In 1979, especially, MCs grew more important, in part because crew size increased, with the most prominent crews having four or five members.[47]

The Galaxy shooting destroyed the reputation of the L Brothers, so Grandwizard Theodore separated from his brothers, Mene Gene and Cordio. As he explains, "they [his brothers] wasn't into it like they once were." He adds, "Also, it got to a point where the style of the DJ was changing. It got to the point where DJs were mixing and scratching now, all kinds of new stuff. [Mene Gene and Cordio] just couldn't keep up with it."[48] Theodore started what would become the Fantastic Four and, eventually, the Fantastic Five. He began playing alongside Kevie Kev and Master Rob, both former members of the L Brothers, and Rubby Dee, the only Puerto Rican MC besides Whipper Whip. Rubby Dee was not the best among the group, but, because he was among four other skilled and popular MCs, he did not face much harassment for being Puerto Rican. At first, his fellow crewmembers paid him less, but that changed when they saw that increasing numbers of Puerto Ricans came to their parties because of Rubby. Around the same time, the Cold Crush Brothers brought in two new MCs, Easy AD and Teddie Ted, to perform with their original two, RC and Cisco.

DJ Grandmaster Caz, who had performed with DJ Disco Wiz (Wiz was in jail at this point), had his own crew, the Mighty Force, composed of DJ Mighty Mike, Whipper Whip, Dota Rock, and JDL (Jerry Dee Lewis). In a richly descriptive manner, JDL recalls the day he met Caz:

> I think I was sixteen or seventeen, I'm not sure. . . . The day I met Caz was one of the best days of my entire life. I can remember it like yesterday. I was on the mic at a jam, Butch Kid was standing next to me keeping them whack emcees at bay, and I'm killing the mic. I mean throwing haymakers, and Butch Kid whispered in my ear, "Yo, Casanova Fly just came in. They coming by the ropes." I looked and Caz, DJ Mighty Mike, and about five girls wearing sweatshirts [that said] "DJ MC Grandmaster Casanova Fly" [were watching him perform]. And Whipper Whip was with them. So they was checkin' me out so I kept on rockin' for about four more records, then Mighty Mike came behind the ropes and said, "Casanova Fly want to talk to

> you." So we walked to the back of the jam and Caz said, "Yo, you was rockin' them," and I said, "Yeah, I try," and Mike said, "We playing at the Audubon on October 6th, wanna rock with us?" and I said, "Yeah, on one condition, let me start off first." See, I said that because I had this new crowd participation rhyme and the Audubon would have been perfect to try it out on. So Mike was like, "Come to Caz's house tomorrow and if you can beat Whip out you [can go on first]." I went to Caz's house the next day[;] Whip and Dota Rock was there with their rhyme books and shit. I brought Butch Kid for back up just in case[,] and Caz put on "Groove To Get Down," and, man, I took off like crazy. I must have rhymed for about 10 or 12 records. I mean rocking 'em, making shit up with Caz name in it on the spot, not missing a beat. Caz cut the music off and I started at the Audubon.[49]

Dota Rock was friends with Charlie Chase, so he and Whipper Whip left Caz and the Mighty Force to MC with the Cold Crush Brothers, a more popular group, which now included Whip, Dota Rock, KG, and Easy AD. (RC, Teddie Ted, and Cisco had dropped out.) With the departure of Whip and Dota, the Mighty Force became the Force Five, featuring Caz, JDL, and two newcomers, Louie Lou and Little G (the fifth member is unknown); they were managed by a guy named Hank, whose significance will soon become clear. In return for a commitment to remain as permanent Cold Crush members, Whip and Dot demanded that Chase get rid of the other MCs (KG and AD) because "they sounded whack." Chase refused, so Whipper Whip and Dota Rock left him to join Theodore's crew. The Fantastic Four, with the addition of the two new MCs, became the Fantastic Five (Whipper Whip, Dota Rock, Kevie Kev, Rubby Dee, and Master Rob) with Grandwizard Theodore as their DJ.

Without Whip and Dot, the Cold Crush Brothers were left with only Easy AD and KG, so Chase decided to hold an audition for new MCs. He invited his good friend, the respected MC Grandmaster Caz, to help him judge, but really he wanted Caz to join his crew. When Caz showed up on the day of the auditions, Chase pleaded with him to get join. Caz agreed and brought with him his long-time MCing partner JDL—they called themselves the Notorious Two. The Cold Crush Brothers thus now featured DJs Tony Tone and Charlie Chase along with MCs Grandmaster Caz, JDL, Easy AD, and KG.

The unifying thread among all these changes is that crews needed more MCs. With each having four or five MCs, the DJ was no longer the star of the crews, and this shift was reflected in small but significant alterations in the scene. For instance, the names of MCs began to appear before the names of

DJs (if DJ names were included at all) on fliers. DJ Breakout and The Funky 4 MCs became the Funky 4 +1 with DJ Breakout; the rearranged L Brothers became the Fantastic Five and DJ Grandwizard Theodore. The Cold Crush Brothers did not even mention the name of their DJ; they were known simply as the Cold Crush Brothers. Amidst the Furious Five camp, this change in crewmember prominence made some tempers flare, especially when one of the MCs began using the title "Grandmaster." Ray Chandler narrates:

> As far as he [Flash] was concerned, this was his group. Then Melle Mel and them started "stepping up to the forefront, and that started a lot of dissension. Melle Mel would rock the crowd so hard that the girls used to come [backstage] to see the Furious Five. It got to the point where Melle Mel said, 'You know, I'm a Grandmaster too.' Flash took offense with that. 'There's only one Grandmaster.' Mel stuck to his guns. He started calling himself 'Grandmaster Melle Mel.'"[50]

Given their increased status, MCs began to demand more money. Now that DJs were no longer a crew's centerpiece, did they deserve to be paid more than MCs were, as was the custom? The Furious 5 did not think so. "We broke up with Flash, 'cause he'd been taking too much of the money," explains Melle Mel.[51] They asked Charlie Chase to DJ for them. "I was the only DJ that [could] match what Flash was doing. You know, because they were so used to that quality in DJing that they needed somebody like that, you know."[52] "I think it was Scorpio who came to Charlie," recalls Charlie's partner Tony Tone. "When Charlie came to me with it, of course I agreed; the Furious was the hottest thing at that time. We cut our MCs off, we took the Furious Five, and Chase was their DJ for three parties."[53] Flash was doing parties on his own, but not even he could last as a DJ without MCs.[54] As Chase puts it, "he was missing what he needed." The Furious Five were doing well with Charlie, but their partnership did not last long because Ray Chandler, their former manager, would not have it. When Chandler asked the MCs to come back to Flash and they refused, he ordered the Casanova Crew to go after them. Melle Mel recounts: "We did a show with Charlie Chase at the PAL. Ray Chandler shows up and takes some of the money and has the Casanovas rough us up. . . . He put the fear of God in your mother-fuckin' heart."[55]Rahiem describes one particular night: "I'm walking down the stairs . . . [to] go to the men's room. The door of the men's room is cracked open a few inches. I'm standing outside looking at the mirror. Through the mirror in the men's room, I could see two members of the Casanovas, Cletus and Football, robbing Scorpio and Kid Creole for their jewelry. And these guys were our security."[56] After the event, they were "convinced" to go back to Flash.

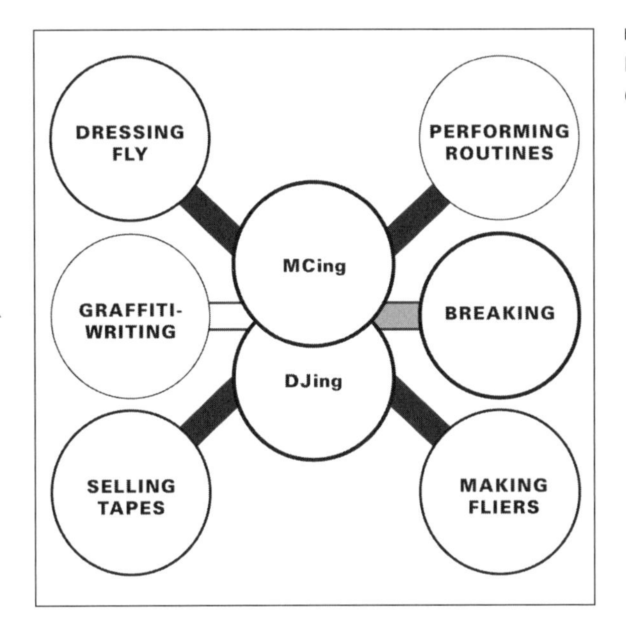

FIGURE 6.1
DJing and MCing as the Central Activities.

As figure 6.1 shows, by 1979 hip-hop focused on MCing, and all other activities revolved around it. This centrality of the MC is one of the conventions of the early days that we still see today. As a result, Jay-Z and T.I. are bigger celebrities than Funkmaster Flex, DJ Clue, or Timbaland. What were some of the effects of this shift? To begin with, MCing changed the atmosphere of hip-hop events. Jams used to feature DJs who spontaneously chose and played music for the audience's dancing pleasure. Moreover, DJs did not pause between songs. They kept the music going, smoothly moving from one break beat to the next. Herc and Bambaataa were accompanied by MCs whose role was to aid the DJ. (Recall that, for Flash, the MC's job was to get the audience to vibe to his innovative mixing technique.) However, when MCs began to rhyme and perform with routines, hip-hop jams began to mimic concerts. The spontaneity of the DJ was gone; he now had a set list. The DJ assumed a role similar to that of a backing band, and the MC became lead vocalist.

With MCs taking center stage, the hip-hop world also inched closer to the club scene outside the Bronx. Important distinctions remained—the music in hip-hop relied more on funk records than on popular disco records, and performers from the Bronx were organized into groups while Harlem DJs were individuals—but crews from the Bronx incorporated some of the strategies that Harlem DJs used to garner more profits. "Prior to the year 1979," Flash explains, "we had DJ crews like DJ Breakout and The Funky 4 with a sound system . . . and every other crew aspired to have their own booming sound system. But right about that time, [towards the end of 1979,] DJ Hollywood changed the whole game."[57] In this statement, Flash implicitly recognizes Hollywood as a player in the same "game," even though, just a few years earlier, Hollywood was thought to be part of a different game. He continues: "Hollywood would book himself in five spots in one night, and you would wonder how in the hell he could be in five places at one time." Because each location had its own sound system, Hollywood would play at one place for about an hour and then drive to another venue, and so on throughout the night. "That became the way promoters hired DJs. This made the sound system a dinosaur." The sound system, which had once been an important element of a DJ's status, was now irrelevant in achieving or maintaining that status. "Everybody started putting their stuff away because you could be at two or three parties in one night and make triple the money, you know?"[58] Here, we observe a subtle and complex aspect of boundary-work. The boundary between hip-hop DJs was "bright"—thus there was no ambiguity in the location of individuals with respect to it—when South Bronx DJs wanted to assert their autonomy. But it was "blurry"—the location with respect to the boundary was indeterminate or ambiguous—when they wished to generate more economic capital.[59] In other words, although the Bronx hip-hop scene overlapped with DJing scenes in other parts of the city, it retained many of its own unique attributes.

To capitalize on the blurring boundary, Sal Abbatiello of Disco Fever in the Bronx booked hip-hop crews and Harlem DJs to play concurrently at his club. The club had been opened by Sal's father, who already owned a jazz spot in the Bronx called Salt and Pepper. Sweet Gee, a Disco Fever DJ, recalls, "When Ally [Sal's father] bought [Disco Fever] I was there when it was being built, I'm talking literally. I mean I had a hammer and nails and was helping them build that place." Abbatiello's goal was to attract an older clientele, so he hired an older white DJ to play R & B music at the spot. Sweet Gee continues:

> Well, this white guy, he used to get tired and want to quit early, it would be 3 or 4 o'clock in the morning and he'd be ready to go. . . . So when he would leave, or take a break, I would take over. Now, I'm not a great deejay or nothing, but I had watched Flash and all of those guys and knew all of the hot break records from that time like Cheryl Lynn's "Got to Be Real." I would turn down the music and talk between her singing. Like, she would sing, "*What you find*," I'd say, "Sweet Gee"; she'd sing, "*What you feel*," I'd say, "DJ Junebug"; "*What you know*" "Disco Fever," and that was my routine.[60]

Gee continued to emulate what he saw hip-hop MCs doing at their parties, and he gradually started to draw a crowd. "Well, one night," Sal relates, "I'm there at the club and I see Gee go into this routine, and I'm saying, 'What in the fuck is Gee doing?' He was saying things like, 'Throw your hands in the air and wave 'em like you just don't care,' and all of this other stuff, and I'm looking at the crowd, and I'm noticing that he's bringing people together, and then it clicked."[61] The way to get a larger clientele was to cater to the younger crowd. Sal's father initially opposed the idea of having his establishment accommodate teenagers, but he allowed Sal to try it for just one night.

Sal invited Flash and the Furious Five. "I tried to promote other nights there before I got Flash, I even had Harold Melvin and the Blue Notes there, but people didn't come, you know why? Because no one believed that Harold Melvin and the Blue Notes would be in some club in the South Bronx." However, the faithful followers of the most popular DJing and MCing crew did not disappoint; they packed Sal's club that night. "We charged a dollar and there were only four of us working the whole club. Six hundred people showed up that night. I was calling home and Salt and Pepper Lounge pleading with my dad, 'Dad, please send more people; we're swamped in here.'" The Disco Fever made $1,000 that first night.[62] Because Flash and the Furious Five brought in such a huge crowd, Sal changed the schedule permanently. "Instead of having this one night, I went and found another rapper, Love Bug Starski, [and] put him on Monday. I found Eddie Cheeba, put him on Sunday. Reggie Wells [and Junebug], Thursday. And then finally Friday, Saturday, with Sweet Gee as the MC."[63] The venue's popularity forced Sal and his father to build an additional room and a new bar.[64]

The new lineup made the Disco Fever *the spot* in the Bronx for young people, because it brought together the best MCs from both the Bronx and Harlem. The club did not simply take advantage of the blurring lines between the two scenes, it further blurred those lines and wove the scenes together. "The older crowd started drifting out, and the younger crowd started coming in," Sal remembers. "Now every kid knows that they could come and hear their sound, their school sound, their street sound, in this club, and it's a major club with a great sound system, being properly run . . . right in the middle of the South Bronx."[65] Hip-hop enthusiasts loved it. "The Fever wasn't just a club," writes Mark Skillz, a prolific historian of hip-hop, "it was *the* club; not only was it the place to be, but it was an experience. If you performed at the Fever, and you rocked it, that meant that you were somebody. You were among the elite. For legions of rap fans at that time, it was the Mecca of the South Bronx."[66]

With the opening of Disco Fever and collaborations with Harlem DJs, hip-hop was moving beyond the South Bronx. What was once an insular and independent scene was now stretching at the seams. It was no longer primarily governed by the conventions that participants had created. The informal style of dress, for example, was no longer acceptable. Dan Charnas explains: "Street kids showing up in sneakers and jeans would destroy the club's reputation as a nice place for a respectable clientele... [so] Sal started charging $5 for anyone wearing sneakers."[67] It was now part of a bigger and a more lucrative party scene.[68] Mark Skillz describes the effect of Disco Fever's popularity on hip-hop:

> For me, the Fever was a metaphor for that time. When it opened in 1978, the culture was young, street wise and naive. It was the first time the stars of [of the Bronx] got to rub elbows with the ghetto celebs of that time, under the spinning lights and glitz and glamour of a real club. The Fever was close in style to the midtown clubs but at its heart, at its root, it was a raunchy ghetto club that had the spinning disco ball and plush carpet, but it catered to pimps, hookers, drug dealers, gangsters and b-boys. It was a recipe for disaster. Though the [Bronx] artists were street kids, none of them were gangsters. They got swallowed up in the action if you will. As the club degenerated into a cesspool of sex, drug abuse, and disillusioned dreams, so did that generation's hold on the culture. The Fever is the place where the original Bronx groups made their last stand. They lost their grip on the culture at the Fever. It was the place that the acts from the outer boroughs came to stake their claim in the game.[69]

The developments I have described are important because they were the precursor to more fundamental changes in hip-hop. Particularly after the rise of the MCs, the scene became more open to influences from without. Hip-hop was able to withstand the influence of the DJing scene in Harlem and merge with it. What would happen, though, when more established social institutions, such as radio and the recording industry, began to interact with hip-hop?

The Spoof and the First Death of Hip-Hop

The Sugar Hill Gang entered the scene in 1979. As mentioned earlier, the success of their song "Rapper's Delight" popularized hip-hop outside neighborhoods in the Bronx. More importantly, and especially as it relates to the study of boundaries, this group almost single-handedly transformed the logic of the hip-hop scene. The remainder of this chapter grapples with how this occurred.

One day when Sal Abbatiello was in his office, around eleven o'clock in the morning, he heard someone in the club rhyming over music. "I'm like, 'who the hell's here so early rapping on the mic?' "[70] He walked out to see who it was, but no one was there. He then realized that the music was coming from the radio and was shocked. It was unthinkable that hip-hop would be recorded and played on the radio. To begin with, it was a performative musical genre. While people listened to hip-hop on tapes, an overwhelming majority participated in the scene by going to shows. Additionally, the music was not the proper length for radio play. Even though MCs now performed routines with breaks between them, the routines were several times longer than the average song on the radio. And finally, who would be interested in recording and selling these songs? Who in the recording industry even knew that hip-hop existed?

When Flash heard the song on the radio, he, too was perplexed but for a different reason. "'To the hip-hop the hibby dibby. . . .' I'm like hold off," Flash recalls. "This is not AJ. It's not L Brothers. It's not Herc. It's not Bam. It's not Breakout. Who are these people?" The artist's name on the record was the Sugar Hill Gang, and the song was called "Rapper's Delight." According to Love Bug Starski, Sylvia Robinson got the idea from him. "I was 'Rapper's Delight.' I did her birthday party at Harlem World, and that's where she got the idea."[71] Robinson, a singer (her single "Pillow Talk" reached number one on *Billboard*'s R & B Chart in 1973) and record executive (she was the previous owner of All Platinum Records and co-owner of Sugar Hill Records), put the group together and signed them to her label. The crew included two MCs from New Jersey and one from the Bronx. The way they came together is worth exploring because it illustrates their unlikely rise to prominence. Moreover, the process shows how radio, a more established entity than the hip-hop scene, imposed its will on hip-hop.

"In 1979," Sylvia's son Joey Robinson explains, "my mother had a birthday party in New York City at a famous place called Harlem World. That's when she first saw a rapper, like spinning records and talking on the mic, and seeing the people respond to it. That's where she got the idea to do a rap record."[72] According to Love Bug, Sylvia approached him with the idea of recording the music. "She said, 'I've got to have him' [Love Bug Starski]. She'll tell you that," Starski recalls. "But I wasn't interested in doing no record back in them days, 'cause I was getting so much money for just DJing."[73] When he passed on the idea, Robinson reached out to others, including Eddie Cheeba and DJ Hollywood and then Grandmaster Flash and the Furious Five. They all turned her down because, at that time, it simply did not make sense to try to record hip-hop.[74]

As Robinson attempted to recruit MCs to record a song, Fatback Band had already recorded and released a song that some writers (mistakenly, in my view) refer to as the first hip-hop song. Drummer Bill Curtis founded the band and assembled a group of musicians to play funk—the band's name is a reference to the drumming term "fatback," a syncopated pattern in 4/4 time with a particularly loud backbeat, a *fat back*beat. In fact, "Fatbackin,'" a record they released in 1973, found its way into the crates of South Bronx DJs, who featured the breaks in the song's second minute for b-boys. They called their version of funk "street funk." However, like most other musicians, they were caught in the inescapable popularity of disco. By the end of the 1970s, now signed with Perception Records, they played as much disco as they did funk and jazz, often times blurring the lines between the genres—their hit single, "Street Dance," which landed on *Billboard*'s Top 30 R & B chart, exemplifies their genre bending. Always keeping his ear open to innovations in black-music traditions, Curtis included rapping on a song that was released on the B-side of their 1979 record, "You're My Candy Sweet." The song "Catch the Beat," which was added to the record as an afterthought, featured an invited Harlem radio DJ, Tim Washington, who went by King Tim III. The B-side of the record caught the attention of radio DJs more than the A-side, so the band rereleased it and renamed it "King Tim III (Personality Jock)," after its main feature. The Fatback Band inadvertently put out a song that is sometimes considered the first commercially released hip-hop song, but its release did not impact the inner workings of the South Bronx scene. Part of the explanation for this might be that even though the song had similar musical elements to music in the Bronx, it was not connected to the Bronx scene in any significant way. King Tim III himself was not in any way connected to the South Bronx hip-hop world. Sylvia Robinson was more intentional in her efforts and her attempt had a more lasting impact on the hip-hop scene. Even though she was culturally further removed from the Bronx than was the Fatback Band, she managed to find a more direct connection to it.

When the South Bronx MCs turned down his mother, Joey Robinson proposed another MC who could make the record: someone named Casper from a crew called Sound on Sound. Casper initially agreed but later changed his mind. His father advised him against it because Robinson's company, All Platinum Records, was involved in litigation with Polygram Records. Warren, a friend of Joey's, suggested yet another rapper, Henry "Hank" Jackson, who worked in a pizza parlor near his house. Hank was a native of the South Bronx and had grown up two buildings away from Kool Herc. "Coke La Rock, Kool DJ Herc [*sic*], we all went to high school together," Hank explains. "We all lived within one minute of each other, and every party we was always together. . . . Then I hooked up with a person by the name of Caz." Grandmaster Caz recalls that Hank was a doorman at Sparkle, a popular venue in the Bronx. "He worked the door, and I'd kick it with him. He had a genuine interest in hip-hop and seemed to have his head on straight."[75] Hank was neither an MC nor a DJ, but Caz believed he could manage his crew, the Mighty Force. "We had the records but lacked a good sound system. . . . Hip-hop was still at a time where it was about the DJ and the sound system. You had to have a big sound system to be competitive."[76] Hank asked his parents for a loan so he could buy a sound system and a power amp for Caz's crew, and they agreed. However, without a strong reputation in the scene, the Mighty Force did not make money as quickly as they had hoped, so Hank got the job at the pizza parlor to start repaying his parents.

"I'm making pizza, and Joey and his mother walk in. I don't know these people at all, right? It's like somebody walking up to you and saying, 'I want you to make a record for me.'" Hank thought they were joking. "Picture this: I'm full of pizza dough, and I'm like 'Okay, they want me to come outside and audition in the car?' I'm like oookkkkaaayyy." He kicked the patrons out of the restaurant and got into the car to rhyme over the instrumental that was playing in the car. "I did my thing," he recalls. By that, he means he recited popular rhymes that most partygoers in the South Bronx would have recognized. Joey adds, "I was like 'Wow! He's rocking!'" The commotion in the car caught the attention of passersbys.[77] Another friend of Joey's, Mark, knocked on the car's window and introduced Guy O'Brien (aka Master Gee). Guy was an active member of the hip-hop scene in New Jersey, around Englewood, Teaneck, and Hackensack. He got into it around 1977 and was part of a two-man crew called Phase 2.[78] Guy recalls his serendipitous audition for the Robinsons: "Mark knew Sylvia and them, and he stopped to talk to Joey. Joey told him that they were looking for rappers, and Mark told them that I could rap, so I got in the car and started rhymin'. . . . I was in the right place at the right time with the right shit."[79] Hired on the spot, Master Gee and Hank met at the Robinsons' house that night to work on the track. Sylvia called them the Sugar Hill Gang.[80]

Wonder Mike, another MC from the New Jersey hip-hop scene was also at the house that night and hoping to make a song for Mrs. Robinson's label.

(Like Casper, Wonder Mike was a member of Sound on Sound, one of the premier New Jersey crews.) Because Sylvia Robinson was unhappy with Wonder Mike's performance, she refused to include him in the new group. After Hank and Gee finished their session that night, Wonder Mike made one final appeal to get into the Sugar Hill Gang. Master Gee recounts: "It was late at night and Mrs. Robinson was about to go to bed. She had actually put her slippers on, and was on her way. Then Mike said, 'Mrs. Robinson you didn't hear me . . . yet.' She almost said no because she was obviously tired, but she told him to go ahead." Wonder Mike's recollection continues the narration, "So I start, 'the hip . . . hop . . . the hibbit, the hibby dibby hibby habba . . . ,' and I kept going, incorporating everything I saw in the room, from the dog to the statue to the library books."[81] Sylvia was sold, and Mike was in. Hank, Master Gee, and Wonder Mike became the Sugar Hill Gang. Ironically, Hank, the MC from the South Bronx, was the least experienced.

The crew was put together on a Friday. By Monday, the record was done, and a few weeks later, the song was released on the radio. "When we released the record, it was massive," Joey reminisces. "I mean people were waiting in the stores for weeks upon weeks. We couldn't sell the record fast enough; we couldn't press it fast enough."[82] Radio stations were bombarded with calls asking that the record be played. "I mean one minute you're walking down the street. The next minute you've got bodyguards and being chased down the street," Hank recalls.[83]

The Sugar Hill Gang's quick rise to fame sent waves through the hip-hop scene. For one thing, the group members were virtually unknown. "I'm wondering why don't I know about them," Flash thought to himself when he first heard the record, "because I was real particular about who was doing what, at least the ones that was rocking, you know what I mean?" He did not know who they were, but he knew the rhymes. "I'm saying, 'Well damn, I heard these rhymes said by Caz.' But this guy, who was a bouncer at the club, is saying these rhymes on record. These other guys, I didn't have a clue who they were."[84] Apparently, Hank did get his rhymes from Caz. He had asked Caz for them.[85] It is not clear if Caz knew how Hank planned to use the material, but Caz freely gave it to him. "It wasn't like, 'How much you gonna pay me?' or none of that," Caz remembers. "I just threw the book on the table and said, 'Use whichever one you want.'"[86]

What is more, the success of "Rapper's Delight" made the radio, once irrelevant to the hip-hop scene, an important instrument, one that unexpectedly imposed itself and powerfully undermined many hip-hop conventions. "'Rappers Delight' just set the goal to [a] whole 'nother level. It wasn't rule the Bronx or rule Manhattan, or rule whatever. It was now 'how soon can you make a record?'" Flash explains.[87] It was a new beginning. MCs were now called rappers, and the music they produced became known as rap music.

Some resented the Sugar Hill Gang's ascension to the top of the hip-hop scene without properly paying their dues. Afrika Bambaataa and his Zulu Nation were unhappy for this reason, and also because they thought putting hip-hop on vinyl would "kill the culture."[88] Others, however, celebrated the Sugar Hill Gang's success. Whipper Whip remarks, "When 'Rappers Delight' first came out, I was proud. I had no idea what the money was like, but just the fact that you got a record that's being played on every radio station everywhere you go, and you know it was written by your people, said by your people, this was a great thing."[89] "Putting it on vinyl did change things a lot, and I think it changed it for the best," comments Sha-Rock. "What recording did was open it up. A lot of people that didn't have the opportunity to listen to it in New York, when it first started, could see that it was something good."[90]

Indeed it was.

Conclusion

I was waiting for my return flight to the United States, after spending the spring semester of my junior year in college in Ecuador, when, to my surprise, the television above me started playing a video by Common. It was a video I had never seen, a new single from his highly anticipated album produced by fellow Chicagoan Kanye West. The video, also directed by West, opens with shots of the skyline of their hometown on a dreary winter day, one of those days when the wind coming off Lake Michigan is so cold people can see their breath. After showing Common riding through the streets of the South Side in an Oldsmobile, the video zooms down to the rapper standing on a street corner reciting his rhymes:

> Memories on corners with the fo's and the mo's
> Walk to the store for the rose talking straightforward to hoes,
> Got uncles that smoke it some put blow up they nose,
> To cope with the lows the wind is cold and it blows.[1]

As his verse continues, the video cuts to images of people who live in the surrounding neighborhoods where life seems gritty and unsympathetic:

> Corners leave souls opened and closed, hoping for more
> With nowhere to go, niggas rolling in droves
> They shoot the wrong way, cause they ain't knowin' their goals
> The streets ain't safe cause they ain't knowing the code
> By the foes I was told, either focus or fold
> Got cousins with flows, hope they open some doors.

The texture and color scheme of the video are such that one can feel the bleakness of this section of Chicago:

> These are the stories told by Stony and Cottage Grove,
> The world is cold the block is hot as a stove,
> On the corners.

And then we see the Last Poets standing around a barrel of fire as they perform their segment of the song. At the time, I knew very little about this group, except that many scholars considered them a precursor to hip-hop:

> We underrated, we educated,
> The corner was our time when times stood still,
> And gators and snakes gangs and yellow and pink,
> And collared blue profiles glorifying that.

Though their rhymes did not line up with Kanye's hard-hitting beat as precisely as Common's did, I could hear the similarity. It was a nice juxtaposition, I thought, of the very beginning and the current state of hip-hop.

Seeing the video was a pleasant going-away gift of sorts, since, being outside the United States, I had been starved of new hip-hop music. It was fitting, too: I was headed to Chicago for a summer research program at the University of Illinois at Chicago (UIC), where I would read about the history of hip-hop for the first time. A few weeks into my studies at UIC, and after engaging with seminal works on the topic, I returned to this video because it conveyed to me so much about how hip-hop started, save the fact that it was set in Chicago and not New York. It portrayed the dire socioeconomic conditions, the perilous tenor of life on the streets, the creativity and ingenuity of young people making do with resources available, and the strong presence of previous African American cultural traditions. These were, in the accounts I read, the main features of the history of hip-hop.

One of the main objectives of this book has been to add to and challenge some of these taken-for-granted assumptions about how hip-hop was created. In the final sections, I consider this book's potential impact on scholarship about hip-hop, sociological work on boundaries, and beyond. Finally, I present a potential implication of this work for understanding the American Ghetto.

Looking Forward

Obviously the story of hip-hop does not end where I ended my narrative. I chose to bring my narrative to a close at that particular juncture because, in my view, it represents an end to one stage. It represents the end of a time when much of the internal logic of the scene was determined by those involved and those who lived in and immediately around the Bronx. Much of the literature on hip-hop focuses on its history after 1979, but more can be added to the contributions of that literature.

Anyone interested in using the theoretical framework developed in this work to continue the story would need to take several steps. First, they would need to track the impact of the release of "Rappers Delight." How wide an audience did this single actually reach? If we were to go back to 1979 or 1980 and wanted to hear this song, where and when would we hear it? Which stations played it? How did it expand the boundaries of hip-hop? Did hip-hop become just like other DJing scenes or other musical scenes in New York City, or did it retain its unique attributes? The second important step would be to investigate how "Rappers Delight" changed the conventions of the scene. How did it change how people consumed hip-hop? Did hip-hop remain, as it once was, a performative enterprise? How did it change performance conventions? Were crews still important? Were DJs still important? Which new conventions were introduced? Third, it would be important to determine how those involved in the scene accumulated and expended symbolic capital after "Rapper's Delight." How did the record shift the distribution of capital? How did it change the principles of hierarchization? What mattered most in the struggle to gain a name? How did new members become part of the scene? What dues did they have to pay? And how did newcomers, especially those from other boroughs, challenge those who were already established in the scene?

All these questions are easily answerable because there has been quite a bit written about hip-hop of the post–Sugar Hill Gang era, though most of it focuses on the entity's expansion into Manhattan. (Thanks to Troy Smith's tireless work, we also have the stories of those who continued the traditions of the original scene in the Bronx.) Revisiting this literature, to add empirical data from Smith's archive, and applying the theoretical approach developed in this book can yield new insights into how hip-hop continued to grow and how other social and cultural entities endure. By looking closely at the biography of the participants who became part of the scene, we get a better sense of the skills, talents, and dispositions that they brought with them. And through this, we can understand that hip-hop's expansion into the clubs of Manhattan, for example, was not something that was inevitable but something that can be explained if we look at the creativity, ambition, and drive of a figure like Fab 5 Freddy. Likewise, by looking at the networks to which various participants belonged, we see that the participation of someone like Special K, a member of the Treacherous 3, or someone like Debbie Harry of Blondie were not destined to happen, but were the result of contingent processes of social interaction and association. We can also better understand, when we organize empirical details around theoretical concepts like symbolic boundaries, conventions, and accumulation and expenditure of cultural capital, why some participants, such as Afrika Bambaataa, initially resisted the urge to record hip-hop; how photography and film, as much as the radio, contributed to the growth of hip-hop; and how breaking, graffiti-writing, DJing, and MC intertwined, once again, to define hip-hop in the mid-1980s.

The theoretical arguments in this book can also travel beyond the world of hip-hop in several ways. Let me point out just three. First, they could be used to enhance existing scholarship on other social and cultural entities. This applies to writing about music and race. Let's consider two particular texts. Craig Werner's *A Change Is Gonna Come*, a book about the history of black music and American racial politics, artfully displays how various forms of black popular music—blues, gospel, soul, rock and roll, and hip-hop—emerged over several decades and developed certain attributes based on participants brought with them into the respective musical scenes and on political context in which the form of music came to be. Detailed and concise, Werner weaves together stories about the actors, the political times, and musical tastes to explain how "Soulsville USA" (Memphis) for example, differed from "Hitsville USA" (Detroit). Werner does not use any of the sociology terminologies that this book employs, but he uses all of the same underlying ideas. For example, Werner provides biographical information on Sam Cooke and how, transitioning from gospel music to more secular music, Cooke became a part of the making of "soul music." Essentially, he described the making of a new genre of music. Adding to his rich historical survey the concepts I have developed and refined in this text, I think, enriches this already significant text."[2]

Second, the theoretical arguments developed in this work provide tools for investigating the rise of new social and cultural entities. If someone were interested in writing about the rise of food trucks in Los Angeles, the theoretical framework developed here could prove helpful. (I am purposely choosing an entity that is fairly distant from music to make the point that the framework is applicable beyond the realm of musical entities.) Why has the number of food trucks exploded in recent years? (There are more than 2,000 in Los Angeles.) To best answer this question, one needs to first get a sense of the "street food" scene before this new generation of food vendors came about. Then, one might consider how these new vendors sought to, if at all, distinguish themselves from those who already existed. And, finally, they might look at how these new street vendors came up with standards or conventions for the new food truck scenes. Using this approach, one can put forth a compelling and comprehensive account of what several writers are calling a "food truck revolution."

In *Racial Formation in the United States*, Michael Omi and Howard Winant present the socio-historical process by which racial categories are created, inhabited, transformed, and destroyed, a process that takes place on both macro socio-structural levels and in micro everyday practices.[3] Unlike works about race that came before it, where race was subordinated to other paradigms (ethnicity, class, and nation), *Racial Formation* treats race as a project, an entity of sorts, with its own internal logic. Again, this work may not explicitly deploy theoretical arguments about the making of symbolic boundaries and the creation of social and cultural entities, but in many ways it addresses those processes. Laying the theoretical framework developed in this work on top of these existing works, in my view, enhances the theoretical arguments that the authors make. It does so by giving their rich empirical details more explanatory power. In the case of Omi and Winant, for example, we are able marshal all that we know about the development of an internal logic, from works as diverse as hip-hop and food trucks, to corroborate their argument. And as such, even though race exerts more power on our lives, and more heavily structures inequalities, it becomes an entity to be explained, just like hip-hop, food trucks, or soul music. Race, then, can be seen as truly a social construct.

By deepening what we know about the creation of symbolic boundaries and the making of social and cultural entities, I have contributed to a theoretical language that can bring into closer proximity bodies of literature that are perceived to be distant from one another. This is the third way that theoretical arguments in this book can travel beyond the world of hip-hop. What I have developed here is not really about hip-hop. It helped to explain hip-hop, and it can help to explain other new social and cultural entities, like food trucks, and it can enhance explanations for other existing social and cultural entities, like black music and race. But my real aim all along has been to provide a better sense of how fundamental distinctions are created between people. Studying symbolic boundaries, and the entities they birth, may allow us to address fundamental questions of how we create an "us" and a "them." It reminds us that the social processes that go into the making of real and imagined distinctions between New York Yankees fans and Boston Red Sox fans are the same social processes that go into the making of real and imagined distinction between Republicans and Democrats, white Americans and black Americans, or Muslims and Christians. Understanding these fundamental processes is useful if we have any hope of curbing some of the increasing polarization in today's world.

Hip-Hop and the American Ghetto

Finally, this work may prove useful in how we consider poverty-stricken urban spaces. In public conversations and sociological research, the neighborhoods from which hip-hop arose are often characterized as "ghettos." One of the attributes of such neighborhoods is that they are socially disorganized, to borrow the phrasing of early-twentieth-century Chicago School sociologists. By this, they meant ghettos were places where intense societal inequalities shape the behaviors of its inhabitants. In other words, the actions of ghetto dwellers, often characterized as socially deviant and incongruent with widely held mainstream norms and values, are partially a consequence of the harsh socioeconomic context in which they lived. W. I. Thomas and Florian Znanieck, for instance, argued that behaviors of new Polish immigrants were intimately related to the social circumstances they faced in their new worlds.[4] Various subsequent scholars, from Edwin Sutherland, Clifford Shaw and Henry D. McKay down to Robert J. Sampson, have relied on versions of this concept to explain crime, especially, in urban spaces.

Loïc Wacquant argues we ought to "[forsake] the trope of 'disorganization'" and "[retrieve] an institutionalist conception of the ghetto." He proposes that we begin our analysis of life in ghettos not with the behaviors of its inhabitants but with an examination of the extreme depravities.[5] "To say that they are ghetto because they are poor," he writes, "is to reverse social and historical causation: it is because they were and are ghettos that joblessness and misery are unusually acute and persistent in them—not the other way around."[6] What is more, an institutional understanding of the ghetto rejects any attempt to blame the victim. Wacquant writes that ghettos are environments with "high levels of interpersonal and institutional mistrust, dog-eat-dog world view and high densities of social predators," but, in his view, all of this makes sense given the context. The "broken habitus and ambiguous strategies of the professional hustler in the south side of Chicago," for instance, is to be expected especially if one considers the "structure of political, economic, and symbolic domination that predetermine their availability, attraction and differential payoffs."[7] Further, he adds that the actions of ghetto dwellers are indeed organized but in a distinctive manner: "The entropy characteristic of street life at the heart of the ghetto is in fact patterned and obeys a distinctive, if unstable, social logic."[8]

Various other works have illustrated that the worlds of the ghettos are highly organized and, revising Wacquant's analysis, not with a distinctive social logic but with ones that are widely shared.[9] Randol Contreras' *The*

Stickup Kids, a book about South Bronx youth who rob drug dealers to make a living, illustrates the patterned and routinized nature of conducting robberies.[10] Their actions, the author adds, are based in their belief in the widely held American Dream. Some of the stickup kids tried to find different routes, but, as they did for other family members, drug dealing and robbery presented themselves as the best routes to pursue the American dream, despite the danger they pose to both victim and perpetrator. A few decades prior to this work, Elijah Anderson, in trying to make sense of senseless violence in poverty stricken urban neighborhoods in Philadelphia, presented a similar argument in *Code of the Street.*[11] He illustrates that campaigning for respect, which includes showing and performing one's toughness through verbal sparring and physical fights, is not just about creating and maintaining a healthy sense of self but also about protecting oneself from others. Again, the underlying motive for such behaviors are not unique to inhabitants of poor neighborhoods. As Anderson writes, "Adolescents everywhere are insecure and trying to establish their identities. Young people from the middle and upper classes, however usually have a wider variety of ways to express the fact that they consider themselves worthwhile. . . . In poor inner-city neighborhoods, verbal prowess is important for establishing identity, but physicality is a fairly common way of asserting oneself."[12]

The present work adds to this conversation. It argues that spaces like the South Bronx of the 1970s are indeed not disorganized—they were organized and were organized on a social logic common to most of American life. Even in the midst of urban decay in the 1970s, the inhabitants of the South Bronx were beholden to cultural and social expectations that organized their lives. The cultural and social aspects of life in the Bronx differed from those in other parts of the country, but they shaped lives just as cultural and social aspects of lives shape the lives of other Americans. (It is for this reason that I argue above that the theoretical insights from this work can be used to understand underlying processes in the creations of various other social and cultural entities, such as occupations, genres of music, racial categories or nations.)

As described above, gang culture had its own set of social and cultural dictates. Gangs' underlying logic was to organize themselves and to give meaning to their lives in the midst of a depressed social context. This principle of forming a group to protect and guard oneself is commonplace in American life—recall that Alexis de Tocqueville once described the country as a nation of joiners.[13] The social and cultural aspects of their gang organizations shaped what they did, what they believed, what they thought of each other, and how they organized their days. The efforts towards these ends, which were significantly shaped by rampant inequalities in their lives, included destructive, violent behaviors. The hip-hop world also had its own set of rules, which shaped the behaviors of its participants within the particular social world and beyond. Adolescents share the goal of gaining status among and respect from their peers. In the midst of urban decay, hip-hop provided a productive means of engaging in the chase for neighborhood fame.

An institutional understanding of the ghetto, as Wacquant proposes, moves us towards explaining how the constraints of their lives shape their action. But an understanding of the cultural and the social aspects of the social worlds in ghettos reveal that the actions of the participants are not being governed by principals that are remarkably different from those of mainstream Americans. In the worst of cases, navigating ghetto life with these same principles results in the kind of destructive and tragic violence the South Bronx experienced in the early 1970s or that present-day residents of Chicago's South Side experience. The case I investigate in this book suggests that, in poverty-stricken neighborhoods, there existed and continue to exist profitable avenues to live out widely shared principals in ways that do not result in tragedies. In our studies of impoverished neighborhoods, we would do well to pay as much attention to these more productive ways of social life.

Acknowledgments

The idea for this book was not mine—it was yours, Mustafa Emirbayer. I'm the second of your students to begin the acknowledgments of their first book with such a sentence. We, your students, are a testament to how wonderful you are as an advisor. Thank you for your unending support for my intellectual growth. If I can do for just one student what you have done for so many of your students, I will consider my career a success. And, most important, thank you for your friendship.

Mr. Troy Smith, this book is as much yours as it is mine. Your hard work is on just about every page. Thank you for your trust and your friendship. You and I both know there is still more of the story to be told. I can't wait for what you add to what we know. This work is dedicated to your relentless devotion to hip-hop's history.

Ron Radano, you believed in this book long before it was well polished. Thank you for that. Craig Werner, Alexander Shashko, and Charles Hughes, hanging out with you all and talking endlessly about black music made me believe more and more in this work. Af Am 156 was so important for my growth—much respect to the entire Afro-American Department. Matthew Desmond, you started counting the number of books I would write before I had an idea worthy of a book. Tessa Lowinske Desmond, I learned from you to keep in mind that scholarship is a means to a much more important end. Thank you.

My teachers at Ithaca College, you sowed the seeds for this project and for my career. Sean Eversley Bradwell, you introduced me to hip-hop scholarship and, more important, showed me (and several of my peers) that it was cool to be young, black, and intelligent. Jeff Claus, you taught me to believe in my academic potential. Stephen Sweet, you saw the sociologist in me before I knew anything about the field. Thanks for encouraging me to pursue my graduate studies at Wisconsin. Peyi Soyinka-Airewele, thank you for opening up my mind about how we think and talk about the African continent and the diaspora. Julian Euell, you taught me to chase footnotes, a lesson that has led me to many discoveries. Roger Richardson and David Speller, I attended Ithaca College because of your MLK Program. Shout out to all past and present MLK Scholars and to OMA Class of 2006. Vivia Hill,

Stephanie Adams, Nicole Everseley-Bradwell, you lovingly pushed us to be our best selves, especially outside of the classroom. Thank you!

To the sociology department at the University of Wisconsin-Madison, thank you for a nurturing intellectual environment. And to Anna Haskins, Steven Alvarado, Adrienne Pagac, Rob Chiles, Peter Hart-Brinson, Calivna Ellerbe, Toni Schulze, and Patrick Brenzel, thank you for your kindness through the journey. Chad Golberg and Mara Lovemen, you both were encouraging when you saw the very beginnings of this project—thank you. Alice Goffman, you were encouraging through the lows—thank you. Alyn Turner, Sarah Bruch, and Megan Shoji, thanks for letting me into your writing group. I made so much progress on this manuscript during that time. I'm also grateful for the friendship that developed from working together.

My dear friends and colleagues in different corners of the country, thanks for all the conversations: Regina Baker, Victor Ray, Maliq Matthew, Edwin Ackerman, Justin Schupp, Celso Villegas, and Ethan Caldwell. Special shout-out to Matthew Hughey—thanks for all the tips. To my counsel of wise black men who saw me through the end of my graduate school and through the job market—Glenn McNair, Hewlett McFarland, Ennis Edmonds, Chris Kennerly, Reggie Sanders—thank you for everything. And thank you to the Kenyon College. I completed this manuscript as a Marilyn Yarbrough Dissertation Fellow. My sincerest gratitude to the Sociology Department for granting me a warm working environment.

Shout-out to my UW-Madison crew—you all kept me sane: Edward Cole, Greg Okotie, and Kwadwo Owusu Ofori (the 1850 Squad), Torsheika Maddox, Michelle Robinson, Brian Peret, Patrick Brown, Gil Jose, Milton Jones, Andrew Sterling, Travelle Franklin-Ford, Tezeta Stewartz, Andrea Ashwood, Crystal Moten, Sherry Johnson, Bukky Akinsiku, Heather O'Connell, Valencia Edochie, Shatina Williams, Shameka Powell, Zerandrian Morris, Adrienne Duke, Mya Warren, Margatha McClean, and Vanity Gee.

Zahida, you were there from the very beginning—thank you. Ms. Charlotte Sherman, the first sentence is what it is because of you.

CJ Harmon, Courtney Peck, Lonna Dawson, Tashonda Frazier, Dalayna Tillman, and Enrika Williams, along with the 1850 Squad, you all know, or should know, that I made it through because of you—and I'm not just talking about this book. Camille Rogers, what more can one ask for in a friend? You challenge me to be the best version of myself. Thank you Bestie! And thanks for helping me put the final touches on this book.

To my new friends and colleagues at Davidson College, especially my Africana and sociology colleagues, you have been wonderful. Caroline

Fache, Hilton Kelly, Laurian Bowles, Tracey Hucks, Gayle Kaufman, and Alice Wiemers, your comments during our brown-bag made this book better.

To all my students who have read various portions of this book in Introductory Sociology and in Hip-Hop and Urban Sociology at Kenyon College and at Davidson College—thank you. Special shout-out to the Spring 2017 Davidson College Qualitative Research Methods class for reading the entire manuscript.

I thank former UNC Press editor Joe Parsons for believing in this project as soon as he heard about it. And thanks to the whole team in Chapel Hill.

Mama, I've always believed that you gave me the sensibilities to be a sociologist. Dad, you taught me to love the pursuit of knowledge. Ce, it has been inspiring watching you come into your own. When you first read this work, you paid me a wonderful compliment that kept me going through the difficult moments. I love you all dearly, and I thank God for you. My extended family in Brooklyn, Bronx, Atlanta, and in various parts of the world—Ghana (Jukwa, Takoradi, Swedru, Benso, Ankamu, Accra), England (London and Northampton), Australia (Sydney [Penrith] and Perth)—I hear all your prayers. Richard Ewoodzie and Jerry Ewoodzie, you introduced me to hip-hop, so, in some ways, you're responsible for all of this.

Finally, I thank the Ford Foundation, the American Sociological Association's Minority Fellowship Program, the Harvey Fellowship, and Davidson College for their support as I finished this manuscript.

Mrs. Mercy Edzii, this book is dedicated to you. Your spirit guided me through graduate school. *Da Yie*!

Glossary of Terms

ACTION JACKSON. DJ Plummer's partner.
AFRIKA BAMBAATAA. Former member of the Black Spades; DJ; founder of the Zulu Nation.
AJ. DJ who performed with Love Bug Starski.
AJ LESTER. Popular department store where the most fashionable performers purchased their clothing.
ARTHUR ARMSTRONG. Hip-hop promoter and owner of the Galaxy 2000 and the Ecstasy Garage.
AUDIO EXCHANGE /HARVEY SOUNDS. An electronic store where DJ Plummer worked.
BABY DEE. DJ and member of the Mercedes Ladies.
BARON. DJ and member of the Funky 4.
THE BLACK DOOR. Popular venue in the Bronx owned by Ray Chandler.
THE BOSTON ROAD CREW. Security crew loosely affiliated with Grandmaster Flash.
BREAKOUT. DJ and founder of the Funky 4.
THE BRONX BOYS (TBB). All Latino b-boy crew.
BUDDY ESQUIRE. Former graffiti writer; most well known flier maker.
BUSY BEE STARSKI. MC who began playing with the Funky 4; member of the L Brothers.
CASANOVA FLY (GRANDMASTER CAZ). Former B-boy; DJ; MC; played with Disco Wiz; founded the Mighty Force; member of the Cold Crush Brothers.
CASANOVAS (SECURITY). Security crew for Grandmaster Flash and his MCs; promoters for Ray Chandler's Black Door Productions.
CASPER. MC who was initially selected to record "Rappers Delight."
CINDY CAMPBELL. Kool Herc's sister who hosted the party at 1520 Sedgwick Avenue.
CISCO. Flier-maker and MC who played with DJ Charlie Chase.
CLUB 371. Famous venue in the Harlem DJing scene.
COKE LA ROCK. MC who worked Kool Herc.
CORDIE-O. DJ who was a founding member of the L Brothers.
CORNBREAD. Graffiti writer in Philadelphia during the 1960s who became famous for writing his name at the airport.
COWBOY. MC who performed with Grandmaster Flash.
THE CRAZY COMMANDER CREW. All Latino b-boy crew from Burnside Avenue.
CRAZY LEGS. B-boy who was a member of Rock Steady Crew.
D SQUAD. Dance group, made up of Melle Mel, Scorpio, and Kid Creole, who performed with Grandmaster Flash during the early 1970s.
DISCO BEE. MC who performed with Grandmaster Flash.
DISCO FEVER. Famous venue in the South Bronx DJing scene owned by Sal Abbatiello.

DISCO KING MARIO. DJ in the South Bronx scene famous for his powerful sound system.

DISCO TWINS. DJing duo in Queens famous for their sound system.

DISCO WIZ (CASANOVA FLY). Former B-boy; DJ (the first Latino DJ) who performed with Grandmaster Caz.

DIXIE CLUB. Famous venue in the South Bronx DJing scene.

DONALD BIRD. Former gang member; member of Boston Road Crew; Tracy Tee's brother.

DONALD D. MC and member of the Cold Crush Brothers.

DOTA ROCK. MC and member of Grandmaster Caz's Mighty Force and the Cold Crush Brothers before joining Grand Wizard Theodore and the Fantastic Five; he and Whipper Whip called themselves Salt and Pepper.

DOWNSTAIRS RECORDS. Famous record store where the likes of Herc, Tony Tone, and Charlie Chase purchased their break beats.

E-Z MIKE. B-boy; Flash's childhood friend.

EASY AD. MC for the Cold Crush Brothers.

THE ECSTASY GARAGE. Popular venue in the Bronx owned by Arthur Robinson.

EDDIE CHEEBA. DJ in the Harlem club scene; often performed at Club 371 with DJ Hollywood, DJ June Bug, and Reggie Wells.

THE EXECUTIVE PLAY HOUSE. Popular venue in the Bronx where Kool Herc battled Pete DJ Jones.

THE FANTASTIC FIVE. DJing and MCing crew anchored by DJ Grandwizard Theodore.

FRANCIS GRASSO. DJ in the Manhattan club scene during the 1960s known for his innovative techniques.

THE FUNKY 4. DJing and MCing crew founded by DJ Baron.

FURIOUS FIVE, THE. MC crew that performed with Grandmaster Flash.

GALAXY 2000. Famous venue in the South Bronx scene owned by Arthur Armstrong.

GRANDMASTER FLASH. DJ famous for his "Quick Mix Theory" and making MCing an important part of his performance.

GRANDMASTER FLOWERS. Famous DJ in Brooklyn.

GRANDWIZARD THEODORE. DJ and founding member of the L Brothers and the Fantastic Five.

HANK. Manager of the Mighty Force and member of the Sugar Hill Gang.

HOLLYWOOD. DJ in the Harlem club scene known for his smooth talking voice; often performed at Club 371 with Eddie Cheeba, Reggie Wells, and DJ Junebug.

JAZZY DEE. Breakout's brother; financed equipment for the Funky 4.

JAZZY JEFF . MC and member of the Magnificent 7 and Funky 4+1.

JDL. MC and member Grandmaster Caz's the Mighty Force and the Cold Crush Brothers.

JOEY ROBINSON. Son of Sugar Hill Records founders Sylvia Robinson and Joe Robinson, Sr. who initiated the formation of the Sugar Hill Gang.

JUNEBUG. DJ in the Harlem club scene; often performed at Club 371 with Eddie Cheeba, Reggie Wells, and DJ Hollywood.

KEITH KEITH. MC and member of the Funky 4.

KENNY GEE. MC who performed with DJ AJ.

KEVIE KEV. MC and member of the L Brothers and the Fantastic 5.
KID CREOLE. MC who performed with Grandmaster Flash.
KK ROCKWELL. MC and member of the Funky 4.
KOOL HERC. DJ who popularized break beats, coined the term "b-boy," and founded the Herculoids.
THE L BROTHERS. DJing and MCing crew founded by Mene Gene and his brothers, Theodore and Corie-O.
LADYPINK. Most famous female graffiti writer during the late 1970s.
LIL BIT. Member of the Mercedes Ladies.
LISA LEE. MC and member of the Zulu Nation; held a leadership role in the Zulu Queens.
LITTLE G. MC and member of the Mighty Force.
LOUIE LOU. MC and member of the Mighty Force.
LOVE BUG STARSKI. DJ and MC; performed with Pete DJ Jones and DJ AJ.
MASTER GEE. MC who was a member of the Sugar Hill Gang.
MASTER ROB. MC and member of the L Brothers.
MEAN GENE. DJ who founded the L Brothers, along with his brothers Theodore and Corie-O.
MELLE MEL. MC who played with Grandmaster Flash.
THE MERCEDES LADIES. First all-female DJing and MCing crew.
MISTER T. MC and member of the Cold Crush Brothers.
THE MIGHTY FORCE. DJing and MCing Crew founded by Grandmaster Caz.
MIGHTY MIKE. DJ and member of the Mighty Force.
THE MIGHTY MIGHTY SASQUATCH. The name of the Funky 4's sound system.
THE MONTEREY CREW. A lesser-known DJing and MCing Crew.
NEICY. Cowboy's sister.
PEANUT. Respected member of promoter Ray Chandler's Casanova Crew security team.
PETE DJ JONES. Disco DJ who played in clubs that catered to an older crowd.
PHASE 2. Former graffiti-writer instrumental in the creation of South Bronx party fliers.
PLUMMER. DJ in Brooklyn who was known for his powerful sound system.
QUICK MIX THEORY. Grandmaster Flash's innovative mixing techniques.
RAHIEM. MC and member of the Funky 4 and the Furious Five.
RAY CHANDLER. Party promoter and owner of the Black Door.
REGGIE WELLS. DJ in the Harlem club scene; often performed at Club 371 with DJ Hollywood, DJ June Bug, and Edie Cheeba.
RIIS BEACH. Radio DJ in Brooklyn who popularized DJ Plummer.
RODNEY. MC and member of the Funky 4+1 More.
RUBBY DEE. MC and member of the Fantastic Five; one of few Puerto Rican MC.
SAL ABBATIELLO. Party promoter and owner of Disco Fever.
SCORPIO. MC who performed with Grandmaster Flash.
SHA-ROCK. Female MC who performed with the Funky 4+1.
SHERI SHER. MC and founding member of the Mercedes Ladies.
SMILEY, RD. DJ and managing member of the Mercedes Ladies.
SOUND ON SOUND. MCing crew to which Casper belonged.
SPECIAL K. MC for the Treacherous 3, along with Kool Moe Dee and L.A. Sunshine..

SPY. B-boy and member of the Crazy Commander Crew; known as "the man with a thousand moves".

STAY HIGH 149/VOICE OF THE GHETTO. Most famous graffiti writer in the Bronx.

THE SUGAR HILL GANG. MCing crew put together by Sugar Hill Records's owner Sylvia Robinson and son Joey Robinson who recorded "Rapper's Delight" in 1979.

SUGAR HILL RECORDS. Record label that released "Rappers Delight".

SWEET GEE. DJ at Disco Fever.

SYLVIA ROBINSON. Co-owner, with husband Joe Robinson, of Sugar Hill Records and founder of the Sugar Hill Gang.

TAKI 183. Famous graffiti writer in New York City during the 1970s.

TEDDIE TED. MC and member of the Cold Crush Brothers.

THE 3 MCS. Grandmaster Flash's MC crew.

TONY AND RUEBEN/ TOM AND JERRY. DJing duo who introduced Charlie Chase to DJing.

TONY TONE. Sound man for the Funky 4 and founding member of the Cold Crush Brothers.

TRACY TEE. Member of the Mercedes Ladies.

TREVOR. Manager for the L Brothers and the Mercedes Ladies.

PHASE 2. Two-man MCing crew in New Jersey to which Master Gee belonged.

VAN SILK. Party promoter.

WHIPPER WHIP. MC who began his career with Grandmaster Caz, formed the Salt and Pepper MCs with Dota Rock, was briefly a member of the Cold Crush Brothers, and then joined Grand Wizard Theodore's Fantastic Five.

WONDER MIKE. MC and member of the Sugar Hill Gang.

THE ZULU NATION. An organization founded by Afrika Bambaataa dedicated to DJing, MCing, and activism.

Notes

Introduction

1. Noreaga, "SuperThug," on *N.O.R.E.* (Penalty Records, 1998).

2. One writer eloquently describes the matching of words and instrumentation, the two rhythm-creating elements of hip-hop music, as follows: "It's been said that the thing that makes rap special, that makes it different both from pop music and written poetry, is that it's built around two kinds of rhythm. The first kind of rhythm is the meter. In poetry, the meter is abstract, but in rap, the meter is something you literally hear: it's the beat. The beat in a song never stops, it never varies. No matter what other sounds are on the track.... But the beat is only one half of a rap song's rhythm. The other is the flow. When a rapper jumps on a beat, he adds his own rhythm. Sometimes you stay in the pocket of the beat and just let the rhymes land on the square so that the beat and flow become one. But [other times,] the flow chops up the beat, breaks the beat into small units, forces in multiple syllables and repeated sounds and internal rhymes, or hangs a drunken leg over the last *bap* and keeps going, sneaks out of that bitch." Jay-Z, *Decoded* (New York: Spiegel & Grau, 2010).

3. Jeff Chang, *Can't Stop, Won't Stop: A History of the Hip-Hop Generation* (New York: Picador, 2006), 3.

4. Alex Ogg and David Upshal, *The Hip Hop Years: A History of Rap*, Pap/Com ed. (London: Macmillan UK, 1999), 13.

5. Nelson George once remarked that every rapper who ever successfully dropped a verse on a tape owes part of his or her career to Kool Herc.

6. Chang, *Can't Stop, Won't Stop*; Jim Fricke and Charlie Ahearn, *Yes Yes Y'all: The Experience Music Project Oral History of Hip-Hop's First Decade* (Boston: Da Capo Press, 2002); Ogg and Upshal, *The Hip Hop Years.*

7. See Cheryl L. Keyes, *Rap Music and Street Consciousness* (Urbana: University of Illinois Press, 2004); Tricia Rose, *Black Noise: Rap Music and Black Culture in Contemporary America*, 1st ed. (Middletown, Conn.: Wesleyan University Press, 1994); and Chang, *Can't Stop, Won't Stop.*

8. Also see Ed Piskor, *Hip-hop Family Tree, 1975–1983*, 1st ed. (Fantagraphics, 2014).

9. This is not to suggest that hip-hop was fully cooked, once and for all, by 1979. Others in the United States and around the world have tasted and offered, and continue to offer, their own versions of the meal.

10. *Black Noise* sets out to cover four key topics: (a) the history of rap and hip-hop in relation to postindustrial New York City; (b) rap's music-technological innovations; (c) rap's racial politics, its critiques of social institutions, and media and institutional responses to it; and (d) rap's sexual politics, particularly as these relate to female rappers.

11. Ibid., 34.

12. To take another example, she writes: "Rappers, DJs, graffiti artists, and breakdancers all [took] on hip-hop names and identities that speak to their role, personal characteristics, expertise or 'claim to fame.'" Again, she does well to point out this unique attribute of the emerging entity but does not explain why the use of pseudonyms became part of hip-hop in the first place. As a historical approach, attempting to understand present conditions by tracing them to their origins inherently stifles part of the narrative, mostly because this approach does not sufficiently consider the present as an outcome of a range of possibilities. We learn significantly less about the process of making hip-hop—instead we hear about outcome of the process. Unfortunately, this characteristic method of discussing hip-hop's emergence—description without analysis—prevents us from fully understanding what occurred after the rise of the so-called founding figures.

13. As French social theorist Michel Foucault puts it, "The traditional devices for constructing a comprehensive view of history and for retracing the past as a patient and continuous development must be systematically dismantled." Michel Foucault, "Nietzsche, Genealogy, History," in *Language, Counter-Memory, Practice* (Ithaca, N.Y.: Cornell University Press, 1977), 153. We must move beyond this linear approach or else risk obscuring the creative and conflictual social process from which the characteristics of present outcomes emerged.

14. Andrew Abbott, "Things of Boundaries," *Social Research* 62, no. 4 (1995): 865. The "present to past" vs. "past to present" contrast is a slight variation on Andrew Abbott's discussion of the differences between "back to front" and "front to back" approaches.

15. Paul Gilroy, *The Black Atlantic: Modernity and Double-Consciousness* (Cambridge, Mass.: Harvard University Press, 1993).

16. See Cheryl L. Keyes, *Rap Music and Street Consciousness* (Urbana: University of Illinois Press, 2004). Keyes is not the only one to begin her narrative in this fashion. Anthropologist John F. Szwed frames it as follows: "Does Rap have a beginning? Where does the credit or (some might say) blame lie? The quick answer is to say that it is an African-American form for which, on a diasporic flow chart, you could plot an unbroken line from Africa to the Caribbean and on to the United States." Szwed highlights the similarities between rap music and other African American cultural forms such as the rhyme scheme of children's songs like "Little Sally Walker"; songs from "Double Dutch" games (a jump-rope competition often played by African American girls); Dr. Martin Luther King Jr.'s rhythmic oratory skills; the boasting of black radio DJs (such as Dr. Hep Cat from Austin and Dr. Daddy-O from New Orleans); and the tauntings of Muhammad Ali. See John F. Szwed, "The Real Old School," in *The Vibe History of Hip Hop* (New York: Three Rivers Press, 1999), 3–11. Raquel Rivera usefully points out that these authors' emphasis on the African, African American, and Caribbean "roots" of hip-hop ignores the role of Puerto Rican cultural traditions, especially music and dance, in the creation of the art form. She also highlights the influences of bomba, plena, and boogaloo. See Raquel Rivera, *New York Ricans from the Hip-hop Zone* (London: Palgrave, Macmillan, 2003).

17. Nelson George describes the early 1970s as the "post-soul era" and the youth who grew up during this period as "post-soul kids": "Post-soul kids grew up with the Vietnam War. Their fathers came back with drugs and bad dreams—if they came back at all. As they grew up, both the black middle class and the black lower class expanded; they grew up with the Wall Street greed, neo-con ideology, Atari Gameboys, crack, AIDS, Afrocentricity,

and Malcolm X as a movie hero, political icon, and marketing vehicle. They saw Nelson Mandela walk out of jail and Mike Tyson walk in." See Nelson George, *Hip Hop America* (London: Penguin, 1993), xi. Prior to George, Tricia Roase had put forth an interpretation of the rise of hip-hop that focused on the role played by social conditions in post-industrial New York City. In similar fashion, the authors of *Yes Yes Y'all,* with their unique first-hand account of hip-hop's early years, begin their narrative with a description of the negative impact of gang culture on South Bronx communities. The opening pages of their book are filled with vivid photographs of gang life and urban decay.

18. Chang, *Can't Stop, Won't Stop.*

19. Karl Marx, *Capital : A Critique of Political Economy,* reprint ed. (Penguin Classics, 1867); Max Weber, *Economy and Society: An Outline of Interpretive Sociology* (Berkeley: University of California Press, 1978); Émile Durkheim, *The Elementary Forms of The Religious Life* (New York and London: Free Press; Collier Macmillan, 1965). More recently, during the 1960s and 70s, Frederik Barth and Pierre Bourdieu made "boundaries" a central concept in their works. Barth broke with the canon in anthropology by arguing that ethnic groups are hardly made of "aggregates of people" with "discrete" cultural forms; see Fredrik Barth, *Ethnic Groups and Boundaries; the Social Organization of Culture Difference* (New York: Little, Brown and Company, 1969). Contrary to this view, he asserted that ethnic groups are categories of ascription and identification. As such, they are best understood not with typologies, but by exploring different processes that go into generating and maintaining groups. This, according to Barth, requires that scholars shift their attention from studying the internal constitution of ethnic groups to studying the creation of ethnic boundaries.

Bourdieu's work provides analyses of the inner workings of boundaries. First, he argues that the process of boundary-creation involves contestations between various actors—he calls "the space of ongoing historical contestation" a *field.* (When I use the terms "scene" and "DJing world" throughout the text, I refer to something similar to Bourdieu's concept of a field.) Second, he explains that the positions the actors take up in their struggles are not based only on rational choice but also on "previous condition(ing)s"—what, roughly speaking, he calls *habitus.* Third, Bourdieu maintains that the contestations in the field are over different forms of assets or *capital.* (These three concepts—*field, habitus,* and *capital*—constitute the core of Bourdieu's work.) In *Distinction,* Bourdieu's seminal study of class boundaries, he puts these concepts to work. He demonstrates that class boundaries are not sustained with economic capital alone; taste also matters. With rich empirical details about the artistic preferences of people from different social classes, such as schoolteachers, ministers, technicians, bakers, and foremen, he shows that taste is an acquired disposition that differentiates people. Differences in taste then become "principles of division, organizing the image of the social order," and "the social order [becomes] progressively inscribed in people's minds." There, it comes to "present every appearance of objective necessity." See Pierre Bourdieu, *Distinction: A Social Critique of the Judgement of Taste,* (Cambridge: Harvard University Press, 1987), 473, 471, 473. Like Barth, though perhaps even more relentlessly, Bourdieu insists that boundaries do not come ready-made; they are created. To understand these social divisions, he insists that we do away with "taxonom[ies] based on explicit and explicitly concerted principles." In a Durkheimian spirit, he argues that "forms of classification [are not a] universal (transcendental) . . . [but are] *social forms*, that is, forms that are arbitrary (relative to a particular group) and socially determined" (Pierre Bourdieu, *Language and Symbolic Power* [Cambridge: Harvard University Press, 1999], 164.)

Contemporary scholars have built upon these foundations. Thomas Gieryn, for example, has detailed the process of boundary creation in his analysis of how actors demarcate science from non-science. Unlike those before him, who relied on a list of characteristics, Gieryn argues that the differences are "not . . . inherent or possibly unique, but [are the result of] ideological efforts by scientists to distinguish their work and its products from non-scientific intellectual activities." See Thomas F. Gieryn, "Boundary-Work and the Demarcation of Science from Non-Science: Strains and Interests in Professional Ideologies of Scientists," *American Sociological Review* 48, no. 6 (December 1983): 781–95, doi:10.2307/2095325.

For his part, Rogers Brubaker has shown that, in order to understand how boundaries are created, we must avoid groupism—"the tendency to take for granted discrete bounded groups as basic constituents of social life." In particular, he has distinguished between groups and categories. While groups constitute a "mutually interacting, mutually recognizing collectivity with a sense of solidarity, . . . a category is at best a potential basis for group formation." Rogers Brubaker, *Nationalist Politics and Everyday Ethnicity in a Transylvanian Town* (Princeton, N.J.: Princeton University Press, 2006), 11. Thus, categories are the basis for group formation. In "The Making and Unmaking of Ethnic Boundaries," Andreas Wimmer goes even further, specifying strategies of ethnic boundary-making such as boundary expansion, boundary contraction, boundary inversion, boundary repositioning, and boundary blurring. Andreas Wimmer, "The Making and Unmaking of Ethnic Boundaries: A Multilevel Process Theory," *American Journal of Sociology* 113, no. 4 (January 1, 2008): 970–1022. Perhaps the strongest proponent of symbolic boundaries research today, Michèle Lamont has in *The Dignity of Working Men* provided an empirical example of how working-class men in France and the United States draw racial and class boundaries. Like Gieryn, she discards explanations that rely on a list of inherent national characteristics. She demonstrates that racial boundaries are not always based on black versus white antagonisms. While white French workers, for example, use language that evokes solidarity with poor blacks, they reject African immigrants on grounds that the latter "lack civility, violate the principles of republicanism, and are culturally incompatible with the French." Michèle Lamont, *The Dignity of Working Men: Morality and the Boundaries of Race, Class, and Immigration* (Cambridge, Mass.: Harvard University Press, 2000), 242.

20. Michèle Lamont and Virág Molnár, "The Study of Boundaries in the Social Sciences," *Annual Review of Sociology* 28 (January 2002): 167–95.21. Abbott, "Things of Boundaries," 857. A similar approach can be found in Priscilla Parkhurst Ferguson, "A Cultural Field in the Making: Gastronomy in 19th-Century France," *American Journal of Sociology* 104, no. 3 (November 1998): 597–641 where the author explains the rise of the field of gastronomy in France during the nineteenth century. Her main objective is to use her empirical case to explain how cultural fields arise. Ferguson argues that there are two major phases: emergence and consolidation. The first section of her article deals with the first stage. In it, she describes the foundations of the field: "first, abundant, various, and readily available foodstuffs; second, a cadre of experienced producers (chefs) in a culturally specific site (the restaurant), both of which are supported by knowledgeable,

affluent consumers (diners); and third, a secular cultural (culinary) tradition" (603). Next, she deals with how these various developments consolidated to form a culinary discourse which led to the field of gastronomy. "The new element in early 19th-century France was the particular configuration of culinary discourse, the multiplication of culinary genres, and the sheer volume of apposite writing, with the whole very much a function of the rapidly expanding publishing and journalistic market" (611). Her theoretical arguments are similar to Abbott's and are convincing. I prefer Abbott's framework, however, because he provides important concepts, like "sites of difference" and "proto-boundaries" that make it easier to apply his approach to the present empirical case.

22. Ibid., 860.

23. Andrew Abbott, "Boundaries of Social Work or Social Work of Boundaries? The Social Service Review Lecture," *Social Service Review* 69, no. 4 (December 1995): 545–62.

24. Abbott, "Things of Boundaries," 869–70.

25. Mustafa Emirbayer, "Manifesto for a Relational Sociology," *The American Journal of Sociology* 103, no. 2 (1997): 304.

26. Abbott, "Things of Boundaries," 863.

27. Ferguson, "A Cultural Field in the Making," 598.

28. Abbott, "Things of Boundaries," 873.

29. Abbott's framework is an alternative to the present-to-past approach common in most historical accounts of hip-hop. It prompts an account that begins in the past and traces events forward and, by doing so, avoids some of the pitfalls in current scholarship. In particular, it opposes the conventional notion that hip-hop began with four elements; instead, it urges us not to assume hip-hop had inherent qualities. Hip-hop begins with participants carving something new out of what already existed—it begins with proto-boundaries and sites of differences. From this approach, the story starts with a sense of what the South Bronx was like before hip-hop and it illustrates how black and Latino youth began to differentiate some activities from others. This theoretical orientation moves away from a heroic narrative, because the focus is not on describing particular people but on analyzing the creation of boundaries. Popular stories about Herc, Flash, and Bambaataa become situated in a larger narrative about how a dynamic process unfolded. This approach also pays closer attention to other actors involved in drawing the boundary lines that birthed hip-hop, including those who were part of other social activities from which the emerging entity distinguished itself. Accordingly, the narrative features DJs in Manhattan, Brooklyn, Queens, and Harlem; graffiti writers in Philadelphia and New York City; gang members from various parts of New York City; and MCs, breakdancers, party promoters, flier makers, security crews, club owners, neighborhood hustlers, family members, radio DJs, record company executives, and political figures. All of them contributed to hip-hop's creation. Finally, the narrative does not prioritize the influence of past cultural traditions. Nor does it privilege the influence of the dire social context from which hip-hop arose. For the current approach, there are no theoretical reasons to do so. To attend to my agenda, I draw on a large amount of data—described in the next section—to construct various story lines that feature both the social and cultural elements contributing to hip-hop.

30. Pierre Bourdieu and Loïc J. D. Wacquant, *An Invitation to Reflexive Sociology*, 1st ed. (Chicago: University of Chicago Press, 1992).

31. Andrew Abbott, *Time Matters: On Theory and Method* (Chicago: University of Press, 2001), 274.

32. Nina Eliasoph and Paul Lichterman, "Culture in Interraction," *American Journal of Sociology* 108, no. 4 (2003): 735–94.

33. Theda Skocpol, *States and Social Revolutions: A Comparative Analysis of France, Russia and China* (Cambridge: Cambridge University Press, 1979).

34. While Harvard and Schomburg do not hold extensive collections about the history of hip-hop, I searched through materials that dealt with the history of the South Bronx. At Cornell's archives, I searched through troves of materials in their "Born in the Bronx" collection donated by Johan Kugelberg. I also looked through Joe Conzoe's 10,000 photographs of life in the Bronx in the late 1970s. Most exciting of all, I dug into three boxes of materials donated by DJ AJ, an important figure in hip-hop's history, which were yet to be processed. And, I searched through six boxes of materials donated by Afrika Bambaataaa, including his rhyme books, address books, notebooks (which included notes from school and notes on the Zulu Nation), and a few fliers from parties in 1977.

35. These interviews were conducted by museum curators as part of EMPSFM's ongoing Oral History Program, which seeks to collect and archive the stories of musicians, authors, filmmakers, producers, and other key figures who have shaped American popular music and science fiction. Interviews were conducted by museum curators using both audio and video devices. In this study, I use transcripts in which interviewees speak of hip-hop as it unfolded between 1973 and 1979.

36. I also rely on transcripts from a few interviews conducted by Jayquan, who, like Smith, also sought out lesser-known founding figures. I use his work with his permission.

37. Take the following example:

TS: So why did ya'll [throw the party] in T-Connection instead of Harlem World? Especially since the Bronx clubs are dying out and Harlem World was the Mecca.

Interviewee: I really don't know[;] it's a good question. The best answer I could give is [that] it is a Ray Chandler the Promoter situation. Everybody knows when Ray Chandler does a party, it's going to be packed; it was packed, and it was nice.

Smith's understanding of the world in which pivotal events occurred allows him to recognize that there were alternative routes to the creation of hip-hop. In the example above, the interviewee implicitly acknowledges that, indeed, "Harlem World was the Mecca," but the event in question took place at the T-Connection instead because of the significance of a promoter named Ray Chandler. Without Smith's knowledge of the popular Harlem World and his question about it not being the venue for the event under discussion, we would know less about Chandler's influence. Because of such questions, this set of interview transcripts greatly enhances the historical narrative I provide.

38. In the example above, the interviewee remarks, "Everybody knows when Ray Chandler does a party it's going to be packed; it was packed and it was nice." Actually, not everyone does know about Ray Chandler. Only those who were in that world recognize his name and know about his parties. Smith, being part of this world, often does not ask the follow-up questions an outsider might.

39. In my effort to be as empirical as possible in this study, I have used many quotations from the interview transcripts provided by my two sources.

Chapter One

1. Dan Charnas, *The Big Payback: The History of the Business of Hip-Hop*, reprint ed. (New York: New American Library, 2011), 16.

2. Tukufu Zuberi, "History Detectives: Birthplace of Hip Hop," *History Detectives* (produced by Lion Television, New York City, 2009).

3. I provide new data about various other actors and the social scene in which they partook.

4. Several authors have written about the rise of historical figures. Michèle Lamont, for example, has written about how Jacques Derrida gained legitimacy in intellectual atmospheres as different as the United States and France because his work managed to serve different purposes for the different contexts. See Michele Lamont, "How to Become a Dominant French Philosopher: The Case of Jacques Derrida," *American Journal of Sociology* 93, no. 3 (1987): 584–622. We see something similar in Robert Caro's book about Robert Moses. While the author painstakingly describes Moses's intelligence, political shrewdness, eloquence, and hands-on management style, the book is highly regarded, not just as an autobiography but also as a historical study, since Caro properly places Moses in a particular time in New York City's history. See Robert A. Caro, *The Power Broker: Robert Moses and the Fall of New York*, 1st ed. (New York: Vintage, 1975).

5. Andrew Abbott, "The Historicality of Individuals," *Social Science History*, no. 29 (2005): 1–13. For more on this, see also Pierre Bourdieu, *Homo Academicus* (Stanford, Calif.: Stanford University Press, 1990).

6. It is significant that what came through him was a musical reflection because, as some scholars argue, music uniquely captures social conditions: "Once in its place, music is a very public way of articulating things that cannot easily, or safely, or effectively be said. It can therefore evoke the subtleties of existence, its unspoken spaces nurturing qualities like 'pleasure, tenderness, delicacy, fulfillment, all the values of the most delicate image-repertoire' (Roland Barthes, *The Responsibility of Forms: Critical Essays on Music, Art, and Representation*, reprint ed. [Berkeley: University of California Press, 1986]:184). And it can tackle the material world as cultural critique (Ingrid Monson, "Doubleness and Jazz Improvisation: Irony, Parody, and Ethnomusicology," *Critical Inquiry* 20, no. 2 [January 1994]: 283–313); as a route to identification (Holly Kruse, "Subcultural Identity in Alternative Music Culture," *Popular Music* 12, no. 1 [January 1993]: 33–41); as a mode of negotiation within a fragmented society (Ron Eyerman and Andrew Jamison, "Social Movements and Cultural Transformation: Popular Music in the 1960s," *Media, Culture & Society* 17, no. 3 [July 1995]: 449–68); and as "the means by which groups represent and signal their collectivity . . . the acoustical projection of their size, unity, and power" (Gage Averill, "Anraje to Angaje: Carnival Politics and Music in Haiti," *Ethnomusicology* 38, no. 2 [April 1994]: 243)." Citations from Susan J. Smith, "Beyond Geography's Visible Worlds: A Cultural Politics of Music," *Progress in Human Geography* 21, no. 4 (August 1, 1997): 502–29, doi:10.2307/851739.

Paul Gilroy and Amiri Baraka, both important theorists of black music, have argued that more than visuals or words, music has been the primary form of expressions black diasporic peoples. See Paul Gilroy, "Between the Blues and the Blues Dances: Some Soundscapes of the Black Atlantic," in *The Auditory Culture Reader*, ed. Michael Bull and

Les Black (Oxford: Berg, 2003), 381–95; Amiri Baraka (as Leroi Jones), *Blues People: Negro Music in White America*, 1st ed. (New York: Harper Perennial, 1963).

7. John Agnew, "Space and Place," in *The SAGE Handbook of Geographic Knowledge*, ed. Agnew, John and David Livingston (London: SAGE Publications, 2011), 316–31.

8. James Mahoney, "Path Dependence in Historical Sociology," *Theory and Society* 29 (2000): 504–49.

9. Ibid., 547.

10. Douglas S. Massey, Andrew B. Gross, and Kumiko Shibuya, "Migration, Segregation, and the Geographic Concentration of Poverty," *American Sociological Review* 59, no. 3 (June 1, 1994): 425–45.

11. Evelyn Gonzalez, *The Bronx* (New York: Columbia University Press, 2006), 4.

12. Denton Tarver, "The New Bronx: A Quick History of the Iconic Borough," *The Cooperator*, April 2007.

13. Gonzalez, *The Bronx*.

14. Kenneth T. Jackson, *Crabgrass Frontier: The Suburbanization of the United States* (Oxford: Oxford University Press, 1985); Douglas S. Massey and Nancy A. Denton, "Suburbanization and Segregation in U.S. Metropolitan Areas," *American Journal of Sociology* 94, no. 3 (November 1, 1988): 592–626.

15. Gonzalez, *The Bronx*, 11; Jill Jonnes, *South Bronx Rising: The Rise, Fall, and Resurrection of an American City*, 2nd ed. (New York: Fordham University Press, 2002), 71.

16. Robert Worth, "Who Saved the South Bronx? The Silent Partner in Community Development," *The Washington Monthly*, April 1999.

17. Gonzalez, *The Bronx*, 16.

18. Worth, "Who Saved the South Bronx?"

19. Jeff Chang, *Can't Stop, Won't Stop: A History of the Hip-Hop Generation* (New York: Picador, 2006).

20. Worth, "Who Saved the South Bronx?"

21. Gary Weis, *80 Blocks from Tiffany's*, documentary (Above Average Productions Inc., 1979).

22. Deborah Wallace and Rodrick Wallace, *A Plague on Your Houses: How New York Was Burned Down and National Public Health Crumbled* (London: Verso, 2001). This work also provides an analysis of how this negatively affected the health of people in the neighborhood.

23. Alan Ehrenhalt, *The Lost City: Discovering the Forgotten Virtues of Community in the Chicago of the 1950s*, 2nd ed. (New York: Basic Books, 1995).

24. Worth, "Who Saved the South Bronx?"

25. Ibid.; Chang, *Can't Stop, Won't Stop*, 13.

26. Chang, *Can't Stop, Won't Stop*, 15.

27. Worth, "Who Saved the South Bronx?"

28. Stephen Steinberg, "The Myth of Concentrated Poverty," in *The Integration Debate: Competing Futures For American Cities*, ed. Chester Hartman and Gregory Squires, 1st ed. (London: Routledge, 2009).

29. Ibid.; Gonzalez, *The Bronx*, 120.

30. Jill Jonnes, *South Bronx Rising: The Rise, Fall, and Resurrection of an American City*, 2nd ed. (Fordham University Press, 2002), 225, 227.

31. For a discussion of the rise, reign, and fall of gangs, see Chang, *Can't Stop, Won't Stop*, 41–65.

32. Scholars cite different reasons for the decline of gangs, including the rise of political organizations like the Black Panther Party and Young Lords (Chang, *Can't Stop, Won't Stop*; Schneider, *Vampires, Dragons, and Egyptian Kings.*). A consequence of the decline, according to some, was the heroin epidemic. Although the use of heroin was present in the early 1960s, it became more widespread towards the end of the decade.

33. Gene Weingarten, "East Bronx Story—Return of the Street Gangs," *New York Magazine*, March 27, 1972.

34. Ibid.

35. Sonia Roccas and Marilynn B. Brewer, "Social Identity Complexity," *Personality and Social Psychology Review* 6, no. 2 (May 1, 2002): 88–106.

36. Weis, *80 Blocks from Tiffany's.*

37. Charles Horton Cooley, *Social Organization: A Study of the Larger Mind* (General Books, 2012 [1909]), 23.

38. Weis, *80 Blocks from Tiffany's.*

39. Jonnes, *South Bronx Rising*, 245.

40. Ibid.

41. Weingarten, "East Bronx Story."

42. Chang, *Can't Stop, Won't Stop*, 49.

43. Weis, *80 Blocks from Tiffany's.*

44. Chang, *Can't Stop, Won't Stop*; Henry Chalfant and Rita Fecher, *Flyin' Cut Sleeves* (Mvd Visual, 2009), DVD.

45. Edward Gray, *American Experience: The World That (Robert) Moses Built*, 1989 (season 1, episode 15; produced by WGBH).

46. Caro, *Power Broker*, 850. This was not the first time that Moses had plowed through already existing communities to erect one of his building projects. For the contruction of the Lincoln Center for the Performing Arts, he had had to evict 10,000 people.

47. Gray, *American Experience.*

48. Ibid.

49. Caro, *Power Broker*, 856.

50. Jonnes, *South Bronx Rising.*

51. Caro, *Power Broker.*

52. Edelstein had never led anything but she became the leader of the battle against Robert Moses' construction plan. "Not only would she lose her apartment, . . . but her mother and sister would lose their apartments, too: they all lived at 867 East 176th Street, Lillian in 2F, her sister in 3F, her mother in 3G" (Caro, *Power Broker* 865.) She was joined by other housewives in the neighborhood. Most men could not afford to take off from work to join the protests.

53. Caro, *Power Broker*, 869.

54. For an analysis of how highway construction affected suburbanization, see Nathaniel Baum-Snow, "Did Highways Cause Suburbanization?," *Quarterly Journal of Economics* 122, no. 2 (May 2007): 775–805.

55. Jonnes, *South Bronx Rising*, 122.

56. Caro, *Power Broker*, 893.

57. Worth, "Who Saved the South Bronx?"

58. Caro, *Power Broker*, 1151.

59. Robert Reisner, *Graffiti: Two Thousand Years of Wall Writing* (Spokane, Wash.: Cowles Book Company, 1971).

60. David Ley and Roman Cybriwsky, "Urban Graffiti as Territorial Markers," *Annals of the Association of American Geographers* 64, no. 4 (December 1974): 497.

61. Jack Stewart, "Subway Graffiti; An Aesthetic Study of Graffiti on the Subway System of New York City" (Ph.D. diss., New York University, 1989).

62. Ibid., 152.

63. Ibid., 152. For a more detailed description of the use of "territorial marker" graffiti, see Ley and Cybriwsky, "Urban Graffiti as Territorial Markers."

64. Stewart, "Subway Graffiti."

65. Ley and Cybriwsky, "Urban Graffiti as Territorial Markers," 500.

66. Stewart, "Subway Graffiti," 156.

67. Donald Janson, special to the *New York Times*, "Spray Paint Adds to Graffiti Damage," *New York Times*, July 25, 1971, http://www.nytimes.com/1971/07/25/archives/spray-paint-adds-to-graffiti-damage.html.

68. Perhaps it was CORNBREAD's protégé, TOPCAT126, who spread graffiti from Philadelphia to New York City when he moved to Harlem during the early 1970s (Stewart, "Subway Graffiti," 158).

69. Ibid., 173.

70. Ibid., 177.

71. Ibid., 169.

72. Ibid., 170.

73. Norman Mailer and Jon Naar, *The Faith of Graffiti*, new ed. (New York: It Books, 2009), 41.

74. The use of crowns on top of tags was to "claim supremacy in quantity of tags, or signatures" (Stewart, "Subway Graffiti," 184).

75. Ibid., 169.

76. "'Taki 183' Spawns Pen Pals," *New York Times*, July 21, 1971; Randy Kennedy, "Early Graffiti Artist, TAKI 183, Still Lives," *New York Times*, July 22, 2011, http://www.nytimes.com/2011/07/23/arts/design/early-graffiti-artist-taki-183-still-lives.html.

77. Stewart, "Subway Graffiti," 234.

78. Howard S. Becker, *Art Worlds* (Berkeley: University of California Press, 1984), 29.

79. Stewart, "Subway Graffiti."

80. For an excellent account of the city's efforts to control graffiti on the subway, see Craig Castleman, "The Politics of Graffiti," in *That's the Joint: The Hip-Hop Studies Reader*, ed. Mark Anthony Neal and Murray Forman (New York: Routledge, 2004), 21–30.

81. Stewart, "Subway Graffiti," 215–216.

82. "Bio," *Stay High 149*, accessed March 15, 2007, www.stayhigh149.com.

83. "Stay High 149 Interview," *Subwayoutlaws*, accessed March 8, 2011, http://subwayoutlaws.com/Interviews/stayhigh149%20interview.htm.

84. "Bio," *Stay High 149*.

85. http://nymag.com/guides/summer/17406/index3.html; http://www.nytimes.com/2012/06/13/nyregion/wayne-roberts-stay-high-149-in-graffiti-circles-is-dead-at-61.html.

86. Another important figure in the history of radio DJs is Dr. Conrad, who broadcasted the 1920 presidential election on the first fully licensed commercial station, KDKA, in Pittsburgh. For an exhaustive history of DJing, see Bill Brewster and Frank Broughton, *Last Night a DJ Saved My Life: The History of the Disc Jockey* (New York: Grove Press, 2000).

87. Ulf Poshardt, *DJ Culture* (United Kingdom: Quartet Books, 2000).

88. Brewster and Broughton, *Last Night a DJ Saved My Life*.

89. Brewster and Broughton add: "Over the years, Block's selling prowess grew ever more impressive: one department store reported that his ad-libbed commercials helped them sell 300 refrigerators during a blizzard, and when he made a wartime appeal for pianos to entertain the troops, the USO were offered 1500" (Ibid., 29).

90. A particularly noteworthy Black radio DJ is Al Benson in Chicago. He was instrumental in the careers of both Mahalia Jackson and Muddy Waters (see Adam Green, *Selling the Race: Culture, Community, and Black Chicago, 1940-1955* (Chicago: University of Chicago Press, 2009).

91. For a more extended discussion of Northern Soul, see Brewster and Broughton, *Last Night a DJ Saved My Life*, 76–105.

92. Ibid., 129.

93. Ibid., 136.

94. Ibid., 131.

95. William Sewell, "Historical Events as Transformations of Structures: Inventing Revolution at the Bastille," *Theory and Society* 25, no. 6 (1996): 844.

96. One attendee of the Loft describes his experience: "I would go early and hang out with David in the booth, because I loved hearing the music that started out the night. Some of my favorite music was David's early records. He would make this whole atmosphere when people were coming in. Before people started dancing. Oddball things that he would discover, mostly jazz-fusion records or world music. Things that didn't have any lyrics for the most part, but were just cool-out or warm-up records. . . . It was great to see the mood getting set. Little by little, they would start dancing. I loved seeing the whole theatre get underway" (Brewster and Broughton, *Last Night a DJ Saved My Life*, 146).

97. Bob Casey, founder of the National Association of Discothèque Disc Jockeys, remembers the Gallery fondly: "Every once in a while, everybody would be so together with it, so together—and they'd be singing along—and Nicky would bring it up and then all of a sudden BOOM!, out would drop the center and everybody would be stunned—'Awwwww!'—and then BLAMM!!, in would come this incredible bass. And by that time—and there's essence of amyl nitrate all over the place—it was flawless" (ibid., 153.)

98. "Prefiguring the amazing cut and paste skills later developed by the hip hop DJs, Gibbons would take two copies of a track . . . and work the drum breaks so adroitly it was impossible to tell that the music you were hearing hadn't been originally recorded that way" (Ibid., 159.)

99. A young club goer of this time describes Scott: "He would try things like these long overlays. Back then it was so much harder—people really don't realize how hard it was to mix those records with live drummers. And he would do them much longer than other DJs. . . . He was more into squeezing the last drop out of a record and making it into a hit" (Ibid., 161).

100. Ibid., 127. David Mancuso deserves special attention here for propelling DJing and dancing. For an excellent historic account of his contributions, see Tim Lawrence, *Love Saves the Day: A History of American Dance Music Culture, 1970–1979* (Durham: Duke University Press Books, 2004).

101. Brewster and Broughton, *Last Night a DJ Saved My Life*, 155.

102. On the concept of a "cultural toolkit," see Ann Swidler, "Culture in Action: Symbols and Strategies," *American Sociological Review* 51, no. 2 (April 1986): 273–86.

103. Brewster and Broughton, *Last Night a DJ Saved My Life*, 210.

104. Interview with DJ Kool Herc by Jim Fricke (MoPOP Oral History Project).

105. Brewster and Broughton, *Last Night a DJ Saved My Life*, 206.

106. Chang, *Can't Stop, Won't Stop*, 79. For more on breaks, see also Chapter 1 in Mark Katz, *Groove Music: The Art and Culture of the Hip-Hop DJ* (New York: Oxford University Press, 2012).

107. Brewster and Broughton, *Last Night a DJ Saved My Life*, 208, 209.

108. Nelson George, *Hip Hop America* (London: Penguin, 1993), 15.

109. According to Mr. Wiggles, another pioneering b-boy, the use of back flips by b-boy Frosty directly comes from Kung Fu. Fabel adds that Ken Swift's mougzy (facial expression), comes from Bruce Lee Israel, *The Freshest Kids*, documentary (Image Entertainment, 2002)

110. Interview with Cholly Rock by Troy L. Smith, August 2016.

111. Ibid.

112. Interview with DJ Disco Wiz by Jim Fricke and Taiya Minott (MoPOP Oral History Project, June 28 2000.

113. Interview with DJ AJ by Troy L. Smith, Fall 2006.

114. Interview with DJ Disco Wiz by Jim Fricke and Taiya Minott.

115. Interview with Sha Rock by Jim Fricke (MoPOP Oral History Project), August 25, 2001.

116. Interview with DJ AJ by Troy L. Smith.

117. Interview with Grandmaster Caz by Jim Fricke and Taiya (MoPOP Oral History Project), June 24 2000.

118. Interview with Coke La Rock by Troy L. Smith, September 2008.

119. W. I. Thomas, *W. I. Thomas On Social Organization and Social Personality: Selected Papers*, 1st ed. (Chicago: University of Chicago Press, 1966).

120. Chang, *Can't Stop, Won't Stop*.

121. Interview with Tony Tone by Troy L. Smith and Joseph Ewoodzie, March 2015. Grandwizard Theodore provided an identical answer when we pitched the same question to him. He, too, believed that Herc's choice of music made him stand out from other DJs at the time.

122. Pierre Bourdieu, *Distinction: A Social Critique of the Judgement of Taste*, copyright 1984 (Harvard University Press, 1987), 471.

123. Interview with DJ Kool Herc by Jim Fricke (MoPOP Oral History Project), 1999.

124. Ibid.

125. The use of pseudonyms might also have come from gang culture. In Weingarten's 1972 *New York Magazine* article, he explains why gang members used names other than their own. "Over the years, gangs have learned to cope [with the presence of police in their neighborhood]. They learned, among other things, that police were jotting down names they heard on the street and compiling dossiers at the station house. To make the task

harder, virtually all gang members take a nickname when they join a clique. Even a gang member's closest friends may not know, or care, what his given name is" (Weingarten, "East Bronx Story").

126. Joseph G. Schloss, *Foundation: B-Boys, B-Girls and Hip-Hop Culture in New York* (New York: Oxford University Press, 2009), 20.

127. Chang, *Can't Stop, Won't Stop*, 80.

128. Israel, *The Freshest Kids—A History of the B-Boy* (2002, QD3 Entertainment); George, *Hip Hop America*, 15.

129. When Troy and I interviewed Tony Tone, he confirmed that, before Herc, there was no such thing as breakdancing. From his recollection, many of the young people were still doing the hustle, but, at Herc's parties, they combined different styles to create breakdancing. He also confirmed that the first generation of b-boys were all black. Interview with Tony Tone by Troy L. Smith and Joseph Ewoodzie.

130. Interview with Afrika Bambaataa and Alien Ness by Jim Fricke (MoPOP Oral History Project), October 28 2000.

131. Interview with Richard Cisco by Van Silk (MoPOP Oral History Project), n.d.

132. Chang, *Can't Stop, Won't Stop*.

133. As discussed below, some of the best DJs and MCs of the South Bronx scene started as b-boys at Kool Herc parties Interview with Afrika Bambaataa and Alien Ness by Jim Fricke (MoPOP Oral History Project).). Some notable b-boys who became more popular as MCs or DJs included Melle Mel, Grandmaster Caz, Imperial JC, Jazzy Jay, DJ Breakout, Scorpio, DXT, and Afrika Islam.

134. Interview with Grandwizard Theodore by Troy L. Smith and Joseph Ewoodzie, March 2015.

135. Pierre Bourdieu, "But Who Created the 'Creators'?," in *Sociology of Art: A Reader*, ed. Jeremy Tanner, 1st ed. (London: Routledge, 2003), 96–104.

136. Jocelyne Guilbault, *Governing Sound: The Cultural Politics of Trinidad's Carnival Musics* (Chicago: University of Chicago Press, 2007).

137. George, *Hip Hop America*, 16.

138. Pierre Bourdieu, "But Who Created the 'Creators'?," 100.

139. Pierre Bourdieu, *The Field of Cultural Production* (New York: Columbia University Press, 1993).

140. Mark Naison, "From Doo Wop to Hip Hop: The Bittersweet Odyssey of African Americans in the South Bronx," *Bronx County Historical Journal* XL (2003): 68–81; Mark Naison, "'It Takes a Village to Raise a Child': Growing Up in the Patterson Houses in the 1950s and Early 1960s—An Interview with Victoria Archibals-Good," *Bronx County Historical Journal* XL (2002): 4–22.

141. Naison, "From Doo Wop to Hip Hop."

142. Naison, "'It Takes a Village to Raise a Child.'"

Chapter Two

1. For a superb review, see Kozorog Miha and Dragan Stanojevic, "Toward a Definition of the Concept of Scene: Communicating on the Basis of Things That Matter," *Journal of Sociology, Social Psychology* 55, no. 3 (July 2013): 353–74.

2. Dick Hebdige, *Subculture: The Meaning of Style*, new ed. (London: Routledge, 1979); for an early exploration of the "subculture" concept, see Frederic Milton Thrasher, *The Gang: A Study of 1,313 Gangs in Chicago* (Chicago: University of Chicago Press, 1927).

3. Michaela Pfadenhauer, "Ethnography of Scenes. Towards a Sociological Life-World Analysis of (Post-Traditional) Community-Building," *Forum Qualitative Sozialforschung / Forum: Qualitative Social Research* 6, no. 3 (September 30, 2005), http://www.qualitative-research.net/index.php/fqs/article/view/23.

4. Joseph A. Kotarba, *Baby Boomer Rock "N" Roll Fans: The Music Never Ends* (Lanham, Md.: Scarecrow Press, 2013).

5. Pierre Bourdieu, *The Field of Cultural Production* (New York: Columbia University Press, 1993).

6. Howard S. Becker, *Art Worlds* (Berkeley: University of California Press, 1984).

7. Ibid.

8. John Irwin, *Scenes*, The City and Society, v. 1 (Beverly Hills: Sage Publications, 1977), 23; also see Miha and Stanojevic, "Toward a Definition of the Concept of Scene," 357.

9. Interview with Afrika Bambaataa and Alien Ness by Jim Fricke (MoPOP Oral History)..

10. As quoted in Jeff Chang, *Can't Stop, Won't Stop: A History of the Hip-Hop Generation* (New York: Picador, 2006), 94.

11. For a lengthy discussion of Bambaataa's involvement in gang activities, so Chang, *Can't Stop, Won't Stop:*, chapter 5. My discussion here relies on Chang's excellent work.

12. Interview with Afrika Bambaataa and Alien Ness by Jim Fricke (MoPOP Oral History).

13. Johan Kugelberg, ed., *Renegades of Rhythm: DJ Shadow & Cut Chemist Play Afrika Bambaataa* (Boo-Hooray, 2015).

14. Change, *Can't Stop, Won't Stop*, 96.

15. Tia DeNora, *Music in Everyday Life*, 1st ed. (Cambridge University Press, 2000). Also see William G. Roy and Timothy J. Dowd, "What Is Sociological about Music?," *Annual Review of Sociology* 36, no. 1 (June 2010): 183–203.

16. Interview with Afrika Bambaataa and Alien Ness by Jim Fricke.

17. "The Music World of Afrika Bambaataa," *Official Website of the Universal Zulu Nation*, accessed March 10, 2010, http://www.zulunation.com/afrika.html.

18. Interview with DJ Breakout by Jim Fricke (MoPOP Oral History Project), n.d.

19. As quoted in Jim Fricke and Charlie Ahearn, *Yes Yes Y'all: The Experience Music Project Oral History of Hip-Hop's First Decade* (Boston: Da Capo Press, 2002), 49.

20. Chang, *Can't Stop, Won't Stop*, 93.

21. As quoted in Marcus Reeves, *Somebody Scream!: Rap Music's Rise to Prominence in the Aftershock of Black Power* (New York: Faber & Faber, 2009), 18.

22. Chang, *Can't Stop, Won't Stop*, 102.

23. Grandmaster Flash and David Ritz, *The Adventures of Grandmaster Flash: My Life, My Beats* (New York: Broadway Books, 2008). Most of the data from this section come from his book. Data from other sources are cited accordingly.

24. Ibid., 11, 12.

25. Ibid., 17.

26. Interview with Grandmaster Flash by Jim Fricke (MoPOP Oral History Project), 1999.

27. Ibid.

28. Chang, *Can't Stop, Won't Stop*, 113.

29. Bill Brewster and Frank Broughton, *The Record Players: DJ Revolutionaries* (Grove/Atlantic, Inc., 2011), 180.

30. For an excellent documentary about DJs in Brooklyn, Queens, and Harlem, see Ron Lawrence and Hassan Pore, *Founding Fathers: The Untold Story of Hip Hop* (Highlife Entertainment [2009]), film, https://www.youtube.com/watch?v=x2xR-mc-Ikw&feature=youtube_gdata_player.

31. Ibid.

32. Mark Skillz, "Master Mix Those Number One Tunes," blog, *Hip-hop 101A* (June 16, 2007), http://hiphop101a.blogspot.com/2007/06/master-mix-those-number-one-tunes.html.

33. Lawrence and Pore, *Founding Fathers*.

34. Most of the data about DJ Plummer come from an audio recording of interview with DJ Plummer, conducted by Troy L. Smith, July 2010. All other data sources will be cited accordingly.

35. Interview with the Disco Twins by Troy L. Smith, January 2011.

36. Ibid.

37. Lawrence and Pore, *Founding Fathers*.

38. All the data on DJ Hollywood come from Mark Skillz, "Straight No Chaser: DJ Hollywood," blog, *Hip-hop 101A* (May 9, 2007), http://hiphop101a.blogspot.com/2007/05/straight-no-chaser-dj-hollywood.html.

39. Mark Skillz, "Cheeba, Cheeba Y'all!," *Hip-hop 101A*, blog (September 8, 2007), hiphop101a.blogspot.com/2007/09/cheeba-cheeba-yall.html.

40. Skillz, "Straight No Chaser: DJ Hollywood."

41. Skillz, "Cheeba, Cheeba Y'all!"

42. Skillz, "Master Mix Those Number One Tunes."

43. Ibid.

44. Jim Fricke and Charlie Ahearn, *Yes Yes Y'all: The Experience Music Project Oral History of Hip-Hop's First Decade* (Boston: Da Capo Press, 2002), 56.

45. Travis Gutierrez Senger, *White Lines and the Fever: The Death of DJ Junebug*, documentary (Lincoln Leopald Films, 2010).

46. On the perception of difference as a means of creating boundaries, see Michèle Lamont and Virág Molnár, "The Study of Boundaries in the Social Sciences," *Annual Review of Sociology* 28 (January 2002): 167–95.

47. Interview with DJ Plummer by Troy L. Smith, Summer 2010.

48. Skillz, "Master Mix Those Number One Tunes."

49. Mark Skillz, "Founding Fathers Part Two," blog, *Hip-hop 101A* (November 26, 2008), http://hiphop101a.blogspot.com/2008/11/founding-fathers.html.

50. Ibid.

51. Skillz, "Straight No Chaser: DJ Hollywood."

52. Andrew Abbot, "Things of Boundaries, *Social Research* 62, no. 4 (1995): 857–82.

53. Skillz, "Cheeba, Cheeba Y'all!" Also see Dan Charnas, *The Big Payback: The History of the Business of Hip-Hop*, reprint ed. (New York: New American Library, 2011), 14–15.

54. Interview with Pete DJ Jones by Jayquan, October 2001.

55. Interview with Grandwizard Theodore by Troy L. Smith, 2005.

56. Interview with Tony Tone by Jim Fricke (MoPOP Oral History Project), July 15, 2001.

57. Skillz, "Master Mix Those Number One Tunes."

58. Skillz, "Straight No Chaser: DJ Hollywood."

59. Similar differences are identified in Charnas, *The Big Payback*, 16.

60. Andrew Abbott, "Things of Boundaries," 867.

61. Rogers Brubaker, *Ethnicity without Groups* (Cambridge, Mass.: Harvard University Press, 2006).

62. Lewis A. Coser, *Masters of Sociological Thought: Ideas in Historical and Social Context*, 2nd ed. (Waveland Press, Inc., 2003), 312.

63. Bourdieu, *The Field of Cultural Production*.

Chapter Three

1. Max Weber, *Economy and Society: An Outline of Interpretive Sociology* (Berkeley: University of California Press, 1978), 319.

2. Ibid., 320.

3. Ibid., 322.

4. Howard S. Becker, *Art Worlds* (Berkeley: University of California Press, 1984), 29.

5. Pierre Bourdieu, *Outline of a Theory of Practice*, trans. Richard Nice (London: Cambridge University Press, 1977), 164, 167, 169.

6. This framework is adopted from Victoria Johnson, *Backstage at the Revolution: How the Royal Paris Opera Survived the End of the Old Regime* (Chicago: University of Chicago Press, 2009), 29.

7. Interview with Grandmaster Flash by Jim Fricke (MoPOP Oral History Project), 1999.

8. Downstairs Records was one of the places Herc hunted for records.

9. Interview with Grandwizard Theodore by Troy L. Smith, summer 2005.

10. Interview with Grandmaster Flash by Jim Fricke.

11. Interview with Grandwizard Theodore by Troy L. Smith, 2005.

12. Joseph G. Schloss, *Foundation: B-Boys, B-Girls and Hip-Hop Culture in New York* (New York: Oxford University Press, 2009).

13. Interview with Cholly Rock by Troy L. Smith, August 2016.

14. Interview with Grandmaster Caz by Jim Fricke and Taiya Minott (MoPOP Oral History Project), June 24 2000.

15. Grandmaster Flash and David Ritz, *The Adventures of Grandmaster Flash: My Life, My Beats* (New York: Broadway Books, 2008), 13.

16. Jim Fricke and Charlie Ahearn, *Yes Yes Y'all: The Experience Music Project Oral History of Hip-Hop's First Decade* (Boston: Da Capo Press, 2002), 71.

17. Ibid., 117.

18. Schloss, *Foundation*, 31.

19. Interview with Cholly Rock by Troy L. Smith.

20. Craig Castleman, "The Politics of Graffiti," in *That's the Joint: The Hip-Hop Studies Reader*, ed. Mark Anthony Neal and Murray Forman (New York: Routledge, 2004), 21–30.

21. Fricke and Ahearn, *Yes Yes Y'all*, 74.

22. Dan Charnas, *The Big Payback: The History of the Business of Hip-Hop* (New York: New American Library, 2011).

23. Nina Eliasoph and Paul Lichterman, in "Culture in Interaction," *American Journal of Sociology* 108, no. 4 (2003): 735–94, theorize how culture becomes tools for everyday life.

24. Fricke and Ahearn, *Yes Yes Y'all*, 76.

25. Interview with Kid Creole by Jayquan, n.d.

26. Mustafa Emirbayer and Ann Mische, "What Is Agency?," *The American Journal of Sociology* 103, no. 4 (January 1, 1998): 975.

27. Interview with Coke La Rock by Troy L. Smith, September 2008.

28. Ibid.

29. Interview with Kid Creole by Jayquan, October 14, 2002.

30. Ibid.

31. Emirbayer and Mische, "What Is Agency?," 972.

32. William Jelani Cobb, *To the Break of Dawn: A Freestyle on the Hip Hop Aesthetic* (New York: New York University Press, 2007), 43.

33. In his introduction to *The Anthology of Rap*, Henry Louis Gates explores the similarities between rap and signifying. I am arguing that signifying and other oral traditions is part of the dispositions of the young men and women who created hip hop. See Henry Louis Gates, "Forward," in *The Anthology of Rap*, ed. Adam Bradley (New Haven: Yale University Press, 2010).

34. Pierre Bourdieu, *Pascalian Meditations*, 1st ed. (Stanford: Stanford University Press, 2000), 138.

35. Fricke and Ahearn, *Yes Yes Y'all*, 70.

36. Interview with Melle Mel by Jayquan, 2005.

37. Fricke and Ahearn, *Yes Yes Y'all*, 85.

38. Charnas, *The Big Payback*, 20.

39. Interview with Whipper Whip by Jim Fricke (MoPOP Oral History Project), November 8 2001.

40. Fricke and Ahearn, *Yes Yes Y'all*, 90.

41. Interview with Grandmaster Caz by Jim Fricke (MoPOP Oral History Project), June 24, 2000.

42. Interview with Charlie Chase by Jim Fricke (MoPOP Oral History Project), July 15 2001.

43. Interview with Scorpio by Jayquan, May 16 2002.

44. Interview with Melle Mel by Jayquan, February 15, 2002.

45. Interview with Scorpio by Jayquan.46. Interview with Coke La Rock by Troy L. Smith, September 2008. For an illustration of the incident Coke describes, see Ed Piskor, *Hip Hop Family Tree, 1975–1983*, 1st ed. (Seattle, Wash.: Fantagraphics, 2014). In his criticism of how social scientist have characterized the ghetto, Robin Kelley writes " . . . the biggest problem with the way social scientists employ the culture concept in their studies of the black urban poor is their inability to see what it all means to the participants and practitioners." See Robin D. G. Kelley, *Yo' Mama's Disfunktional!: Fighting the Culture Wars in Urban America* (Boston: Beacon Press, 1997), 41. Thanks to Troy Smith's work, we have passages like these that provide intimate details of the emotional bonds among hip-hop participants.

47. Lewis A. Coser, *Masters of Sociological Thought: Ideas in Historical and Social Context*, 2nd ed. (Long Grove, Ill.: Waveland Press, 2003), 309.

48. Herc also mentions that young members of the Nation of Islam and 5 Percenters served as security for his events. "Interview with Herc by Jim Fricke."

49. Fricke and Ahearn, *Yes Yes Y'all*, 93.

50. Interview with Grandwizard Theodore by Troy L. Smith, 2005.

51. Interview with Grandmaster Caz by Jim Fricke (MoPOP Oral History Project), June 24, 2000

52. Fricke and Ahearn, *Yes Yes Y'all*, 93.

53. Flash was perhaps the first to have his own security crew, but he was not the first to need it. Herc may not have been known to carry his own security crew but, according to his partner Coke La Rock, he carried his own protection: "I had a 12 gauge pump, I had a three seven, Herc had a four five. And that was all we needed." He adds, "We were the first ones to put a rope around our equipment . . . so if you come past that rope we are entitled to shoot you! Point blank; that's the mentality of us at that time" (interview with Coke La Rock by Troy L Smith, Fall 2006). Bambaataa had some members of the Zulu Nation—notorious for including a lot of former gang members—work as a security crew for his parties.

54. AJ describes Harlem Prep on 135th Street and 8th avenue as "the hustler's playground," where famous Harlem hustlers like Nicky Barnes, Bat, Guy Fisher, and Shamecca spent time. Interview with DJ AJ by Troy L. Smith, 2006.

55. Ibid.

56. DJs outside of the South Bronx scene also worked with other personalities, but, unlike South Bronx DJs, they did not work with a constant crew of people.

57. Interview with DJ AJ, Fall 2006.

58. Ibid.

59. Ibid.

60. See, for example, Nelson George, *Hip Hop America* (London: Penguin, 1993).

61. Fricke and Ahearn, *Yes Yes Y'all*, 52

62. Pierre Bourdieu, *Language and Symbolic Power* (Cambridge, Mass.: Harvard University Press, 1999), 221; ibid.

63. Kelley, *Yo' Mama's Disfunktional!*, 45.

64. I make this observation to combat the romanticized notion of a "pre-commodification" era of hip-hop. Tricia Rose writes: "It is a common misperception among hip hop artists and cultural critics that during the early days, hip hop was motivated by pleasure rather than profit, as if the two were incompatible. The problem was not that they were uniformly uninterested in profit; rather, many of the earliest practitioners were unaware that they could profit from their pleasure." See Tricia Rose, *Black Noise: Rap Music and Black Culture in Contemporary America*, 1st ed. (Middletown, Conn.: Wesleyan, 1994), 40.

65. Interview with Coke La Rock by Troy L. Smith, September 2008. He admits that he first went to Herc's parties because it was a good place to sell marijuana.

66. Ibid.

67. Interview with Rahiem by Jim Fricke (MoPOP Oral History Project), November 9 2001. At other times, the tapes helped people build a reputation or get into the scene. The Imperial JC of the Herculords describes how the tapes helped him to get

into the game: "Back then it was about making cassettes. You know cassettes, eight-tracks whatever. Then you went back to school with your tape. I went to Dewitt Clinton High School. So you go into the school with your tape in the box and you played it. If a cat liked what you were doing then they would ask can they buy a tape. So everybody knew that I was good on the West Side. But it was a matter of Herc knowing that I was good, and him believing that I was good." Interview with Imperial JC, interview` by Troy L. Smith, 2006. Herc eventually heard Rahiem's tape, and invited him to be down with his crew.

Tricia Rose adds that the copying and trading of these tapes outside the Bronx was hip hop's first way of spreading. "These tapes traveled far beyond the Bronx; Black and Puerto Rican army recruits sold and traded these tapes in military stations around the country and around the world." See Rose, *Black Noise*, 53.

68. Andrew Abbott, "Things of Boundaries," *Social Research* 62, no. 4 (1995): 878.

69. Schloss, *Foundation*.

70. On "manifest" and "latent" functions, see Robert K. Merton, *Social Theory and Social Structure*, enlarged ed. (New York: Free Press, 1968).

71. On the sociological concept of "effervescence," see Mustafa Emirbayer, ed., *Emile Durkheim: Sociologist of Modernity*, 1st ed. (Hoboken, N.J.: Wiley-Blackwell, 2003), 14; William Sewell, "Historical Events as Transformations of Structures: Inventing Revolution at the Bastille," *Theory and Society* 25, no. 6 (1996): 841–81.

72. For more on how listening binds people together, see Roland Barthes, "Listening," in *The Responsibility of Forms: Critical Essays on Music, Art, and Representation* (New York: Hill and Wang, 1985), 245–60; Gayle Wald, "Soul Vibrations: Black Music and Black Freedom in Sound and Space," *American Quarterly* 63, no. 3 (2011): 673–96.

73. Erving Goffman, *Interaction Ritual - Essays on Face-to-Face Behavior*, 1st Pantheon Books ed. (New York: Pantheon, 1982).

74. Randall Collins, "Stratification, Emotional Energy, and the Transient Emotions," in *Research Agendas in the Sociology of Emotions* ed. Theodore D. Kemper and Randall Collins (Albany: State University of New York Press, 1990), 27–57.

75. "Kool Herc—'The Father of Hip Hop,'" n.d., http://hiphop.sh/koolherc. In an interview, Grandwizard Theodore tells a similar story about Herc "drowning out" the L Brothers with his sound system in a battle. Interview with Grandwizard Theodore by Troy L. Smith and Joseph Ewoodzie, March 2015.

76. "Kool Herc—'The Father of Hip Hop.'"

77. Interview with DJ AJ by Troy L. Smith, Fall 2006.

78. Ibid.

79. Mark McCord, "Kool DJ Herc vs. Pete DJ Jones: One Night at the Executive Playhouse," *Wax Poetics* 17 (June–July, 2006).

80. Ibid.

81. Ibid.

82. Ibid.

83. Interview with DJ AJ by Troy L. Smith, Fall 2006.

84. Pierre Bourdieu, *The Field of Cultural Production* (New York: Columbia University Press, 1993), 16, 38-46.

Chapter Four

1. Howard S. Becker, *Art Worlds* (Berkeley: University of California Press, 1984), 32.

2. Interview with DJ Baron and DJ Breakout by Troy L. Smith, August 2010.

3. Jim Fricke and Charlie Ahearn, *Yes Yes Y'all: The Experience Music Project Oral History of Hip-Hop's First Decade* (Da Capo Press, 2002), 96.

4. Interview with Cholly Rock by Troy L. Smith, August 2016.

5. Interview with DJ Baron and DJ Breakout by Troy L. Smith, August 2010.6. Ibid.

7. Interview with DJ Baron by Jim Fricke (MoPOP Oral History Project), July 15, 2001. To confirm Baron's account of the event, Troy Smith and I asked Tony Tone about the event. Troy asked, "So what happened in that battle?" to which Tone simply responded, "Bam drowned us the fuck out, that's what happened" (Interview with Tony Tone by Troy L. Smith and Joseph C. Ewoodzie, March 2015.)

8. Interview with Tony Tone by Jim Fricke (MoPOP Oral History Project), July 15, 2001.

9. Interview with DJ Breakout by Jim Fricke (MoPOP Oral History Project), n.d.

10. Interview with Rahiem by Jayquan, July 16, 2002.

11. Fricke and Ahearn, *Yes Yes Y'all*, 119.

12. Interview with Grandwizard Theodore, by Troy L. Smith, 2005.13. Interview with Busy Bee Star Ski by Troy L. Smith, June 2006.

14. On the concept of "fictive kinship," see Carol B. Stack, *All Our Kin: Strategies for Survival in a Black Community* (New York: Basic Books, 1997).

15. Interview with Whipper Whip by Jim Fricke (MoPOP Oral History Project), November 8, 2001.

16. Interview with Busy Bee Starski by Troy L. Smith, Summer 2006

17. Ibid.

18. Interview with Grandmaster Caz by Jim Fricke (MoPoP Oral History Project), June 24, 2000

19. Interview with DJ Disco Wiz by Jim Fricke (MoPOP Oral History Project).

20. Ibid.

21. Interview with Grandmaster Caz by Jim Fricke (MoPOP Oral History Project), June 24, 2000

22. Interview with DJ Disco Wiz by Jim Fricke (MoPOP Oral History Project). 23. Interview with Grandmaster Caz by Jim Fricke (MoPoP Oral History Project), June 24, 2000

24. Interview with DJ Disco Wiz by Jim Fricke (MoPOP Oral History Project).

25. In a conversation with Grandmaster Caz, I asked if he still had "the Plate." He shook his head no and explained that after a little while, it did not serve any purpose so they threw it away (Joseph Ewoodzie, Conversation with Grandmaster Caz, March 11, 2015).

26. Mark Skillz, "Master Mix Those Number One Tunes," blog, *Hip-hop 101A* (June 16, 2007), http://hiphop101a.blogspot.com/2007/06/master-mix-those-number-one-tunes.html.

27. Steven Hager, *Hip Hop: The Illustrated History of Break Dancing, Rap Music, and Graffiti* (New York: St. Martins Press, 1984), 19.

28. Interview with Coke La Rock by Troy L. Smith, September 2008.

29. Interview with DJ AJ by Troy L. Smith, 2006.

30. Interview with Afrika Bambaataa and Alien Ness by Jim Fricke (MoPOP Oral History).

31. Sheri Sher, *Mercedes Ladies* (New York: Kensington Publishing, 2008), 69.

32. Ibid., 79.

33. John Borneman, "State, Territory, and Identity Formation in the Postwar Berlins, 1945–1989," *Cultural Anthropology* 7, no. 1 (February 1992): 45–62.

34. Sher, *Mercedes Ladies*, 105

35. Naison, Mark Naison, "From Doo Wop to Hip Hop: The Bittersweet Odyssey of African Americans in the South Bronx," *The Bronx County Historical Journal* XL (2003).

36. On the concept of a "cultural toolkit," see Ann Swidler, "Culture in Action: Symbols and Strategies," *American Sociological Review* 51, no. 2 (April 1986): 273–86.

37. Interview with Rahiem by Jayquan, July 16, 2002..

38. Ibid.

39. Ibid.

40. Interview with Keith Keith by Troy L. Smith, n.d.

41. Interview with Grandmaster Caz by Jim Fricke (MoPOP Oral History Project), June 24, 2000.

42. . Interview with Grandmaster Caz by Jim Fricke (MoPOP Oral History Project), June 24, 2000.

43. Charles P. Sigwart, "Night of Terror," *Time*, July 25, 1977.

44. Peter Goldman, "Heart of Darkness," *Newsweek*, July 1977. For more descriptions of the blackout see the July 25, 1977, issues of *Time* and *Newsweek* magazines. For more about the looting, see Robert Curvin and Bruce Porter, *Blackout Looting!: New York City, July 13, 1977* (New York: Gardner Press, 1979).

45. Anthony Ramirez, "The Darkest Hours of a Dark Time," *New York Times*, July 13, 1977. Popular folklore is that nine months later, New York City saw an unusual increase in the number of newborns.

46. Some hypothesize that the difference in response to these blackouts can be attributed to the weather (a hot July night vs. a cool autumn afternoon), and the socioeconomic conditions (New York City was amidst a harsh financial crisis in 1977). (See the July 25, 1977 *Newsweek* and *Time* magazine articles dedicated to the blackout.) Others argue that the summer of 1977 was already one of high anxiety, especially given the Son of Sam (David Berkowitz) murders, and the high rate of arson in the South Bronx.

47. Curvin and Porter, *Blackout Looting!*

48. Goldman, "Heart of Darkness."

49. Herbert Gutman, denouncing the characterization of the looters as "vultures," argued that the looting was evidence for the desperation of the very poor, especially blacks and Hispanics. See Herbert Gutman, "As for the '02 Kosher-Food Rioters," *New York Times*, July 21, 1977.) Conservative pundit Midge Decter, in contrast, characterized the looters as the "urban insect life." See Joshua B. Freeman, *Working-Class New York: Life and Labor Since World War II* (New York: New Press, 2001), 281–282;

50. Henry Corra, *NY77: The Coolest Year in Hell*, documentary (VH1 Television, 2007).

51. In October 1977, *Time* magazine reported that 40 percent of all arson was for economic profit. See "Arson for Hate and Profit," *Time*, October 31, 1977.

52. Ibid.

53. Lee Dembart, "Carter Takes 'Sobering' Trips to South Bronx," *New York Times*, October 6, 1977.

54. Curvin and Porter, *Blackout Looting*; Wohlenberg, "The 'Geography of Civility' Revisited."

55. Fricke and Ahearn, *Yes Yes Y'all*, 132; Jody Rosen, "A Rolling Shout-Out to Hip-Hop History," *New York Times*, February 12, 2006, Arts/Music section., http://www.nytimes.com/2006/02/12/arts/music/12rose.html.

56. Pierre Bourdieu, *Language and symbolic power*, ed. John B. Thompson (Cambridge: Harvard University Press, 1991), 105.

57. Interview with Melle Mel by Jayquan, February 15, 2002.

58. Interview with Neicy by Jayquan, 2005.

59. Interview with Kid Creole by Jayquan, October 14, 2002.

60. Ibid.

61. Richard Jenkins, *Social Identity*, 2nd ed. (London: Routledge, 2004).

62. Interview with Kid Creole by Jayquan, October 14, 2002

63. Cheryl L. Keyes, *Rap Music and Street Consciousness* (Urbana: University of Illinois Press, 2004), 49.

64. William Grimes, "Michael Martin, Subway Graffiti Artist Iz the Wiz, Is Dead at 50," *New York Times*, June 29, 2009, sec. Arts / Art & Design, http://www.nytimes.com/2009/06/29/arts/design/29martin.html.

65. Craig Castleman, "The Politics of Graffiti," in *That's the Joint: The Hip-Hop Studies Reader*, ed. Mark Anthony Neal and Murray Forman (New York: Routledge, 2004), 21–30.

66. Jeff Chang, *Can't Stop, Won't Stop: A History of the Hip-Hop Generation* (New York: Picador, 2006).

67. Interview with Buddy Esquire by Troy L. Smith, December 2010.

68. Ibid.

69. Ibid.

70. Ibid.

71. Ibid.

72. Fricke and Ahearn, *Yes Yes Y'all*, 153.

73. Ibid.

74. Interview with Cholly Rock by Troy L. Smith, August 2016.

75. Israel, *The Freshest Kids—A History of the B-Boy*, QD3 Production Company

76. Ibid.

77. Ibid.

78. Chang, *Can't Stop, Won't Stop*, 117.

Chapter Five

1. Pierre Bourdieu, *Language and Symbolic Power* (Cambridge, Mass.: Harvard University Press, 1999), 196.

2. Jeff Chang, *Can't Stop, Won't Stop: A History of the Hip-Hop Generation* (New York: Picador, 2006), chap. 5.

3. Max Weber, *The Essential Weber: A Reader*, ed. Sam Whimster (London: Routledge, 2003), 242.

4. Bourdieu, *Language and Symbolic Power*, 195.

5. Patricia Hill Collins, *Black Sexual Politics: African Americans, Gender, and the New Racism*, new ed. (New York: Routledge, 2005).

6. Marcela Raffaelli and Lenna L. Ontai, "Gender Socialization in Latino/a Families: Results from Two Retrospective Studies," *Sex Roles* 50, no. 5–6 (2004): 287–99. Also see Evelyn P. Stevens, "Machismo and Marianismo," *Society* 10, no. 6 (1973): 57–63.

7. Collins, *Black Sexual Politics*; Shirley A. Hill, "Class, Race, and Gender Dimensions of Child Rearing in African American Families," *Journal of Black Studies* 31, no. 4 (2001): 494–508.

8. David Carter, *Stonewall: The Riots That Sparked the Gay Revolution*, 2nd ed. (New York: St. Martin's Griffin, 2010).

9. Susan M. Shaw, "Gender, Leisure, and Constraint: Towards a Framework for the Analysis of Women's Leisure," *Journal of Leisure Research* 26, no. 1 (January 1, 1994): 8–22. Also see Natasha Yurk Quadlin, "Gender and Time Use in College: Converging or Diverging Pathways?," *Gender & Society* 30, no. 2 (April 1, 2016): 361–85, doi:10.1177/0891243215599648.

10. Carol Gilligan, *In a Different Voice: Psychological Theory and Women's Development* (Cambridge, Mass.: Harvard University Press, 1982). For more how the lack of time constrains women's involvement in leisure activities, also see Maureen Harrington, Don Dawson, and Pat Bolla, "Objective and Subjective Constraints on Women's Enjoyment of Leisure," *Loisir et Société / Society and Leisure* 15, no. 1 (January 1, 1992): 203–21.

11. D. L. Samdahl, "Women, Gender, and Leisure Constraints," in *Leisure, Women, and Gender*, ed. Valeria Freysinger et al. (State College, Pa.: Venture Publishing, 2013), 109–26.

12. Tim Lawrence, *Love Saves the Day: A History of American Dance Music Culture, 1970–1979* (Durham, N.C.: Duke University Press, 2004), 93.

13. Kirsten Incorvaia, "Interview with Lady Pink," *Graffiti News EN*, March 2, 2009, http://www.graffitinews.net/en/interviews/146/lady-pink.html.

14. For an elaboration of this argument, see Tricia Rose, *Black Noise: Rap Music and Black Culture in Contemporary America*, 1st ed. (Middletown, Conn.: Wesleyan, 1994).

15. Ibid., 57.

16. Ibid.

17. See Gwendolyn D. Pough, *Check It While I Wreck It: Black Womanhood, Hip-Hop Culture, and the Public Sphere*, 1st ed. (Boston: Northeastern University Press, 2004), 8–9.

18. Judith M. Gerson and Kathy Peiss, "Boundaries, Negotiation, Consciousness: Reconceptualizing Gender Relations," *Social Problems* 32, no. 4 (April 1985): 318.

19. Candace West and Don H. Zimmerman, "Doing Gender," *Gender & Society* 1, no. 2 (June 1987): 129.

20. Judith Butler, in *Gender Trouble: Feminism and the Subversion of Identity* (New York: Routledge, 1990), writes about the relationship between the performances of gender and of sexuality.

21. Interview with Regie Reg by Jim Fricke (MoPOP Oral History Project), November 10, 2001.

22. Interview with Kid Creole by Jayquan, October 14, 2002.

23. Interview with Master Gee by Jayquan, October 2005. Afrika Bambaataa, in an interview with Nelson George, expresses the same thing when he argues that it was the women who helped to bring about the end of gangs and the rise of the DJing culture. "The women

got tired of the gang shit," he explained. "So brothers eventually started sliding slowly off of that 'cause they knew people that got killed." (Nelson George, "Hip-Hop's Founding Fathers Speak the Truth," in *That's the Joint: The Hip-Hop Studies Reader*, ed. Mark Anthony Neal and Murray Forman [New York: Routledge, 2004], 45–56). As gang culture waned, DJs replaced gang leaders as the most desirable male sexual partners.

24. West and Zimmerman, "Doing Gender"; Margaret W. Sallee, "Performing Masculinity: Considering Gender in Doctoral Student Socialization," *Journal of Higher Education* 82, no. 2 (2011): 187–216.

25. Interview with Grandwizard Theodore by Troy L. Smith, 2005.

26. Eric Anderson, "Openly Gay Athletes Contesting Hegemonic Masculinity in a Homophobic Environment," *Gender & Society* 16, no. 6 (December 1, 2002): 860–77, doi:10.1177/089124302237892; R. W. Connell, *Gender and Power: Society, the Person, and Sexual Politics*, 1st ed. (Stanford, Calif: Stanford University Press, 1987).

27. Essex Hemphill, *Ceremonies* (San Francisco: Cleis Press, 1992), 70.

28. The content of this paragraph comes from the following *New York Daily News* article: Michael O'Keeffe, "Hip Hop Legend Afrika Bambaataa Accused of Sex Abuse by Three More Men: 'He Is a Pervert—He Likes Little Boys,'" *New York Daily News*, April 16, 2016, online edition. Additional accounts come from the following sources: Shayna Jacobs et al., "Afrika Bambaataa Sex Abuse Accuser Ronald Savage Details Years of Torment Following Hip-Hop Icon's Molestation: 'He Damaged Me,'" *New York Daily News*, April 9, 2016, online edition; Dan Rys, "Afrika Bambaataa Sexual Abuse Allegations: What's Been Said, Disputed & What's Next," *Billboard*, accessed October 26, 2016, http://www.billboard.com/articles/columns/hip-hop/7364592/afrika-bambaataa-abuse-allegations.

29. According to *Rolling Stone* magazine, after initially questioning the accusers, the Zulu Nation has since distanced himself from Bambaataa, insured an apology to the victims, and removed from the organization any of its members who knew about the alleged molestation but failed to act. See Daniel Kreps, "Zulu Nation Apologizes to Alleged Bambaataa Abuse Victims," *Rolling Stone*, accessed October 26, 2016, http://www.rollingstone.com/music/news/zulu-nation-apologizes-to-alleged-afrika-bambaataa-abuse-victims-20160601.

30. Sharon Jackson and Iesha Brown, *Luminary Icon: The Story of the Beginning and End of the First Hip-hop Female MC* (Virginia Beach, Va.: Outta Da Blue Publishing, 2010).

31. Interview with DJ Breakout by Jim Fricke (MoPOP Oral History Project), n.d.

32. Interview with Sha Rock by Jim Fricke (MoPOP Oral History Project), August 25, 2001.

33. Troy L. Smith, interview with Lisa Lee, 2005.

34. Ibid.

35. Interview with DJ Baron by Jim Fricke (MoPOP Oral History Project), July 15, 2001

36. Sheri Sher, *Mercedes Ladies* (New York: Kensington Publishing, 2008), 80.

37. Ibid., 81.

38. Ibid., 83.

39. Ibid., 88.

40. Interview with RD Smiley by Troy L. Smith, 2009.

41. Sher, *Mercedes Ladies*,, 87.

42. Davey D, *Meet Hip Hop Pioneer Sherri-Sher* [sic] *of Mercedes Ladies*, video, 2009, http://www.youtube.com/watch?v=xIYlznG8nhE.

43. Interview with RD Smiley.

44. Ibid.

45. Ibid.

46. The lineup for the Mercedes Ladies changed over time. Sheri Sher and DJ RD Smiley were the most consistent members.

47. Interview with RD Smiley.48. Ibid.

49. Ibid.

50. Sher, *Mercedes Ladies.*

51. Ibid.

52. Ibid.

53. William G. Roy, "Aesthetic Identity, Race, and American Folk Music," *Qualitative Sociology* 25, no. 3 (2002): 460.

54. Ibid., 461.

55. For examples, see Alan Light, *Vibe History of Hip Hop* (New York: Three Rivers Press, 1999); and Cheryl L. Keyes, *Rap Music and Street Consciousness* (Urbana: University of Illinois Press, 2004).

56. See, for example, Raquel Z. Rivera, *New York Ricans from the Hip Hop Zone* (London: Palgrave Macmillan, 2003).

57. Quoted in Joseph G. Schloss, *Foundation: B-Boys, B-Girls and Hip-Hop Culture in New York* (New York: Oxford University Press, 2009), 20–21.

58. This follows a definition of race by Mustafa Emirbayer and Matthew Desmond. See Matthew Desmond and Mustafa Emirbayer, *Racial Domination, Racial Progress: The Sociology of Race in America* (London: McGraw-Hill, 2009).

59. Interview with Charlie Chase by Oral History Project, 2001.

60. Juan Flores, *From Bomba to Hip-Hop: Puerto Rican Culture and Latino Identity* (New York: Columbia University Press, 2000), 118.

61. Rivera, *New York Ricans from the Hip-hop Zone.*

62. Nathan Kantrowitz, *Ethnic and Racial Segregation in the New York Metropolis*, 1st ed. (Westport, Conn.: Praeger Publishers, 1973); Douglas S. Massey and Nancy A. Denton, "Trends in the Residential Segregation of Blacks, Hispanics, and Asians: 1970-1980," *American Sociological Review* 52, no. 6 (December 1, 1987): 802–25; Rivera, *New York Ricans from the Hip-hop Zone.*

63. Juan Flores, "Puerto Rocks: New York Ricans Stake Their Claims," in *Droppin' Science: Critical Essays on Rap Music and Hip-hop Culture*, ed. Eric Perkins (Philadelphia: Temple University Press, 1996), 85–105; Rivera, *New York Ricans from the Hip-hop Zone*; Douglas S. Massey and Brooks Bitterman, "Explaining the Paradox of Puerto Rican Segregation," *Social Forces* 64, no. 2 (December 1985): 306–31.

64. Rivera, *New York Ricans from the Hip-hop Zone*, 25.

65. Ibid.

66. Flores, *From Bomba to Hip-Hop.*

67. Daniel McCabe, *Latin Music USA*, documentary (2009).

68. Ibid. Even before the birth of boogaloo, Latin American and U.S. Afro-diasporic strains of music were fused to create a new sub-genre of jazz music. In the 1940s, Dizzy Gillespie brought Afro-Cuban percussionist Chano Pozo into his band to create compositions like "Conga Be" and "Conga Bop."

69. During this time, most Puerto Ricans lived in Brooklyn or the Bronx, with the South Bronx containing about 25 percent of all Puerto Ricans in New York (Rivera, *New York Ricans from the Hip-hop Zone*, 23.)

70. Flores, *From Bomba to Hip-Hop*, 119.

71. Interview with Charlie Chase by Jim Fricke (MoPOP Oral History Project), July 15 200172. Flores, *From Bomba to Hip-Hop*, 119.

73. Interview with Charlie Chase.

74. Flores, "Puerto Rocks: New York Ricans Stake Their Claims," 90.

75. Interview with Charlie Chase.

76. Ibid.

77. Ibid.

78. Rivera, *New York Ricans from the Hip-hop Zone, 63*.

79. Interview with Charlie Chase.

80. Flores, *From Bomba to Hip-Hop*, 120.

81. Eminem, a contemporary rapper who is white, expresses the same sentiment when, in his song "White America," he raps, "When I was underground, No one gave a fuck I was white."

82. Interview with Tony Tone by Oral History Project, 2001.

83. Interview with Charlie Chase.

84. Interview with Tony Tone.

85. Interview with Charlie Chase.

86. Ibid.

87. Ibid.

88. Thanks to Troy L. Smith for this insight.

89. Jim Fricke and Charlie Ahearn, *Yes Yes Y'all: The Experience Music Project Oral History of Hip-Hop's First Decade* (Boston: Da Capo Press, 2002).

90. Rivera, *New York Ricans from the Hip Hop Zone*; Fredrik Barth, *Ethnic Groups and Boundaries: the Social Organization of Culture Difference* (New York: Little, Brown and Company, 1969).

91. Another noteworthy Puerto Rican in the founding days of hip-hop is Joe Conzo, a photographer of the early days of hip-hop. His work can be seen in Johan Kugelberg, Joe Conzo, and Afrika Bambaataa, *Born in the Bronx: A Visual Record of the Early Days of Hip-hop* (New York: Rizzoli, 2007).

Chapter Six

1. This was not the first time that another activity had challenged the centrality of the DJ. If we recall from the first chapter, b-boys were once so popular that they became the main attraction at park jams. B-boying was unable to displace DJing because Flash's innovations moved the attention of the audience from the ciphers on the dance floor back onto the stage.

2. David Bruinooge, *100 Greatest Hip-hop Songs* (VH1, October 6, 2008); "The 500 Greatest Songs of All Time," *Rolling Stone*, December 9, 2004, http://www.rollingstone.com/music/lists/the-500-greatest-songs-of-all-time-20110407.

3. Pierre Bourdieu and Loïc J. D. Wacquant, in *An Invitation to Reflexive Sociology* (Chicago: University of Chicago Press, 1992), 69, discuss how fields lose their autonomy.

4. Interview with Grandmaster Flash by Oral History Project, 1999.

5. Interview with Rahiem by Oral History Project, 2001.

6. Interview with DJs of the Funky 4 Plus One More [*sic*] by Troy L. Smith, August 2010.

7. Ibid.

8. Ibid.

9. Interview with Rahiem by Jayquan, July 16, 2002..

10. Interview with Tony Tone by Oral History Project, 2001.

11. In another interview with Troy L. Smith, KK Rockwell mentioned that a crew from the Edenwald Projects were their security that night, but they did not bring any guns. (Interview with DJs of the Funky 4 Plus One More.)

12. Ibid.

13. Ibid.

14. Interview with Rahiem by Jayquan, July 16, 2002..

15. Interview with Kid Creole by Jayquan, October 14, 2002

16. Flash purchased the machine from a drummer who lived on 149th Street and Jackson Avenue. "I think his name was Dennis. He had this manually operated drum machine and whenever he didn't feel like hooking up his drums in his room, he would practice on this machine" (*Last Night a DJ Saved My Life: The History of the Disc Jockey* (New York, NY: Grove Press, 2000), 225–226.)

17. Interview with Rahiem by Jayquan, July 16, 2002..

18. Ibid.

19. Interview with DJs of the Funky 4 Plus One More by Troy L. Smith.

20. Ibid.

21. Alessandro Portelli, "What Makes Oral History Different?" in *The Oral History Reader*, ed. Robert Perks and Alistair Thomson, 2nd ed. (London: Routledge, 2006), 63–74.

22. Interview with DJ Baron by Jim Fricke (MoPOP Oral History Project), July 15, 200123. Interview with DJs of the Funky 4 Plus One More by Troy L. Smith

24. Interview with Sha Rock by Jim Fricke (MoPOP Oral History Project), August 25, 2001.

25. Interview with DJ Baron by Jim Fricke (MoPOP Oral History Project), July 15, 2001

26. Ibid.

27. Interview with Sha Rock by Jim Fricke (MoPOP Oral History Project), August 25, 2001.28. Ibid.

29. Interview with Arthur Armstrong by Troy L. Smith, December 2010.

30. Although Armstrong, in this interview, refers to hip-hop as "rap," there is no evidence that this was what the music was then being called. The use of the term *rap* to refer to hip-hop began after the popularity of Sugar Hill Gang's "Rappers Delight."

31. Interview with Arthur Armstrong, December 2010.

32. Interview with Arthur Armstrong by Jim Fricke (MoPOP Oral History Project), November 9, 2001.

33. Ibid. He speculates that the territoriality of the scene was a residual of the gang culture.

34. Ibid.

35. Interview with Arthur Armstrong, December 2010.

36. Interview with Arthur Armstrong by Jim Fricke (MoPOP Oral History Project), November 9, 2001.

37. Ibid.

38. Interview with Busy Bee Starski by Troy L. Smith, June 2006.

39. Interview with Kevie Kev by Troy L. Smith, Spring 2005.

40. Interview with Busy Bee Starski, June 2006.

41. Interview with Arthur Armstrong by Jim Fricke (MoPOP Oral History Project), November 9, 2001.

42. Interview with Busy Bee Starski, June 2006.

43. . Interview with Grandmaster Caz by Jim Fricke (MoPOP Oral History Project), June 24, 2000.

44. Interview with Busy Bee Starski, June 2006

45. Interview with Arthur Armstrong, December 2010.

46. Ellsworth Faris, "Attitudes and Behavior," *American Journal of Sociology* 34, no. 2 (September 1928): 278.

47. Special thanks to Troy L. Smith (and JDL, indirectly) for help with this portion of the narrative.

48. Interview with Grandwizard Theodore by Troy L. Smith, 2005.

49. Interview with JDL by Troy L. Smith, n.d.

50. As cited in Jim Fricke and Charlie Ahearn, *Yes Yes Y'all: The Experience Music Project Oral History of Hip-Hop's First Decade* (Boston: Da Capo Press, 2002), 170.

51. Interview with Melle Mel by Jayquan, February 15, 2002.

52. Interview with Charlie Chase by Jim Fricke (MoPOP Oral History Project, July 15, 2001.

53. Interview with Tony Tone by Oral History Project, 2001.

54. In fact, according to Troy L. Smith, Flash played Queens, where the MC was significantly less important to the DJ.

55. Interview with Melle Mel by Jayquan.

56. Interview with Rahiem by Jayquan, July 16, 2002.

57. Interview with Grandmaster Flash by Jim Fricke (MoPOP Oral History Project), 1999.

58. Ibid.59. Richard Alba, "Bright vs. Blurred Boundaries: Second-Generation Assimilation and Exclusion in France, Germany, and the United States," *Ethnic and Racial Studies* 28, no. 1 (2005): 23, 25. See also Thomas F. Gieryn, "Boundary-Work and the Demarcation of Science from Non-Science: Strains and Interests in Professional Ideologies of Scientists," *American Sociological Review* 48, no. 6 (December 1983): 791.

60. Mark Skillz, "When the Fever Was the Mecca," *Wax Poetics*, no. 14 (September 2005).

61. Ibid.

62. Dan Charnas, *The Big Payback: The History of the Business of Hip-Hop* (New York: New American Library, 2011), 23.

63. Skillz, "When the Fever Was the Mecca."

64. Ibid.

65. Ibid.

66. Ibid.

67. Charnas, *The Big Payback*, 23.

68. Here again, one thinks of Robin Kelley's term "play-labor" cited in chapter 3. Playing alongside Harlem DJs was, perhaps, the culmination of turning what was once a hobby

into a legitimate source of income. See Robin D. G. Kelley, *Yo' Mama's Disfunktional!: Fighting the Culture Wars in Urban America* (Boston: Beacon Press, 1997), 45.

69. Mark Skillz, personal communication with author, July 14, 2011.

70. Interview with Sal Abbatiello by Bill Adler (MoPOP Oral History Project), July 16 2001.

71. As cited in Fricke and Ahearn, *Yes Yes Y'all*, 181.

72. Ibid., 184.

73. Ibid.

74. Mark Skillz, "Cheeba, Cheeba Y'all!," *Hip Hop 101A*, blog (September 8, 2007), hiphop101a.blogspot.com/2007/09/cheeba-cheeba-yall.html

75. As cited in Fricke and Ahearn, *Yes Yes Y'all*, 184.

76. Ibid.

77. Ibid., 185.

78. Although inspired by the South Bronx scene, his two-man crew, something that would not have been acceptable in the South Bronx around 1977, provides evidence that a New Jersey scene existed, with its own conventions and logic.

79. Interview with Master Gee by Jayquan, October 2005.

80. The name might have been a reference to Harlem's historical Sugar Hill district. See Charnas, *The Big Payback*, 5.

81. Fricke and Ahearn, *Yes Yes Y'all*, 185.

82. Ibid., 185.

83. Ibid.

84. Interview with Grandmaster Flash by Jim Fricke (MoPOP Oral History Project), 1999

85. Joseph Ewoodzie, conversation with Grandmaster Caz, March 11, 2015.

86. Ibid.

87. Interview with Grandmaster Flash.

88. Fricke and Ahearn, *Yes Yes Y'all*, 196.

89. Interview with Whipper Whip by Jim Fricke (MoPOP Oral History Project), November 8, 2001.90. Interview with Sha Rock by Jim Fricke (MoPOP Oral History Project), August 25, 2001.

Conclusion

1. This and the following two excerpts of lyrics are taken from Common, "The Corner" on *Be* (Geffen Records, 2005).

2. Craig Werner, *A Change Is Gonna Come: Music, Race, and the Soul of America*, rev. ed. (Ann Arbor: University of Michigan Press, 2006).

3. Michael Omi and Howard Winant, *Racial Formation in the United States: From the 1960s to the 1990s*, 2nd ed. (New York: Routledge, 1994).

4. William Isaac Thomas and Florian Znaniecki, *The Polish Peasant in Europe and America: A Classic Work in Immigration History* (Urbana: University of Illinois Press, 1918).

5. Loïc J. D. Wacquant, "Three Pernicious Premises in the Study of the American Ghetto," *International Journal of Urban and Regional Research* 21, no. 2 (June 1997): 341–53.

6. Ibid., 343.

7. Ibid., 347.

8. Ibid., 347.

9. Also see Waverly Duck, "'Senseless' Violence Making Sense of Murder," *Ethnography* 10, no. 4 (December 2009): 417–34.

10. Randol Contreras, *The Stickup Kids: Race, Drugs, Violence, and the American Dream* (Berkeley: University of California Press, 2012).

11. Elijah Anderson, *Code of the Street: Decency, Violence, and the Moral Life of the Inner City*, reprint ed. (New York: W. W. Norton, 2000).

12. Ibid., 68.

13. Alexis de Tocqueville, *Democracy in America*, ed. J. P. Mayer, trans. George Lawrence (New York: Harper Perennial Modern Classics, 2006), 189–96.

Index

Page numbers in italics refer to illustrations.